Management of Natural Disasters in Developing Countries

Management of Natural Disasters in Developing Countries

Editors
Dr. H.N. Srivastava
Dr. G.D. Gupta

CENTRE FOR SCIENCE & TECHNOLOGY OF THE NON-ALIGNED AND OTHER DEVELOPING COUNTRIES
(NAM S&T CENTRE)

2020

Daya Publishing House®

A Division of

Astral International Pvt. Ltd.

New Delhi – 110 002

First Published, 2006

Reprinted, 2020

ISBN 978-81-7035-425-3 (HB)

Centre for Science and Technology of the Non-Aligned and Other Developing Countries (NAM S&T Centre)
Core-6A, 2nd Floor, India Habitat Centre, Lodhi Road, New Delhi-110 003 (India)
Phone: +91-11-24644974, 24645134, Fax: +91-11-24644973
E-mail: namstct@vsnl.com
Website: www.namstct.org

Published by : **Daya Publishing House®**
A Division of
Astral International Pvt. Ltd.
– ISO 9001:2015 Certified Company –
4736/23, Ansari Road, Darya Ganj
New DelhiA110 002
Ph. 011A43549197, 23278134
EAmail: info@astralint.com
Website: www.astralint.com

Digitally Printed at : Replika Press Pvt. Ltd.

Foreword

Over the years, study of the interactions among the various components of the earth system–lithosphere, hydrosphere, biosphere & atmosphere has gained considerable importance as these interactions influence global change on a variety of spatial and temporal scales. Recent devastating earthquakes and Tsunami and the heavy loss of life in other destructive events such as floods, volcanoes, cyclones, tornadoes, bushfires, hurricanes, landslides etc. have evoked great interest amongst scientists and researchers to actively seek the reasons and remedies of these physical processes by devising reliable means of attention on disaster preparedness, prevention and recognition of the fact that disaster prevention and pre-disaster planning should be an integral part of the national development policy.

I am happy to note that there has been a growing concern amongst the developing countries about the importance of understanding the causes and exploring possible remedial and preventive measures for various naturally occurring hazardous processes. The efforts of NAM S&T Centre, therefore, are noteworthy in bringing together scientists and policy makers on natural hazards from the developing countries on a common platform to share their knowledge and experiences. I congratulate the NAM S&T Centre for bringing out the book entitled "Management of Natural Disaster (Floods and Cyclone)" based on the papers presented and experiences shared during the International Workshop organised by Centre during 24–27 January 2000 at Bangkok in association with the Asian Institute of Technology (AIT), Bangkok. I am sure, this volume would be extremely useful for all those interested in the subject of disaster management.

I congratulate Dr. A.P. Kulshreshtha, Director NAM S&T Centre for his sustained efforts in promoting mutually beneficial collaboration and cooperation among scientists, organisations and policy makers from Non-aligned and other Developing Countries and transfer of technology.

V.S. Ramamurthy
Secretary
Ministry of Science & Technology
Department of Science & Technology, Govt. of India
Technology Bhavan, New Mehrauli Road, New Delhi – 110 016

Preface

Natural hazards have been occurring since time immemorial causing colossal loss of life and property. In view of this, the focus is now towards management of the effects of such disasters to mitigate their impact on the areas affected. Several methodologies have been evolved in different countries which have been found to be more suitable in specific regions. The present volume brought out by Centre for Science and Technology of the Non-Aligned and other developing countries (NAM S&T Centre) has, therefore, supported and coordinated with other NAM countries to arrange an International Workshop on Management of Natural Disasters during January 24-27, 2000 with the cooperation of Asian Institute of Technology, Bangkok. The present volume has identified and discussed areas of mitigating flood, cyclone storm surge, earthquakes and related landslides through status papers and projected plans to improve mitigation strategies in the participating countries. This volume is a synthesis of 17 papers on the subject from Bangladesh, India, Indonesia, Malaysia, Mauritius, Nepal, Pakistan, Syria, Thailand and Vietnam. The two papers presented by Bangladesh focused their attention on mitigating cyclone and storm surge disasters and the emergency support required to mitigate other natural hazards as well like droughts, earthquakes, tornadoes. Of these, the lead paper was presented by India given emphasis on the management of natural disasters including different flood forecasting and cyclone warning methodologies and some research programmes supported by the Department of Science and Technology covering other natural hazards like earthquakes and landslides as well. The role of Natural Resources Data Management System under the Department of Science and Technology was also highlighted. Another paper on cyclone disaster mitigation covered the methodologies of risk analysis, microzonation, dynamic response analysis and vulnerability analysis besides providing information for design standards. Some other papers by the Department of Science and Technology focused its programmes towards recent infrastructural facilities created and other significant achievements including new initiatives taken. The paper on natural disaster and mitigation in Indonesia laid emphasis on earthquakes, tsunami, floods and hurricane impacts as well as volcanoes and fire monitoring and mitigation.

The Environment and Natural Resources Development Division of ESCAP, Thailand has provided a pivotal role supported by IDNDR Programme of UN for regional surveys about experiences and responses to natural disasters and their significant achievements particularly through the International Decade for Natural Hazard Reduction. It also focused its attention on regional concerns on priority areas. The Crisis and Disaster Management Unit of Malaysia discussed the disaster management and relief mechanism with their programmes at Federal, State and District levels covering various disasters affecting the country which also included intense haze episodes and forest fire. The paper on management of natural disasters in Mauritius gave emphasis on the methodologies for cyclonic storm warnings response and recovery. The main types of natural disasters in Nepal pertain to earthquake, landslides and floods including the impacts of glaciers and some man-induced disasters like fire and epidemic. The development plans related to warning systems in the country were also presented. Floods, thunder storms, tornadoes, avalanches, landslides, tidal waves, droughts, aviation hazards - their mitigation and early warning procedures were discussed by Pakistan Meteorological Department. The Faculty of Civil Engineering presented the procedures to encounter natural hazards in relation to the support required by existing structures, their designing and strengthening. An interesting research project undertaken by Asian Institute of Technology, Bangkok and Research & Development Centre, Japan for Nepal was based on satellite data to understand watershed degradation, flood plain sedimentation, changes of river channels in the Siwalik area of central Nepal. The model proposed also enabled to estimate the average annual soil yield reduced land denudation rate to validate the potential of the methodology. Another paper by the same Institute laid emphasis on cyclone disasters due to heavy rain fall in Thailand in addition to the catastrophic flood during 1988. The third paper by the Asian Institute of Technology, Thailand presented the impact of strong wind and surges due to cyclonic storms in Thailand. The impact of flood and typhoons in Vietnam and their mitigation methodologies were discussed by the Ministry of Science, Technology and Environment, Vietnam.

It is, therefore, an excellent endeavour of NAM CENTRE to bring out a coordinated effort of the participating countries towards mitigation of Natural Hazards.

Editors

Contents

Introduction

Natural hazards are naturally occurring processes forming an experience to human being, depending on where one lives. Floods, volcanoes, tornadoes, bushfires and hurricanes are the possible threats, which affect the environment and thus our lives. Encircling the total area of the Asian and Pacific region, which is 35 million square kilometer, around 60 per cent of world population resides in this area. In this particular region, 50 per cent of the world's disaster was recorded during past two decades. On retrospection around 3 million lives have been claimed and the lives of around 1 million were grimly blown up during the aforesaid period. To find out the outcome of the problem, it requires exploring the reason of its origin and the possible antidotes so that it can dwindle to some extent. Planning, managing and implementing environmentally sound strategies are the supreme measures in this concern. ESCAP (Economic and Social Commission for Asia and the Pacific) has established a Bureau for Flood Control, which is functioning well since 1949. Development of active sub-regional network through the Typhoon Committee in typhoon tracking and flood forecasting, panelized work on tropical cyclones, its cooperation with IDNDR (International Decade for Natural Disaster Reduction) in Asia and activities of Mekong River Commission are important appreciable agendas to its credit. The cooperation from such organizations has amplified the importance of viewing the present driving forces, which are responsible to intensify the severity of their occurrence. For example, increase in population density, rapid economic and social development, deforestation due to urbanization and other global factors contribute to disaster directly or indirectly. Though participation of people and mental preparedness prior to disaster could relief the grief to some extent, to conquer the problem absolutely, there is an urgent need to frame well planned and managed strategies. Regional Haze Action Plan under Asian secretariat is one of the feats in this concern. Under this plan people are trained to fire fighting and haze management. A number of UN agencies, donors and others are in assistance to this plan. Moreover it has received the endorsement by Asian ministers in 1997. Availability of coastal radars and geostationary satellites has turned out to be a boon in detecting and tracking of cyclones over Indian seas. Introduction of Doppler weather radars provides small dynamic changes of tropical cyclone with the effort of the India Meteorological Department (IMD). Nevertheless innumerable attempts are still in progress.

Information exchange in the developing countries has not yet reached the levels of developed countries. In this scenario, it is of utmost importance to gather information at one place, so that needs and problems of other countries could also be interacted and disseminated to national and international research bodies as well as social organizations. In this way developing countries could pool their limited resources to its best in cure procedures. Organizing a series of workshops/ trainings on Management of Natural Disaster could be an aid in consecutive steps.

The International workshop on "Management of Natural Disaster" (Floods and Cyclone) during January 24-27, 2000 was a joint effort of the Centre for Science & Technology of the Non-Aligned and Other Developing Countries (NAM S&T Centre) and School of Engineering; Asian Institute of technology (AIT), Bangkok, Thailand. Mr. M. Fazlur Rahman, Secretary, Ministry of Science and Technology, Government of Bangladesh and the then President of the Governing Council of the NAM S&T Centre inaugurated the workshop. The workshop mainly aimed at identifying areas of mitigating flood, cyclone and storm surge disaster. The main objectives of the workshop were to familiarize the participants from different countries with the latest developments and advanced technologies involved in disaster management, to assess and manage related social and gender issues as well as to identify areas of mutual scientific collaboration. The workshop had four interactive sessions. There were exchange of ideas on current developments, successes, shortfalls, issues and future plans of sustaining disaster management in the participating countries.

The proceedings of the workshop have been arranged in a sequential manner beginning with the Introduction, which touched several aspects of disaster management keeping in mind the objectives of the workshop. The Status Reports from different countries began with the lead paper giving the status of disaster management in India followed by the reports from Bangladesh, Indonesia, Malaysia, Mauritius, Nepal, Pakistan, Syria, Thailand, and Vietnam.

On behalf of the Centre I would like to express our appreciation to the Department of Science and Technology, Government of India for sanctioning a grant of Rs. 1,50,000 for publishing these proceedings. Epitomizing the success of the workshop I am overwhelmed to thank Dr. Ashim Das Gupta, Professor, Water Engineering and Management Program, Asian Institute of Technology (AIT), Thailand and my predecessor Mr. K.N. Johry for coordinating the workshop. I also acknowledge the dynamic involvement of the entire team of the NAM S&T Centre, particularly of the young scientist Dr. V. Sikri, in compiling these Proceedings in a systematic manner. Last but not the least, I pay my gratitude to the eminent resource persons and participants of this workshop as well as those who were involved directly or indirectly in making workshop a grand success.

(Arun P. Kulshreshtha)

Director, NAM S&T Centre

1

Mitigating Cyclone and Storm Surge Disasters

Jamilur R. Choudhury
Professor of Civil Engineering,
Bangladesh University of Engineering and Technology,
Dhaka, Bangladesh

1. Introduction

Cyclones and storm surges are among the most destructive of all natural disasters. The regions of the world which are vulnerable to such disasters include the islands in the South-West Pacific, South-East Asia (*e.g.*, the Philippines, Vietnam), countries adjoining the Bay of Bengal (*viz.*, India, Bangladesh and Myanmar), South-East Africa, the Caribbean and parts of the USA and Latin America around the Gulf of Mexico and Atlantic Ocean.

Bangladesh is among the countries most vulnerable to devastating storm surges which accompany cyclones. During the last three decades, Bangladesh has been trying to develop strategies for mitigating the impact of storm surge hazard. Although the progress has been slow, some of the measures appear to have been successful. The paper presents an overview of the strategy developed in Bangladesh for protection of the vulnerable communities from storm surge hazard. The experience of Bangladesh may help other countries in developing their own strategies for dealing with storm surge hazard.

About 6 per cent of the global total of cyclones originates in the Bay of Bengal and about one-sixth of these have landfall in the Bangladesh coast. The funnel shaped coastline in the northern bay, coupled with a gently sloping continental shelf (the 10 m depth contour ranges from 20 to 200 km from the coastline), results in surge heights up to 7.5 m. These may move up the flat deltaic land or along the numerous rivers and creeks in the coastal zone and affect places as far as 40 km inland from the coastline.

Cyclones and storm surges are not new phenomena in Bangladesh–there are records dating back to 1584, when 200,000 peoples were reported to have been killed in Barisal and Patuakhaii districts due to storm surge. During the last 100 years, a total of sixty-six cyclonic storms have hit the Bangladesh coast, out of which thirty-six have been classified as severe cyclonic storm (*i.e.*, with sustained wind speed greater than 119 km/hr). The most devastating, in terms of human fatalities, was the 12 November 1970 cyclone, which killed around 500,000 people. The official death toll in the 29 April 1991 cyclone was around 140,000. More than 98 per cent of these deaths are due to drowning in the surge water. The average human death toll in Bangladesh due to storm surge during the last thirty years has been around 25,000 per year, which is the highest in the world.

Immediately following the April, 1991 cyclone, the Government of Bangladesh constituted a Task Force to review the efficacy of cyclone shelters and assess the needs for new shelters. The Task Force commissioned a comprehensive study to prepare a Master Plan for Cyclone Shelters. This study had undertaken by a Team of Experts from the Bangladesh University of Engineering and Technology and Bangladesh Institute of Development Studies (BUET -BIDS) (Ref. 1). The study was funded by UNDP and the World Bank acted as the executing agency.

A comprehensive analysis of all available data reveals that there are around 5.8 million people (approx. 4.5 per cent of Bangladesh total) living in an area of 9,182 sq. km (6.4 per cent of Bangladesh total), where the surge height may be 1 m or more. This area has been classified as a high-risk *area* where people are likely to be killed due to drowning if they do not live above the surge level in strong houses or if they do not move to shelter.

2. The Effects of Storm Surge

Storm surge, like any other natural disaster, affects human lives, livestock, agriculture, physical infrastructure and as a consequence, may have devastating effect on national development. In fact, in areas prone to storm surges, sustainable development will remain a myth unless mitigatory efforts are made an integral part of the overall development plan. Unlike many other natural disasters, developments in science and technology have made it possible to predict the areas likely to be hit by a cyclone about 24 hours before landfall and also identify the areas likely to be subjected to storm surge along with probable depths of inundation. Satellite and radar-based techniques are now available even in developing countries and have made possible the detection of a cyclone very soon after its formation and its tracking as it moves towards the coast.

3. Possible Mitigatory Measures

The possible mitigatory measures include:

- Construction of embankments or sea walls to prevent ingress of surge water;
- Construction of strong houses;
- Evacuation to safer places;
- Community shelters for human population;
- Shelter for livestock;
- Afforestation;
- Forecasting and warning system;
- Training and deployment of volunteers;
- Public awareness.

(a) Embankments

Embankments along the coastline and around the offshore islands can prevent the movement of storm surges inland. However, the cost of construction and maintenance of these embankments, along with the drainage structures, is so high that these may be economically justified only if there are large investments (*e.g.*, infrastructure, industries) to be protected. The earthen embankments built in the coastal areas of Bangladesh during the late 1960s were designed to prevent inundation due to high tide only and not to withstand storm surges. In fact, the mistaken belief that these embankments can provide protection against storm surges led to the death of a large number of people during the 1991 cyclone. After the 1991 cyclone, strong earthen embankments with precast concrete or stone riprap, have been built in some of the areas. Even then, these may be over topped in case of storm surges with 50 year return period.

(b) Strong Houses

The ideal solution for protecting human lives is to build the houses above the surge level and make them strong enough to resist the lateral forces due to high wind and the accompanying surge. Since construction of an entire house fulfilling the above requirement would be very expensive, only one room of every house, capable of accommodating the entire family during the few hours of emergency, may be designed to resist the wind and surge (Figure 1.1). However, under the prevailing economic conditions, construction of such an elevated room would require around US$ 2,500 per family which, on an average, is equivalent to around three years income for the entire family. Therefore, for most families, it is almost impossible to construct the houses out of their own resources.

(c) Evacuation

The next option is evacuation to high ground above the surge level. On receiving warning of an imminent storm surge, people can move away from the coastal areas to places above the highest surge level. However, this appears to be a feasible option only in case of a small strip of land along the southeastern coast of Bangladesh. Even in these areas the poor communication system is a severe handicap. The required logistic support and mobilization appear to be formidable obstacles.

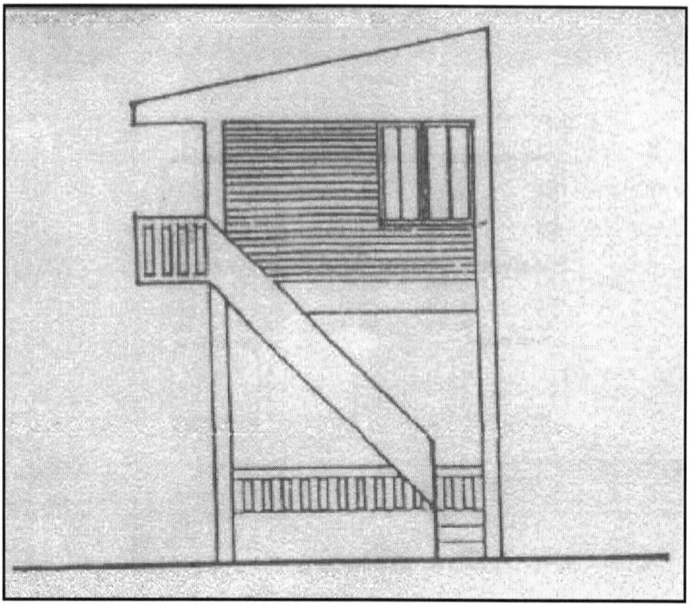

Figure 1.1: Family Shelter (one room on stilt)

(d) Community Shelters

Construction of community shelters capable of providing refuge to the population likely to be affected appears to be a feasible option. The concept of building cyclone shelter in the coastal belt of Bangladesh dates back to the early 1960s. After the devastating cyclones of 1960-61, the Government decided to build a number of two-storey buildings in areas close to the coast, the upper floor of which could be used as shelter during cyclones. These were proposed to be used as office of the Union Council (the lowest tier of local government) and Community Centres during normal times. A total of 132 of these buildings were built, but lack of maintenance resulted in rapid deterioration and many of these have been abandoned. The 226 three-storied shelters constructed during 1972-78 under IDA credit are also in very poor condition due to lack of maintenance. A total of about 1500 shelters have been recently constructed by the Government, Bangladesh Red Crescent Society and various NGOs.

These are usually reinforced concrete framed structures, with brick masonry infill walls. The ground floor is left open to allow the surge water to flow through the building. The upper floors of these two-or three-storied buildings are used as shelters (Figures 1.2 and 1.3). A variety of plan shapes have been used, *viz.* rectangular, arrow shaped, octagonal, or twelve sided polygon; but analysis shows that even for the high design wind speed (around 260 km/hr), the lateral forces do not have a significant influence on the design stresses in 2 or 3 storied buildings. Therefore, the plan shape

Figure 1.2: Community Shelter (Two Storied)

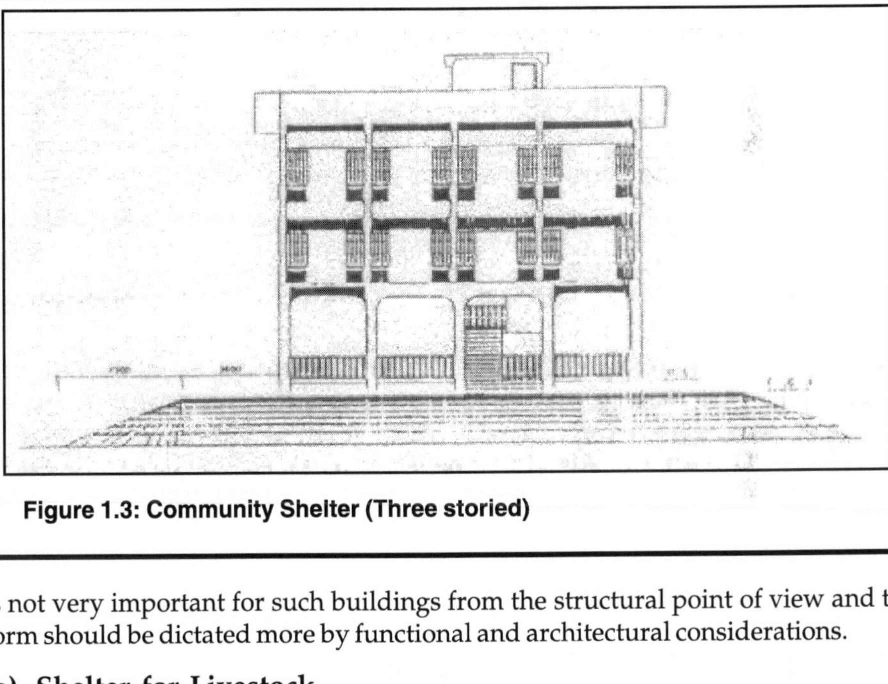

Figure 1.3: Community Shelter (Three storied)

is not very important for such buildings from the structural point of view and the form should be dictated more by functional and architectural considerations.

(e) Shelter for Livestock

Construction of *killas* (earthen mounds) with the top level raised above the maximum height of surges is a possible solution for sheltering livestock. About 250 of these exist in Bangladesh now. These are usually rectangular in plan, varying in size from 24.4 m x 18.3 m to 61.5 m x 30.5 m; a circular plan shape has also been tried. Experience during the recent cyclones shows that standalone killas have very rarely been used for sheltering livestock. The major reason is that the killas are located away from human settlement and people are reluctant to walk a long distance to take their cows, buffaloes, sheep or goat there. Moreover, lack of normal time use and maintenance leads to erosion of slopes and unwieldy growth of grass and shrubs, which make them unusable during emergency.

Normal Time Use of Shelters

The frequency of cyclones and surges is such that the shelters are likely to be used only once in four to five years. Since the shelter buildings are quite expensive structures, it would not be economically justifiable unless some normal time use can be ensured. Moreover, experience shows that unless these buildings are used regularly, it is very difficult to maintain the facilities.

The normal time use of shelters may include the following:

- ❖ Educational institutions (e. g. primary school, secondary school, college)
- ❖ Vocational training Institutions
- ❖ Health and Family Welfare Centres
- ❖ Community Centres
- ❖ Offices
- ❖ Passenger Terminals

Based on a recommendation of the Task Force of the Institution of Engineers, Bangladesh (Ref. 2), the Government has decided that all its office buildings in the surge-prone areas will be at least two-storeyed, so that the upper floors can be used as shelter during cyclones slid accompanying surge.

(f) Afforestation

Coastal afforestation has been found to retard the intrusion of storm surges inland. In some cases, they may help in reducing the depth of inundation.

(g) Forecast And Warning

As mentioned earlier, the technology for detection and tracking of cyclone is quite well developed and the meteorological data can be used in a mathematical model to predict landfall and areas likely to be affected along with probable depth of inundation. Dissemination of warning messages which are clearly understood by the local people appears to be a more difficult task. The traditional system of warning signals originally developed for maritime use led to considerable confusion and is now being replaced by a more easily understood numbering system.

(h) Training and Deployment of Volunteers

Under the Cyclone Preparedness Programme jointly run by the Government and the Bangladesh Red Crescent Society, about 32,000 volunteers have been trained to disseminate the warning among the people (usually through megaphones), to assist the people to move to shelters, to carry out search and rescue operations immediately following a storm surge and to provide first-aid to injured people. These volunteers undergo regular training and have contributed significantly in reducing loss of human lives.

(i) Public Awareness

A programme has been initiated to raise the level of awareness of the vulnerable communities. These are being undertaken by NGOs in cooperation with the

Government. Actions to be taken by individuals and families before, during and following cyclones and storm surges are discussed with the community and training imparted to community leaders. Theatre groups go round villages staging plays based on preparedness measures and what to do during cyclones. Measures have been initiated to include topics related to disasters in primary and secondary school curricula.

4. Planning

The primary consideration in locating a shelter is to ensure that it is easily accessible to potential refuge-seekers. Experience shows that people tend to move to the shelters only a few hours before the water starts rising, by which time the wind speed may be quite high. Under such circumstances, most people are reluctant to walk more than around 1.5 km from their houses. The catchment area for a typical shelter would therefore include the people who live in an area with a radius of around 1.5 km from the shelter. People who move to the shelter carry their valuable assets (which can be hand-carried) to the shelter; some storage space for these must be provided in the shelter.

Experience shows that people who own livestock do not like to take them to a killa which is far away from a human shelter. Based on extensive discussions with the local people, it seems that the preferred solution is an integrated shelter-cum-killa which can be used by livestock as well as human beings (Figure 1.4). During the April 1991 cyclone, the existing shelters on killa were used more efficiently compared to other shelters.

Figure 1.4: Shelter on Killa (One storied)

Till recently, the common practice was to design the building as a cyclone shelter and then try to find out what activities could be carried out during normal times. Experience has shown that this leads to less than optimum use of the facilities. A better methodology would be to design the building for normal time use (*e.g.* school, community centre) and then investigate whether any changes would be necessary to make it function as a shelter during emergencies. This iterative process can be continued till an optimum solution is arrived at. The rationale for the above approach is that for more than 99 per cent of the total usage time of the facility, it would have to be suitable for fulfilling the functional requirement of normal time use. Therefore, the design should be based primarily on this consideration. Of course, to satisfy the functional requirements of a shelter, additional elements may have to be introduced; *e.g.* additional space for storing the belongings of refuge-seekers and storage of food and medicine would be needed. Immediately after the cyclone, the shelters have to operate as relief distribution centres and this must be considered in the design.

The cost of construction of a primary school designed to function as a shelter is relatively more than a normal primary school. Therefore, efforts should be made to utilize these facilities for other purposes as well. For example, during afternoons and evenings, the building may be used for community activities.

The catchment areas (CA) for a typical primary school is found to have a total population of around 2,000 persons. Community development activities, particularly focused towards women, are undertaken for the people within the CA. The following are among the activities which have been proposed in Master plan: training for income generating activities (*e.g.* quilt making, tailoring); vaccination for livestock/ poultry. A family welfare centre/health clinic cannot be justified for 2,000 persons, but the shelter may house a roving centre which provides the facilities in the afternoon on a particular day of the week. A large proportion of the coastal population is engaged in fishing and fish processing. The cyclone shelter could be used for training classes for fishermen, and could also be used for net making. Some of the shelters could house post offices and public telephone facilities, which would also help during emergencies. While planning a multipurpose shelter, compatibility of the various activities which may be undertaken simultaneously must be ensured. For example, it would be difficult to combine a place for religious prayer (*e.g.* mosque), which requires a noise-free environment, with a school.

The vast majority of the rural population does not have access to recreation facilities. The shelter could be used as a community centre and provided with a television set. A review of the available technologies has shown that for meeting the lighting needs (a beacon light at top and room lights) a solar photovoltaic system is the most appropriate. The rural population, most of whom do not have electricity in their homes, would be attracted to this community facility at night and the television may be used not only for entertainment but also for educational purposes.

5. Conclusion

Recent experience in Bangladesh shows that construction of shelters has proved to be successful in protecting human lives in surge-prone areas. In order to maximize the returns from the relatively high investment necessary for shelters, multifarious use of the facilities during normal times would have to be ensured. Besides, experience shows that unless these shelters are used round the year, it would be difficult to maintain them. The Master Plan for Cyclone Shelters prepared by the BUET-BIDS Team estimated that in addition to the existing shelters and shelters under construction (total around 1,500), about 2,500 new shelters would be necessary to provide protection to around 4.3 million people (about 67 per cent of the projected population in the high risk area in the year 2002). Most of the 2,500 shelters necessary would be used as schools. In addition, other uses of these facilities for vocational training, community activities and income-generating activities have been suggested. An integrated solution where a shelter is located on elevated earthen platform *(killa)* which can be used for sheltering livestock, appears to be the preferred solution.

Construction of the network of shelters would prevent the loss of human lives and livestock during future cyclones and storm surges. Moreover, the normal time use of the facilities as educational institutions and other community development and income-generating activities can play a very important role in the socioeconomic development of the coastal areas of Bangladesh. Mitigating the effects of storm surges on Bangladesh and other vulnerable countries by following the strategy outlined above can make a significant impact reducing losses of human lives, properties, livestock, and in ensuring sustainable development.

6. Acknowledgment

The Master Plan for Cyclone Shelters was prepared in 1992 by a multidisciplinary team of experts drawn mainly from the Bangladesh University of Engineering and Technology and the Bangladesh Institute of Development Studies, under the overall guidance of an Interministrial Task Force of the Government of Bangladesh. The author was the Team Leader for the study.

7. References

1. Bangladesh University of University of Engineering and Technology (BUET)–Bangladesh Institute of Development Studies (BIDS), Multipurpose Cyclone Shelter Programme, Final Report (Dhaka, 1993), 12 vols.

2. Institution of Engineers of Bangladesh (IEB), Report of the Task Force on Cyclone and Storm Surge (Dhaka, 1991).

2

Management of Natural Disasters

Aminul Kawser Khan
Coordinator,
Emergency Support Corps, Bangladesh

1. Introduction

Bangladesh, a growing delta of 164000 sq. kilometer with 120 million people lies in the northeastern part of South Asia. India borders the Country in the west, north and northeast sides and Bay of Bengal in the South.

The country offers interesting trips through the rural countryside on boats plying on its innumerable myriad rivers, reputedly the longest beach in the world and the largest mangrove forest in the world, archaeological site of cultures dating back over 2000 years. It also has a fascinating architectural heritage, which includes the remains of ornately carved temples, beautiful centuries-old mosques and decaying mansions of 19th century maharajas.

The country is mostly riverine plain and flat, there are two major hilly areas. One is in the northeastern part, where tea estates dot the countryside. The other hilly area lies in the southeast side of the country, which is on the east of Chittagong and Cox's Bazaar, known as the Hill tracts, it is a surpassingly large of rolling hills covered with verdant tropical forests, populated with colorfully dressed tribal people.

2. Brief History

The history of Bangladesh has been one of extremes: of turmoil and peace, prosperity and destitution. It has thrived in the glow of cultural splendor and suffered under the ravages of war. Throughout its tumultuous history it has known internal warfare, suffered the rise and fall of mighty empires and several religions, and benefited from the trade and culture brought from foreign lands. Some medieval European geographers located paradise at the mouth of the Ganges, and although paradise was not found here, amazingly enough, Bengal was probably the wealthiest part of the subcontinent until the 16th century.

Stretching from the lower reaches of the Ganges River on the Bay of Bengal and to the north almost to the foothills of the Himalayan, the Bengal region of the subcontinent is the gateway to Myanmar (Burma) and South East Asia, controlling over it, vital to successive Indian empires. Its strategic position has ensured a place in the political, cultural and religious conflicts and developments of the subcontinent through the millennia.

3. Geographic Location and Environment

Bangladesh is geographically located in the delta region of three enormous rivers, only 8 per cent of whose catchment areas lie within her political boundaries. Most of the catchment areas of our rivers lie in the foot of the Himalyas. As a result by the time the rivers reach Bangladesh they have passed a long way. For various reasons including siltation the flow the rivers is reduced. Strikingly the flow of the Ganges down river during the dry season has dropped to about 15 per cent of its former level. If the situation continues to remain like this experts predict that in near future the flow during the dry season may completely stop.

The environmental consequences for Bangladesh are severe. Some rivers draining from the Ganges are now completely silted up in the dry season, losing all navigability. Reduced flow also increases saline intrusion from the Bay of Bengal in to the southwest, threatening the fragile ecology of the Sundarbans and reducing ground water levels. The most immediate effect is that thousands of hectors of land, which could formerly be irrigated for a third crop, now lay dry during the winter.

4. Disasters in the Country

We have experienced natural calamities of different proportions in the past. Bangladesh have a reputation of being a disaster prone country. It is evident that due to the geographical location Bangladesh is vulnerable to various natural disasters. One contributing factor to the vulnerability of the country is that more people occupy marginal and exposed land. Historically the country has four major climate- related hazards.

- Cyclone
- Flood
- Drought
- Tornado

Tornadoes strike occasionally and the devastation they bring is largely localized. Drought is more persistent and its effects are more extensive. Past experience prove that it has been a major killer. Floods are yearly occurrences. Cyclones and tidal surges are considered the most dangerous hazards.

The major natural & man made disasters which strike Bangladesh are given below:

Year	*Disaster*	*Death*
1644-45	Floods	+
1648	Floods	+
1769-70	Drought	+
1783-84	Drought	+
1797	Cyclone	+
1833	Earthquake	+
1822	Cyclone	40,000
1865-66	Drought in West Bengal, Present Bangladesh largely escaped	135,000
1871	Floods (Rajshahi)	+
1873-74	Drought	+
1876	Cyclone	100,000
1885	Floods (Rajshahi/Dinajpur)	+
1892	Floods (Rangpur/Dinajpur)	+
1896-97	Drought	+
1897	Earthquake	
1897	Cyclone	+
1898	Cyclone	175,000
1906-7	Floods in East Bengal	+
1901	Cyclone	+
1909	Cyclone (2)	+
1911	Cyclone	+
1917	Cyclone	+
1918	Earthquake	+
1918	Fl`oods	
1919	Cyclone	+
1922	Cyclone	+
1922	Flood	
1923	Cyclone	+
1926	Cyclone	
1936	Cyclone	+
1941	Cyclone	I
1942	Cyclone	+
1943-44	Drought, irregular rain, transport	
1943-44	dislocation and war, includes	3,000,000

Year	*Disaster*	*Death*
1943-44	West Bengal	
1947	Earthquake	+
1950	Earthquake	+
1954	Earthquake	+
1955	Floods	+
1957	Earthquake	+
1960	Cyclone (2)	11,149
1961	Cyclone	11,468
1963	Cyclone	11,520
1964	Cyclone	196
1965	Cyclone	19,270
1965	War	+
1966	Cyclone (2)	850
1969	Cyclone	75
1969	Tornado	922
1970	Cyclone	300,000
1971	Liberation war	3,000,000
1972	Drought	+
1973	Cyclone (2)	103
1974	Cyclone	20
1974	floods followed by famine	30,000
1975	Cyclone	5
1975	Floods	+
1977	Cyclone	I
1978-79	Drought	+
1981	Cyclone	2
1982	Drought	+
1983	Cyclone (2)	343
1984	Floods	+
1984	Cyclone	
1985	Cyclone	11,069
1986	Cyclone	14
1987	Floods	1,657
1988	Floods	2,379
1988	Cyclone	5,708
1989	Drought	+
1989	Tornado	800
1991	Cyclone	138,868
1994	Cyclone	+
1996	Tornado	545
1997	Cyclone	550
1998	Flood	1050

5. Seasonal Floods

During the monsoon seasons, around 70 per cent of the country appear to be under water. It is assumed that the flooding is due to heavy rainfall in the country during that time of the year. However, it has little to do with local rainfall because water comes mainly from Ganges, Meghna and the Bramhaputra rivers. For Bangladeshis, annual flooding is a fact of life. Wading through waist high water to the nearest tube well for drinking water is just part of living in difficult circumstances. Farmers regard much of the flooding, which affects about one third of the country, as beneficial replenishing soils with nutrients. It is when the rivers rise above their normal limits that problem arise.

In the devastating flood of 1988, all three of the country's major rivers reached flood levels at the same time. The devastation was enormous: some 2000 people drowned. The worst hit area was the small island near the edge of the Jamuna River, where hundreds of people were totally submerged. Even in Dhaka the capital city houses on fairly high ground were inundated and ZIA international airport was covered with water and had to be shut down.

It is observed that the climatic events seem to be worsening in intensity, duration and frequency in recent years. In 1998 the country experienced its worst flood since 1954. The floodwater covered about two-thirds of the country for three months, directly affecting the lives of more than twenty million people in both urban and rural communities. The flood caused major damage to the infrastructure and crops. Rice crops worth about $300 million were destroyed. People in the flood hit areas became homeless and faced acute shortages of food, shelter and employment. Many livestock died. There were widespread health epidemics and infectious diseases. Dhaka Metropolitan City was overrun with displaced families from rural, urban and peri-urban communities, most of whom were forced to live in temporary shelters.

This time the flood started much earlier than normal, beginning in mid-June and continued longer than normal, lasting for a total of three months. The intensity and duration of the flood did not only surpass previous floods but its course was quite unpredictable. Communities living in riverine areas and lowland depressions were most affected ones by the flood.

6. The Cyclones of 1970, 1991 and 1997

Bangladesh is in the worst area in the world for cyclones because of a unique combination of factors. They are: a large tide (five meter near Sandwip island) a funneling coast configuration which increases the height of waves, low flat terrain, and frequent severe tropical storm produce an average of one major cyclone every three years. The cyclone seasons are May to June and October to November, and the area where damage tends lo occur most frequently is in the east around Chittagong and Cox's bazaar.

The 1970 cyclone claimed 300,000 to 500,000 lives. Whereas the 1991 cyclone occurred at midnight when the month's peak high tied was very strong that affected over twice as many people and destroyed four times as many houses. However the death toll of between 140,000 to 200,000 was less than half that of 1970.

A major reason for the reduction of fatalities was the presence of storm shelters: a number of which had been constructed since 1970.

The 1997 cyclone is considered to be the worst Fortunately, the number of causality is relatively low.

7. The Great Indian earthquake of 1897

Bangladesh did not have an earthquake for so long that no one seems to take it seriously, but it is one of tile world's major earthquake zones and that a 'big one' is just waiting to happen.

This century Bangladesh has experienced seven earthquakes measuring more than seven on the Richter scale. The whopper is the 1897 earthquake, which had an epicenter 230 km. from Dhaka and reached 8.7 on the Richter scale. It was felt all over Bangladesh.

The wide swath of destruction leaves no doubt that Bangladesh is indeed in a major seismic zone and that earthquakes are high on the list of potential disasters for the country.

Recently two major issues are becoming alarming for the country. They are:

- Arsenic contamination in drinking water
- Earthquake

There is also one silent disaster which make a number of families homeless every year and that is **River erosion**.

8. Importance of Disaster Preparedness in Bangladesh

The scale of disaster in Bangladesh almost defines comprehension. Floods damage crops and other properties in some part of the country every year. Floods in 1988 captured world media headlines as the worst on record, but these were preceded by series of flood in 1954, 1955, 1956, 1962, 1963, 1968, 1970, 1971 1974, 1977 1980, 1984 and 1987. The 1974 flood was followed by a famine in which 30,000 people (GOB figure) died. Droughts occurred in 1972, 1978-79, 1982. A developing drought in April 1989 ended catastrophically for several villages northeast of Dhaka with a Tornado, which killed over a thousand people. Northern part of the country experienced drought most recently in 1995. The April 1991 cyclone again claimed worldwide attention as 138,000 persons perished along the Chittagong-Cox's Bazar coastline in the southeast part of the country. But it was not a unique event; thirteen tropical cyclones struck coastal areas between 1960 and 1970. In the November 1970 cyclone and storm surge an official report of 250,000 (unofficial figures of up to 500,000) people were dead.

The government has the primary responsibilities for making necessary arrangements in coping with disaster. It recognizes that additional assistance is needed from NGOs, private sectors, general public and donors. The Government of Bangladesh simply does not address effectively all the issues involved in disaster management due to lack of resources and skills. On the other hand the less literacy rate especially among the people staying in the vulnerable areas adds another hindrance for less awareness of the community on different disaster issues and coping system. Due to the lack of awareness and absence of functional structure the communities are not participating in the disaster preparedness and response at a larger rate. All the above threats and consequence extract a heavy tool that falls mostly on the poor–if they are not killed in the disaster itself they are likely to lose what few assets they have carefully accumulated. They have no access to the food during the disaster.

Even with the shortage of resources Bangladesh has developed a very good system in terms of disaster management. However a coordinated approach is needed to make it more efficient.

9. Early Warning

Bangladesh have good early warning system for cyclone. Two organizations named as "Bangladesh Meteorological Department" and "SPARRSO" is well connected with satellite system. They use NOA radar. Also within the country Bangladesh has established 14 observatory centers and five-radar centers to monitor the depression. Government centrally can announce the warning from the meteorological department. The warning is disseminated though radio and television. The local dialogue is also used for disseminating the warning. At the community level "The Cyclone Preparedness Program" disseminates the warnings to the community level using simple flag system. The standing order for cyclone of Government of Bangladesh supplements to evacuate the people to the safe places and shelters.

"Flood Forecasting Center" under the ministry of water management can provide warning 48 hour's ahead. It may be mentioned here that in country rain contributes only 8 per cent to the flood and the rest 92 per cent is due to water from the Himalayan region.

10. Coping with Flood: A Report

A roundtable discussion on "Coping with Floods: Relief, Rehabilitation and Rebuilding the Economy" was jointly organized by the Center for Alternatives and the Daily Star on 15 September at the IBA auditorium, DU. The objective of the roundtable was to bring together people from various sections to share their ideas, perceptions, and views on flood management. Since Bangladesh is a flood prone country and severe floods are likely to occur every few years, it is high time that flood management mechanisms, institutions and strategies are developed based on participatory process. The roundtable was divided into two sessions. The first session focused on strategies for relief distribution and post-flood rehabilitation. The second session was on reconstruction of Bangladesh economy. In both the sessions the floor was open for discussion and suggestions, which contributed much to the success of the roundtable. The recommendations that were made at the roundtable discussion can be divided into three categories: short-term, mid-term and long-term steps. However, these categories are closely interrelated and should be implemented simultaneously. These steps should not be viewed in isolation-they are parts of an integrated process needed for flood management

Immediate Steps

(a) Identifying Vulnerable Groups

The participants pointed out that it is often the adult and able-bodied men who form lines and take up positions at the front of the line, while the vulnerable groups stand at the end. Thus, it is the women, children and the elderly, who receive less or no aid and so on. As a result they become victims of various diseases. Participants urged that the relief workers should be aware of this.

(b) Need for People's Participation

Atiur Rahman of BIDS suggested that people's participation in the whole process of relief distribution is important in alleviating the miseries of the flood-affected people. Bangladesh do not have a social security system. But if a middle class family, which is not directly affected by the flood, could provide just one meal for five flood-affected families a day including some necessary items, it could generate a feeling of empathy and this example would motivate others to come forward.

(c) Need for Social Mapping

The participants pointed out the need for creating a 'social vulnerability map', containing basic facts about flood affected areas. As the magnitude of loss is not the same in the entire flood affected areas the need will vary accordingly. Moreover, a social vulnerability map also helps in identifying remote areas, which are often left out or neglected by relief workers. Absence of social vulnerability maps creates chances of distribution or misuse of relief goods. Therefore, such a map would help in assessing the appropriate needs of the people.

(d) Preventing Politically Motivated Use of Relief

Regarding relief distribution, the participants identified another problem, *i.e.* the 'politically motivated use of relief.' The politicians have a tendency to divert relief indiscriminately to their respective constituencies without considering whether or to what extent relief is needed. In this process, sometimes the more needy areas are often neglected and granted less aid than the less needy areas.

(e) Scarcity of Safe Drinking Water

Participants mentioned that ironically the acute shortage of safe drinking water was the main cause of sufferings for the flood victims. Efforts were taken to distribute water-purifying tablets (WPT) among the flood-affected people by government and NGOs. However, very little information was provided to the flood victims about the potency, methods of using WPT (water quantity, contact time). Some of the participants (from Oxfam, Red Cross) pointed out that most of the WPT distributed were ineffective because their expiry date was over. In all the cases the recipients were not aware of this and the expiry labels were torn off from the bottles. So awareness needs to be raised about the proper use and shelf life of WPT.

(f) Combating Water Borne Diseases

The scarcity of safe drinking water is inter-linked with water borne diseases, which are common phenomena of the flood-affected regions. Diseases like diahorrea, dysentery, scabies, skin diseases are already evident in relief centers. While confronting the challenges, several problems were identified in this field. First of all, there was a shortage of adequate ORS, WPT and other related medicines. Apart from resource constraints, participants stated that there was a shortage of skil1ed medical persons for treating the afflicted persons. Participants stressed that the people need to be made aware of the proper ways of using WPT, bleaching powder and water cans. They also need to be made aware of ways to prevent water borne diseases and prepare cures at home. The electronic and the print media can play a vital role in this regard.

(g) Including A Gender Perspective

Some of the participants drew attention to some specific gender needs such as being aware about tile needs of women and the socio-cultural constraints which they face while receiving relief. Women do not push and shove with men, insecurity of women in the flood shelters and violence against women. Women are the worst victims of flood, and they suffer the most because of gender biased relief and rehabilitation strategies and plans. Several participants pointed out that there was a lack of adequate security measures for women living in flood shelters. (Flood center run by the imam of Tara Mosque can serve as a model, the women slept separately– the older women from and circle around the younger women). Hasna Hena of World Food Program spccifical1y mentioned the lack of sanitation facilities for women in flood-affected areas. The women in the flood-affected areas had to wait till dark to respond to the call of nature as the toilets and bushes all had gone under water. The relief workers, rehabilitation and disaster management planners should take these facts into account.

11. Impact of the Socio-Economic Structure of the Country

All the disaster has a negative impact on the socio-economic structure of the country. Flood cyclone, tornado devastate the infrastructure, cause a great loss in the agricultural sector, make people homeless and cause unemployment. All these effect the economy of the country. It is the prime responsibility of the government to assist the people to go back to their normal life, which includes emergency support and rehabilitation.

12. Impact on Environment and Ecology

Cyclone has the most diversified and dramatic impact on environment and ecology. During cyclone the water surges from the sea brings huge saline water in to the main land. The saline water destroys the agricultural land, damages the fish culture and contaminates the water sources. Also, the heavy wind during the cyclone uproots trees.

13. Mitigation/Protectation Measures

Mostly the dam and embankment had been constructed to save the main land from water surge and flood. However, these measures some times create the adverse environmental problem. The increased number of river erosion is one of the outcomes of that. Rivers are changing their course.

14. Regional Initiative

A number of regional initiatives had been initiated by the private sectors. Most of them are working in research and advocacy. The Governments of India and Bangladesh also established the joint river commission, which is working only in water sharing. One initiative had been taken by "South Asian Regional Cooperation" (SARC) which is SARC meteorological department. Unfortunately the outcomes are not effective in disaster management

15. Government of Bangladesh

The Government of Bangladesh established Ministry of Disaster Management and Relief to look after the whole disaster paradigm. The Disaster Management Bureau had been established under the ministry to take care of preparedness issues. Number of disaster management committees had been formed from central level to local level for awareness, evacuation, and emergency support and rehabilitation activities.

16. NGO Activities

Non Government Organizations (NGO) are actively working in the process of management of various forms of natural disasters. The work is done in various levels. NGOs are working in constructing and reconstructing embankment. They are working at the community level in forestation and also working on building awareness regarding disaster in the community levels. They are working on mobilizing the volunteers and also skill building for them. Even small groups are developing their skills in facing disaster effectively. As disaster preparedness measure NGOs are working in land rising programs and construction of shelter. In the post flood relief and rehabilitation phase NGOs are working in distributing food, medicine and seed at the community level. They have programs on drinking water and sanitation.

17. Recommendation

- Upgrading the existing satellite image receiving and analyzing facilities.
- Use GIS in risk analysis and need assessment
- Establishment of countrywide radio networks from vulnerable union to thana to district and to central level
- Identify and established user friendly warning system.
- Integration of disaster analysis in ongoing development activities.
- Establishment of effective system of coordination between Government and NGOs.

3

S&T Initiatives for Natural Hazard Mitigation

K. R. Gupta and R. K. Midha
Earth System Science Division,
Department of Science and Technology, New Delhi, India

1. Introduction

Over the years, study of the interactions among the various components of the earth system–lithosphere, hydrosphere, biosphere & atmosphere has gained considerable importance as these interactions influence global change on a variety of spatial and temporal scales. Recent devastating earthquakes and the heavy loss of life in other destructive events like cyclones, floods and landslides, make it imperative for us to actively seek the reasons and remedies of these physical processes by devising reliable means of understanding of natural hazards and their mitigation. There has been a growing awareness of the need to focus more attention on Disaster Preparedness and Prevention, and recognition of the fact that Disaster Prevention and Pre-disaster planning should be an integral part of the national development policy.

In the recent times, the Indian landmass has been severely affected by various natural disasters like floods, cyclones, droughts, earthquakes and landslides. These disasters have taken a heavy toll of life and property and have adversely affected the economic and social development of the country. The Himalayan terrain is prone to earthquakes and landslides, the coastal belt to cyclones and the Indo-Gangetic-Brahamputra plains to recurring floods. The annual losses in India due to natural disasters are estimated to exceed Rs. 10,000 crores.

The Government through its various departments and agencies like India Meteorological Department, Central Water Commission, Ministry of Agriculture, Department of Space, Ministry of Science and Technology and National Informatics Centre have taken advantage of the new developments in science, technology and communication facilities to upgrade the preparedness and mitigation strategies and thereby reduce the impact of natural disasters (Mandal, 1992; Sudhindra, 1992; Seshagiri, 1992). A National Centre for Disaster Management has been set up under the auspices of the Ministry of Agriculture to train the State and district level officials in the modem methods of response and relief. The Department of Science &. Technology (DST) has evolved national coordinated programmes on the study of earthquakes, landslides and atmospheric sciences/ climate research. Initiatives of DST in Natural Disasters Mitigation have been highlighted recently (Midha,1998; Midha, 1999). The India Meteorological Department is upgrading the cyclone monitoring capabilities through the deployment of Doppler radars along the coastal tracts. Information dissemination facilities are being upgraded using satellite communication network.

The present paper gives a glimpse of the studies carried out on various Natural Hazards in India such as cyclones, floods, seismic and landslide hazards etc. The S&T initiatives by the Department of Science &. Technology in various fields of earth system science have also been highlighted. The present paper has heavily drawn from the recent publications of Department of Science &. Technology, Government of India as well as from Midha (1998, 1999).

2. Geological Framework

The Indian sub-continent is made up of 3 major physiographic provinces; the Himalaya, the Indo-Gangetic Plain (IGP), and the Peninsular Shield, all of which are characterised by distinctive geomorphic, structural, stratigraphic and deep crustal features. While the Himalaya is a region of dominant compressional tectonics belonging to continent to continent collision regime, the IGP is a region of recent sedimentation which has witnessed Quaternary movements. The peninsular India is marked by early Archaean cratonisation with associated Proterozoic mobile belts. The distinctive characteristics of these physiographic divisions are reflected in the diverse geologic history of the regions, Mahadevan (1994). These distinctive characteristics have great bearing both on the origin and impact of natural hazards which affect the Indian subcontinent.

3. Cyclone Hazard in India

Tropical Cyclones (TCs) are the intense atmospheric vortices with their genesis related to warm tropical oceans. They are like big heat engines transporting energy from oceanic surface to the upper atmosphere and surroundings. The primary energy source for tropical cyclones is provided by underlying seawater in the form of latent heat.

Indian Coast particularly the eastern coast is highly prone to tropical cyclones and associated surges. These cyclones are the worst natural hazard, affecting the Indian coastal regions, some of which have proved to be devastating in terms of loss of life, cattle and destruction of property.

Tropical cyclones, affecting the Indian subcontinent are generally formed over the south-east Bay of Bengal in the pre-monsoon (March-June) and the post-monsoon periods (October-December). The Bangladesh cyclone of 1970 and the Andhra cyclone of 1977 caused huge loss of life and property. Enormous potential of TCs for damage and loss of life is due to copious rainfall (250-500 mm) and violent winds (50m/s and higher) occurring in its eye-wall; in coastal regions it is mainly due to induced storm surges (1.5-5m). Immense social and economical benefits can be derived by accurate predictions of track, intensity, land-fall and the region of heavy rainfall associated with tropical cyclones.

After the great killer Andhra Pradesh cyclone of November 1977 and on the recommendation of the National Committee on Science & Technology, the DST had constituted a Cyclone Review Committee (CRC) at the national level to review present status of cyclone prediction. Cyclone warning system, telecommunication facilities to disseminate the warnings, community preparedness and suggest a National Cyclone Code and Cyclone Plan for the country. This Committee submitted a comprehensive report in May 1984 with a large number of recommendations. The main report of the CRC (DST, 1986) has been divided in a number of sections covering the following aspects:

- Organisation for formulation, implementation and periodic review of the Cyclone Plan for India.
- Demarcation of cyclone prone areas of coastal India and consideration of terrains and seasons.
- Cyclone detection, observation and tracking methods and facilities in India.
- The Cyclone Warning System (CWS) in India
- Suggestions for formulation of a National Cyclone Code (NCC) for India and Cyclone Emergency Action Plans (CEAPs) for the coastal states. .
- Suggestions for a Community Preparedness Plan against Cyclone (CPPC) threats and hazards for coastal communities in India
- Cyclone Research and Training.

The Scientific Advisory Committee to the Cabinet (SACC) considered the above report during December 1984 and directed DST to implement the recommendations. It was suggested that for the convenience of concerned Central and State Government agencies the report may be split into a number of operative parts relevant to various Central and State Government agencies.

Accordingly, the Report was split into three operative volumes incorporating only the essential write ups and the recommendations to be implemented by the Central Government Ministries/Department's (Vol. I), Coastal State Governments (Vol. II) and India Meteorological Department (Vol. III). A number of follow up actions have been taken by the concerned Departments both at the central level and the state level and the recommendations are at various levels of implementation.

The super cyclonic storm that struck the coast of Orissa on 29 October 1999 has taken a toll of more than 9600 human lives. It is termed as one of the most severe cyclonic storms that hit India's coasts in this century with high winds estimated upto 260 km/hr. In terms of damage it has surpassed the Orissa cyclone which hit the coast near Paradip on 30 October 1971 and the Andhra cyclone of 19 November 1977, each killing about 10000 people. Among natural calamities, tropical cyclones are known to claim a high share of deaths and destruction the world over. About 3,00,000 lives were lost in one of the most severe cyclones that hit East Pakistan (now Bangladesh) in November 1970.

India Meteorological Department holds the responsibility for issuing advance warnings on tropical cyclones, an adverse weather phenomenon affecting the country. Nature of cyclonic disturbances, their destructive features, the observing system employed for their detection and study, the telecommunication network used for transmission of observed data in real time and disseminating the meteorological data, the techniques used in forecasting intensity and track of a cyclone and the cyclone warning systems have been discussed in a recent paper (Bhatnagar, 1999).

The IMD supports a country-wide network of stations for Collection for synoptic meteorological data consisting of 559 surface observations and 100 upper air observations (65 pilot balloon and 35 radiosonde/radiowind observatories). There are 71 current weather observatories and 17 X-band radars mostly at the airports specifically for aviation meteorology. The frequency of observations is twice daily, 3 hourly or depending on the requirement.

To help detection and tracking of cyclones, IMD maintains a network of ten Cyclone Detection Radars, each with a range of 400 km covering the entire coastline of India.

The main facility at present being used by IMD for monitoring cloud imagery is based on INSAT Application Programme which includes meteorological support for meeting IMD's requirement of weather analysis and forecasting.

Operational track prediction is done in IMD using statistical models based on climatology, persistence, CLIPER, analogue, synoptic techniques and Numerical Weather Prediction (NWP) model.

Keeping in view the complex nature and present state-of-the-art understanding and prediction of TCs, the following topics have been identified as thrust areas for future research in the vision paper on atmospheric sciences:

- Installing of Doppler radar along the Indian coast.
- Development of a three-dimensional cyclone model for simulation and prediction.
- Study of the organisation of meso-scale moist convection and its interaction with cyclones.
- Determination of the physical factors or synoptic features favourable for the development of cyclone over Indian seas.
- Deeper study for understanding recurvature and looping of cyclones.
- Enhancement of knowledge of the formation, and maintenance of the cyclone eye.

- Improved storm surge estimates using more realistic models; and
- Possible acquisition of multi-sensor instrumented aircraft for cyclone probing in order to determine its three-dimensional dynamic and thermodynamic structure over the Indian seas.

An adequate chain of coastal radars and geostationary satellite (INSAT) are available for detecting and tracking of cyclones over Indian seas. IMD has a programme to install Doppler weather radars along the coasts, which would produce extremely valuable detailed information about the dynamical changes in die evolving tropical cyclone as it approaches the coast. An accurate three-dimensional structure of TCs while over the Indian Ocean is a pre-requisite for a better understanding of their evolution and or accurate numerical predication of their track and intensity. It can be only obtained by multi-sensor aircraft probing, but at present lacking in the country. The availability of coastal Doppler radars would, for the first time produce data on the changing circulation of tropical cyclones.

4. Flood Hazards in India

Flood hazards has long been recognized as, one of the most recurring, widespread and disastrous natural hazards affecting several densely populated regions of India. Since the time immemorial, monsoon floods in the Ganga and the Brahmaputra Basins have brought severe havoc resulting in loss of life, cattle standing crops and property. India is subjected to some of the World 's most intense flood-generating rainfalls. Moreover, physiographic factors locally enhance the transformation of this rainfall into high-magnitude run off events.

With significant variability in monsoon rainfall from year to year and region to region, India is known as the land of floods and droughts. Estimates indicate that about 40 million hectares of land is prone to floods (RBA 1980), and annually about 7.5 million hectares of land experiences devastation due to monsoon floods. Floods in India usually occur during the summer monsoon months and cause extensive damages in terms of life and property. The Indian states of Uttar Pradesh, Bihar, West Bengal, Orissa and Assam experiences floods and flood related devastation frequently.

Systematic records of floods are available for only a few Indian rivers since the beginning of this century (or slightly earlier), but for most rivers gauge data are available since 1940s or since 1970s. These records are too short to analyze the flooding characteristics of the Indian rivers. Nevertheless the limited systematic records along with historical records suggest that some of most severe floods have occurred in the last few decades. In this regard, the 1962 flood on Brahmaputra, the 1978 flood on Ganga, the 1982 flood on Mahanadi, the 1970 flood on Narmada and the 1986 flood on Godavari are noteworthy (Kale, 1998).

Although floods are an integral feature of the Indian rivers, available data indicate that some rivers experience floods more frequently than the others. From the standpoint of frequency of large floods as well as the extent of flood damages, the river systems in India have been broadly divided into two major groups Rashtriya Barh Ayog or National Flood Commission (RBA, 1980)

1. Rivers of the Himalayan region which experience heavy floods more frequently, and
2. Rivers of the Indian Peninsula that experience devastation floods less frequently

The high Himalayan Mountains form an effective barrier to the southwest monsoon. This is responsible for massive and intense precipitation in the catchment areas of the rivers of the Himalayan region, such as the Ganga and Brahmaputra and their tributaries. Often, therefore, the river channel carrying capacity is exceeded and the rivers overflow their banks causing inundation, bank erosion and extensive damages to crops and structures on the floodplains. In comparison, the rivers of the Indian Peninsula have adequate channel carrying capacity and therefore experience floods less frequently.

Since early 1950s state-wise data regarding area affected by floods, population affected by floods, crop area affected by floods, number of cattle and human lives lost, etc. have been collected. These data indicate that while there bas been a noteworthy increase in the population affected by floods, the flood-affected area does seem to have increased either in terms of frequency or magnitude (Agarwal and Narain, 1991; Kale, 1998). This is contrary to the widely held view that the flood situation in India is deteriorating. Statistical analysis or the available data also do not suggest that the frequency or flooding has increased in recent years (Kale, 1998).

5. Causes of Floods

The occurrence of floods is attributed to meteorological, geomorphic and anthropogenic causes.

(a) Meteorological causes

Large floods on Indian rives are a direct result of excessive rainfall during the monsoon season (Ramaswamy, 1987). Such intense precipitation is associated with active monsoon conditions or intense cyclonic storms. Cyclones and depression have been responsible for some of the most unusual floods that have occurred in this century. For example, the 1978 catastrophic flood on Ganga, the 1968 flood on Teesta and Tapi and the 1970 flood on Narmada were associated with cyclonic storms developed over the Bay of Bengal.

In the Gangetic basin particularly in the parts of eastern U.P. and north Bihar plains overbank flooding is a very dominant and frequent phenomenon. This particular phenomenon influences other fluvial processes operating in the area such as bank erosion, channel morphology changes, sediment transport behaviour and the overall floodplain evolution (Sinha & Jain, 1 998). Many of these processes add to the severity of the flooding effects in the region.

(b) Geomorphic Causes

The Himalaya constitutes one of the most geomorphica1ly dynamic landscape and the rivers flowing through such a dynamic environment have a potential danger of catastrophic floods due to breaching of natural dams. Landslides, triggered by heavy rains and earthquakes or surging glaciers are known to block rivers that cause massive floods when they fail. Breach floods have been recorded on many Himalayan rivers such as Indus, Shyok, Sutlej, Bhagirathi, Alaknanda Brivehganga, Teesta & Subansini (Khan, 1969; Starkel, 1972; Wadia 1975; Mohan, 1982; Sharma, 1992; Sahai *et al.*, 1997). Channel migration, meander growth and avulsion may also affect water levels during peak: floods.

Natural changes in the elevation of river channels due to variations in sediment transport can also increase or decrease the flood levels and/or area affected by floods.

Earthquakes can have a dramatic effect on the conveyance of water and sediments and in turn, can affect the water levels during peak floods. Earthquakes have also resulted for changes in the river courses and profiles of some rivers. The 1897 earthquake m Assam, for instance, raised the river bed by several meters and caused extensive flooding. A similar disturbance after the 1950 earthquake led to increased flooding in the following period (Kale, 1998). It is evident that the lowest water level rose by about 3 m as a result of earthquake (Goswami, 1998).

(c) Anthropogenic Causes

As a part of developmental activities, there have been considerable anthropogenic effects on the riverine environment particularly by way of changes in land use, large-scale deforestation in the catchment areas and the building activity in the flood plains. Construction of dams, barrages, embankments and other engineering work has not only modified the natural behaviour of the rivers, but it has also added a new dimension to the problem of flooding *e.g.* dam failures and breaching of dam in MP, AP, Rajasthan etc.

In addition to meteorological causes, floods in the Indian region have been generated by failure of man-made and natural dams. Floods related to failure of landslides and glacial dams are quite common in the Himalayan region. Apart from these factors, earthquakes in the Himalayan region have also contributed to flooding by raising the bed-level of the river channels.

6. Flood Disaster Management Strategies

In the last fifty years several programmes to control floods and to minimise the flood damages have been implemented. The programmes include structural and non-structural measures. The structural measures that have been adopted so far include:

- Construction of embankments and dikes
- Widening or deepening of channels to increase the carrying capacity of rivers.
- Construction of diversion channels to carry excess flood water
- Construction of dams to store flood waters

Available data indicate that while during the pre-independence period only about five thousand kilometers of embankments existed in India, the length of embankments has increased by three times to about sixteen thousand kilometers by mid-1990s. In addition to these, over 5000 villages have been raised or protected from floods. As a result of these flood management and control programmes about 14 million hectares of land has benefited.

However, the experience of past five decades in India has indicated that the structural measures have not been able to effectively control floods on some of the most flood-prone rivers in India. Goswami (1992 a and 1992 b) has stressed that as a national approach to flood problems in the northeast region posed by Brahmaputra River System, zonal planning based on the concept of watershed management appears to hold much promise.

7. Flood Damage

The Central Water Commission has been collecting flood damage data since 1953 annually. It has been reported than as an average area affected by flood annually is about 7.5 ha, of which crop area is about 3.5 ha an average 1,5 29 human lives and 9,40 00 heads of cattle every year (Chaudhuri and Rajan, 1999). It has been estimated that the total loss an account of flood damage in Rs. 52660 crores during the period 1953 to 1998 (yearly average; Rs. 1155 crores).

8. Flood Forecasting & Warning

In recent years non-structural measures of flood management and control have been adopted. These measures include flood forecasting, flood inundation mapping and flood zoning. Efforts have been made to map the areas affected by floods in different parts of the country. The Central Water Commission (CWC) and the National Atlas and Thematic Organization (NATMO) have prepared and published such maps.

The Central Water Commission (CWC) of India has established a flood forecasting and warning network. This organisation is presently responsible for issuing flood forecasts at 157 stations of which 132 stations are for riverstage forecast and 25 for inflow forecast (Chaudhuri and Rajan, 1999). The 62 streams covered by the above flood forecasting are located in the major river systems as given below:

Sl. No.	*River System*	*No. of FF Stations*
1	Ganga- Brahmaputra-Meghna System	109
2	West flowing rivers	15
3	The Krishna Basin	8
4	Mahanadi Basin	3
5	Eastern Rivers	9
6	The Godavari Basin	13
	Total	**157**

The warning system has significantly aided in reducing the flood damages in the last fifteen years.

Remote Sensing techniques have proved to be very useful in providing information on the areas inundated by floods and in the estimation of flood damages in recent years. Indian Remote Sensing Satellites (IRS) series and ERS satellite data have been used successfully to monitor and map floods in near real-time as well to asses the damages caused .by floods, especially in the Ganga and Brahmaputra Basins (Rao *et al.*, 1998).

In spite of the numerous structural and non-structural measures adopted in the last fifty years, floods have continued to cause severe damages to life and property. It bas therefore been suggested that river-friendly schemes that recognize the environmental value of floods deserve greater attention in all the future flood control programmes (Kale, 1998).

Ministry of Agriculture, Govt. of India has prepared a contingency action plan for natural calamities including floods. In this action plan, duties and responsibilities of each Govt. department and non-governed organisations have been defined.

Proper integration of flood forecasting system with disaster mitigation measures can go a long way to flood damage reduction. Community participation is a vital element in any flood disaster mitigation strategy.

9. Some Issues

- ❖ Strengthening of flood forecasting and warning systems through application of sophisticated technologies like satellite remote sensing, computer based mathematical watershed modelling and telemetric methods of real time data collection and transmission etc. are essential for meeting the challenge posed by flood hazard. Flood plain zone based remotely sensed data using modern techniques like GIS provides an effective tool for management of floods (Goswami, 1998).
- ❖ With the availability of multiple satellite data from IRS series Landsat and ERS, it is now possible to monitor flood situation in a particular basin. Remote sensing has emerged as the most powerful tool to prepare flood inundation maps in near real-time, which can be effectively used for relief management (Rao *et al.*, 1998).
- ❖ The flood hazards are very diverse complex and multi-disciplinary problem and the scientific understanding of the phenomena has been severely hampered by short or non-existent data. Availability of reliable and upto date hydrological data base is very crucial for carrying out realistic assessment of the flood hazard and formulation of effective remedial measures.
- ❖ Floods can be studied in a naturalistic/interpretative manner, reading the natural indicators of their occurrence (Baker, 1998). Accordingly. Palaeoflood studies in different basins need to be accelerated.
- ❖ Need for regional and international cooperation for taking flood hazard is very important.

10. DST Initiative in Atmospheric Sciences/Climate Research

For the last one decade, DST's Earth System Science (ESS) Division has supported Research & Development (R&D) projects in a number of areas of atmospheric sciences, such as Atmospheric and Oceanic Modelling, Numerical Weather Prediction (NWP), Upper Ocean Layer Thermal Monitoring using XBTs Climate Studies, Glaciology, Land Surface Process and Modelling, Agrometeorology and Atmospheric Development Programmes (such as Radio Acoustic Sounding System (RASS), Doppler Radars, LIDARs, etc.). Two major field experiments, *viz.* Monsoon Trough Boundary Layer Experiment (MONTBLEX; 1989-90) and the Land Surface Process Experiment (LASPEX; 1996-97), were hailed as successful multi-agency and multi-disciplinary coordinated field observational programmes. DST established in 1987 the National Centre for Medium Range Weather Forecasting (NCMRWF) with supercomputing facility, specially targeted to provide agromet forecasts on scale. All these efforts have produced excellent results not only in the form of research publications and observational advancements; but also helped the atmospheric and oceanic science research scientists/organisations in India to work in a multi-agency and multi-disciplinary coordinated manner.

The following major thrust areas in atmospheric sciences have been identified in the Vision Paper for R&D in Earth & Atmospheric Sciences (DST, 1998):

- Climate: Observation, Theory and Modelling,
- Severe Weather Systems,
- Middle and Upper Atmosphere,
- Boundary layer and Land-Ocean Surface Processes,
- Observing Systems, Data Archival and Dissemination

Observations, analyses, computer simulation, modelling and theoretical studies on the Indian climate system need due emphasis. In this Context in-depth research is envisaged in the following areas with emphasis on climate variability over the Indian region on intra-seasonal interannual and decadal scales.

- Climate modelling
- Monsoons
- Climatic teleconnections
- Predictability of weather and climate
- Climatic changes,
- Socio-economic impact of climate change

Recognising the importance of climate research in the country, the Department of Science & Technology has nurtured research and development in this field for over two decades. Recently, **INDIAN CLIMATE RESEARCH PROGRAMME (ICRP)** has been concretised by the DST. The ICRP Science Plan (DST, 1996) reviews in detail the outstanding problems in meteorology, physical oceanography and the large-scale air-sea interactions that need to be addressed to understand and ultimately predict the intra-seasonal inter-annual and decadal scales of climate variability over the Indian region. The broad objectives of the ICRP are:

1. Understanding the physical processes responsible for variability on sub-seasonal, inter-annual, decadal, centennial and longer time-scales of the

monsoon, the oceans (specifically the Indian seas and the equatorial Indian Ocean) and the coupled atmosphere-ocean-land system by:

(*a*) Analysis of existing observations from conventional and space-based platforms

(*b*) Development and implementation of new surface-based and space-based observational techniques.

(*c*) Special observational experiments over critical regions such as the Bay of Bengal and the monsoon trough zone, and

(*d*) Development and investigations of a hierarchy of models of atmosphere, ocean and coupled ocean-atmosphere systems

2. Study of the space-time variations of the monsoon from sub-seasonal to inter-annuals scales for development of methods for prediction for appropriate scales.
3. Study of change in climate and its variability generated by natural and anthropogenic factors.
4. Investigation of the links between climate variability and critical resources such as agricultural productivity to provide a basis for deriving agricultural strategies for maximising the sustainable yield in the face of climate variability and for realistic assessment of impact of climate change.

After an exhaustive overview of monsoon variability, ocean variability, climate change, variability and impact, the ICRP Science Plan lists the outstanding problems in the atmosphere (nature of convection over the ocean and convection over land, ocean fluxes and sea surface temperature, ocean dynamics, heat and fresh water transport and climate change variability and impact. Following the Science Plan, the Implementation Plan (1998) of the ICRP focuses on observational programmes and observational experiments linked with monsoon variability (MONVAR) modelling and diagnostic studies, past climate and climate variability and Agriculture (CLIMAG).

After a series of meetings concerning the implementation of the ICRP with regard to the observational experiments on Monsoon Variability (MONVAR) component of the ICRP, the following field programmes have been proposed.

1. Bay of Bengal Monsoon Experiment (BOBMEX)
2. Arabian Sea Monsoon Experiment (ARMEX)
3. Off Shore Trough Experiment (OSTEX)
4. Continental Tropical Convergence Zone (CTCZ)
5. Circulation, Hydrology and Thermodynamics of North India Ocean (CHATNI) consisting of SECTIONS on deep circulation and trace western boundary currents (DWBC).

The ICRP Ocean-Atmosphere draft implementation plan has been concretised with the following major objectives:

- To document and understand the interaction between the upper-oceans and the monsoonal atmosphere in the Indian region.

- To understand the circulation, hydrology and thermodynamics of the north Indian ocean, including the coastal and deep ocean, and the role of the atmosphere in the heat and water balance.

To meet these objectives, the observation programme will rely on continuous monitoring and specific field experiments. Satellite data form an important part of the observations, and a major goal of the ocean-atmosphere *in-situ* measurements is to provide sea truth for the remotely sensed data. A combination of satellite and *in-situ* observation is essential for meeting the two major objectives listed above.

The Bay of Bengal and Monsoons Programme (BOBMON), recently initiated by DST with the involvement of a number of scientists and institutions, has two major parts, namely a study of air-sea coupling over the Bay, and study related to full depth circulation including the heat and slat balance of the Bay.

The Recent initiatives by DST in atmospheric sciences and climatic research will greatly help in understanding the physical processes thereby helping in efforts in cyclone, floods and other climate related hazards.

11. Seismic Hazard

The Himalayan region is unique in this respect, having been the site of 4 great earthquakes of magnitude between the period 1897 and 1950; Shillong earthquake, 1897, Kangra earthquake, 1905, Bihar-Nepal earthquake, 1934 and the India-China border earthquake, 1950. Several damaging earthquakes of magnitude 7 and above have occurred in the Himalayan terrain.

The major structural feature appearing to control the seismicity of Himalayan region consists of a series of NW-SE trending linear thrust belts; the most important of them being the Main Boundary Thrust (MBT) in the South and the Main Central Thrust (MCT) in the North. The small to moderate magnitude earthquakes tend to get concentrated in this 50-KM wide belt. The NW-SE trending thrust belts are intercepted by a series of NE-SW trending faults; dividing the terrain into discrete crustal blocks with similar seismic behaviour, Narula *et al.* (1992). Many plate tectonic models have been proposed to explain the evolution of the Himalaya and related seismic characteristics. The common elements of these models, characterised as steady state and evolutionary, are a subducting slab, the Indian Shield; the overriding slab, the Tethyan slab and a sedimentary wedge contained between and decoupled from the two converging slabs. The great earthquakes occur at the detachment surface between the under-thrust Indian plate and the upper Himalayan blocks.

The Indo-Gangetic plains, a zone of thick sedimentary sequence and high population concentration, have borne the impact of earthquakes originating in the Himalayan terrain. The thick sedimentary pile inhibits location of seismic observatories in the region and, therefore, the seismicity of IGP is not well investigated. However, the NE-SW trending structural features abutting against the orthogonal Himalayan trend have been the locale of several low magnitude earthquakes. The contiguity to the Himalayan region, the nature of the sediments and the observed neo-tectonic activity, Singh (1996), make the region highly vulnerable to earthquake damage, especially through local site effects like soil liquefaction, witnessed in the great Bihar earthquake, 1934 and subsequently in the smaller 1988 Bihar earthquake.

The peninsular India has long been thought to be stable and generally seismic although the zone of Narmada-Son rift running across the peninsular India has a history of earthquake activity. However, since the occurrence of magnitude 6.3 earthquake at Koyna on 10th December 1967, the long held 'stable' notion about the peninsular shield has been under review by the earth scientists. It is now being increasingly recognised that peninsular India has had its share of earth movements, in Tertiary and Quaternary, although somewhat different from those, which have affected the extra-peninsular region. While the lateral operating forces were responsible for folding, thrusting and rise of the Himalaya, the youthful character of the Western ghat has suggested the operation of epi-orogenic forces causing vertical uplift of the rigid continental mass as a whole leaving the cover rocks undisturbed, giving the impression of apparent stability Radhakrishna (1993). The occurrence of Latur earthquake in Maharashtra on September 29,1993 and the 21st May, 1997 earthquake in Jabalpur, Madhya Pradesh have strengthened the emerging impression that weak to moderate seismic activity has been prevalent in Peninsular Shield, Ramalingeswar Rao *et al.* (1984).

It is thus apparent from the foregoing that the entire Indian landmass is prone to seismic hazard of varying degrees. A macro level seismic zoning map has been prepared by the Bureau of Indian Standards; IS 1893-1984. This map has classified the country into five seismic zones based on experienced as well as expected probable intensities on the 12 point MM intensity scale. Zone V with probable intensity of IX and above covers an area of 12 per cent, Zone IV with probable intensity of VIII covers 18 per cent and Zone III with probable intensity of VII covers 26 per cent of the land area of India. In these three zones, destruction and substantial damage to structures and systems is probable. Thus about 56 per cent of India is susceptible to earthquake damage.

It may be noted that the Latur earthquake of 30th September 1993 occurred in Zone I of the Zonal Map and had a maximum intensity of VIII. It was thus a very unexpected event. Since the occurrence of this earthquake there have been discussions about revising the Seismic Zoning Map, which was last revised in 1970. Since 1970, major upgradation in the instrumental coverage of the Himalayan and Peninsular Shield areas has taken place, principally through the initiatives of DST, generating both, weak and strong motion data. It is, therefore, considered appropriate that advantage is taken of the new data to review the Seismic Zoning. In addition, an account has to be taken of the collateral physical, socio- economic and demographic data to arrive at a more realistic assessment of the distribution of seismic hazard; not forgetting at the same time that upgrading the seismicity of any region has important economic connotations. Increasing population and rapid urbanisation have considerably enhanced the vulnerability and the associated seismic risk to human life and property, Arya (1989), Khattri (1992,1998). There is, therefore, an urgent need to translate the results of studies on seismology into civil engineering practices. The Ministry of Urban Affairs, GOI has recently prepared a Vulnerability Atlas giving State and district-wise hazard to buildings and other infrastructure due to natural disasters. Guidelines for hazard resistant constructions and land use zoning have also been suggested, Arya *et al.* (1997,1998).

Initiatives By DST

12. Earthquake Studies

(a) Himalayan Region

As outlined above, the Himalayan region is unique in its geologic evolution, seismic history and earthquake, risk potential. Recognising these features, the Department of Science and Technology has evolved a national coordinated programme on the Seismicity and Seismotectonics of the Himalayan Region, Gupta, (1992). The studies are concentrated in the NW and NE, Himalaya covering partly the gap areas between the 1905 and 1934 great earthquakes and the Assam gap. Well designed seismic networks have been set up in Himachal Pradesh, the hills of Uttar Pradesh, Bihar and North-East Region so as to lower the detection and location threshold to magnitude 3.5 earthquakes. This complements the activities of India Meteorological Department (IMD), which maintains the national network of seismological observatories at an average spacing of about 300 Km and provides operational service to the Government. Under DST support, observatories have been established in the form of dense local networks. A major step has simultaneously been taken to set up strong motion arrays in these critical areas to generate near-source acceleration data, a primary requirement for designing earthquake resistant structures. About 200 strong motion accelerographs (SMA) and 300 Structural Response Recorders have been deployed in six arrays.

These strong motion instruments have recorded a number of earthquakes since their installation, generating more than 100 accelerograms. The analysis has provided, quantitative estimates of the peak acceleration, attenuation relationships, predominant frequencies and equivalent ground motion parameters, specific to the local geological conditions, Figure 3.1, Chandrasekran, *et al.* (1992). A scientific basis has thus been established for pursuing earthquake engineering studies and design of earthquake resistant structures in the country.

Collateral geophysical studies like Deep Electrical Resistivity investigations using magnetotellurics, gravity observations and radon monitoring have provided additional insights into the earthquake processes operating in the Himalayan Region. A first order earthquake risk map for Himalaya bas been generated.

(b) Latur Earthquake and Follow-Up

The Latur earthquake of September 30, 1993, which occurred in Zone-I of the Seismic Zoning Map of India, was a very rare event. This earthquake took a toll of more than 7000 lives and caused widespread damage to property in some 80 villages. This earthquake is rated as one of the deadliest earthquakes in the stable continental regions, which have occurred, in the recorded history, Gupta *et al.* (1993). Most of the local houses and other buildings were not engineered to withstand the earthquake vibrations which resulted in unusually high loss to property. The event, however, provided a unique opportunity to the scientists to mount a coordinated effort to study

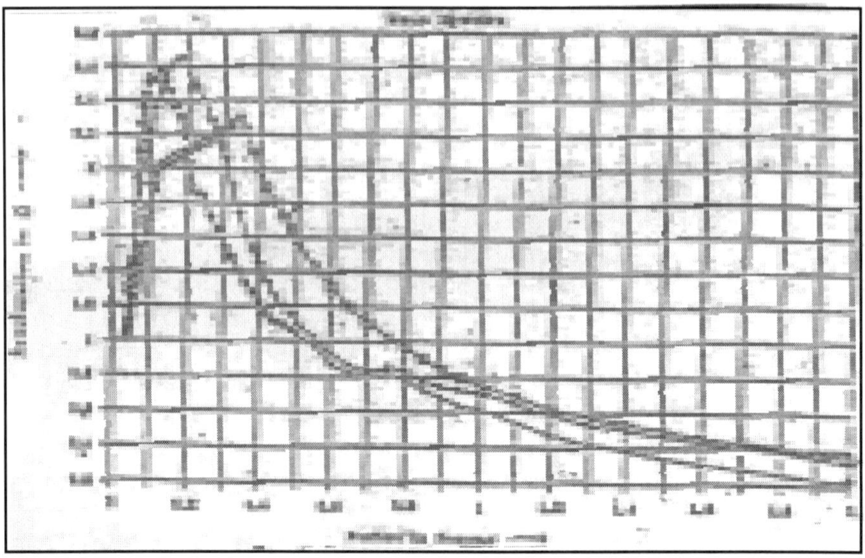

Figure 3.1: Mean Spectra of Horizontal (H) and Vertical (V)

the various aspects of the earthquake. Thus both national and international efforts were launched to monitor the after-shock activity and record the other associated effects like surface deformation, gas emanations, measurement of ground temperature, investigation of water table variations etc.

The Government took note of the unusual happening. In consultation with national experts and a UNDP team, a major programme of upgrading and strengthening the earthquake monitoring facilities was launched in 1994 with World Bank support. Under the project the following activities have been initiated, refer Figure 3.2.

Upgrading the 20 observatories of IMD with three component Broad Band digital instruments, 10 of these with GSN type equipment.

- ❖ Setting up of 10 new digital seismic observatories. .
- ❖ Setting up of 3 multi-element telemetered clusters.
- ❖ Installation of SMAs for free-field and structural response studies in multi-storeyed buildings.
- ❖ Upgradation of facilities for after-shock monitoring.
- ❖ Setting up of a National Seismological Data Centre at IMD headquarters
- ❖ Setting up of a GPS observational network.
- ❖ Collateral geophysical studies to map seismogenic structures.

The Project is being implemented in a consortium mode with the participation major scientific organisations like IMD, National Geophysical Research Institute,

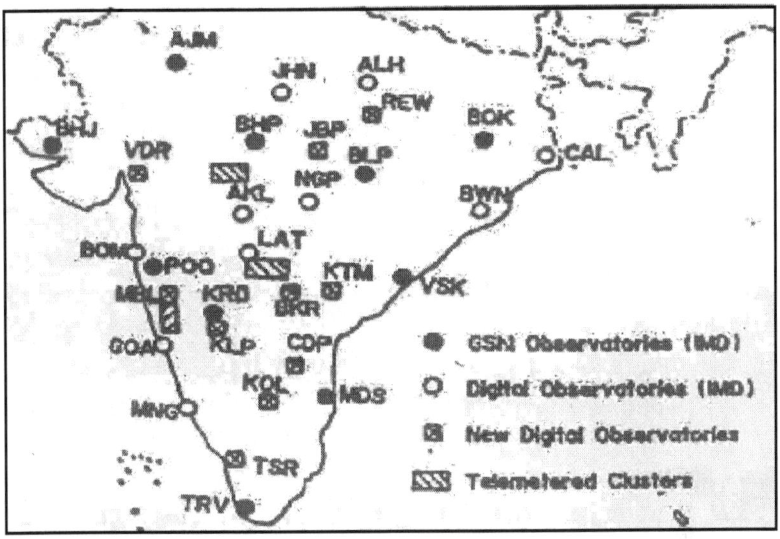

Figure 3.2: Seismological Network in Peninsular Shield

Survey of India, Indian Institute of Geomagnetism etc. Active participation of the academic institutions has been encouraged.

The upgraded network has already proved its efficacy in improving the operational services being provided by IMD. The Jabalpur earthquake of 21 May 1997 was faithfully recorded by 10 GSN observatories producing a unique broad-band data set. The data could be automatically downloaded at IMD, New Delhi within 15 minutes of the earthquake occurrence. The parameters of the earthquake were announced within half an hour a significant improvement over the earlier practices.

The availability of high quality digital data has opened up new possibilities for seismological research in the country. New thrust areas like seismic tomography, palaeo-seismology and earthquake precursory studies are being promoted. A strong component of training and manpower development has been in-built into the programme.

(c) Landslide Studies

The Himalayan terrain, because of its continued evolution is fragile in nature and prone to mass movements causing landslides and associated damage. Similarly, the Western and Eastern Ghats in the peninsular shield area are prone to landslides, mostly triggered by heavy rainfall events. Since landslides tend to coincide with events of heavy rainfall, which could be followed by floods, the local populace acutely feels the impact of dislocations caused by landslides.

DST has conceptualised a multi-disciplinary coordinated programme to study the various aspects associated with the landslide phenomenon Figure 3.3.

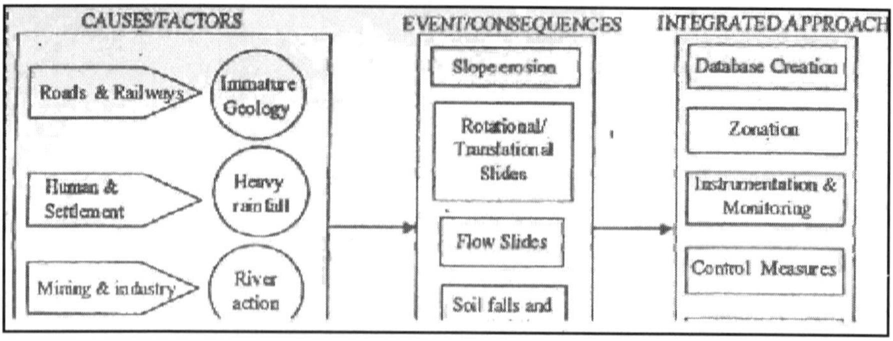

Figure 3.3: Integrated Studies on Landslides (adapted from Indian Geo-technical Journal, January, 1987. Slope instability in the fragile Himalaya and strategy for development by Dr. R K. Bhandari)

Test sites have been selected in Himachal Pradesh, Garhwal and Kumaon Himalaya; Sikkim and Western Ghats for pilot studies. A close interface with the local development agencies and Border Roads Organisation is maintained at various stages of the studies. A methodology has been framed for assigning weights to different parameters like slope, soil condition, geology, hydrology etc. to develop a rating scheme for hazard zonation, Anbalgan (1992), DST (1994). Pilot exercises on landslide monitoring and control measures have also been taken up. Plantation of grasses and shrubs to restore the vegetative cover on slopes has helped in arresting the erosion landslides. The utility of coir, jute netting and geo-textiles has been demonstrated. However, various considerations, including financial, have constrained the application of scientific control measures on a large enough scale. It is to be recognised that the problem of landslide occurrence is closely linked with the general issue of land use. Unplanned construction on unstable slopes, deforestation and other cultural activities has accentuated an already difficult situation. It is disconcerting to find that disasters due to landslides are-repeating in different parts of the country with increasing frequency. The Bureau of Indian Standards has taken steps to develop a code of construction on hilly slopes.

13. Natural Resources Data Management System

It is now appreciated that natural hazard mitigation measures have to be embedded in the strategies of local level development to make them sustainable. The government has adopted the 73rd and 74th Constitutional Amendments to promote district level planning and empower the local populace for participation in the decision making. To operationalise this concept, DST has initiated a programme on Natural Resources Data Management System to develop decision support models based on the concept of Geographic Information System (GIS). Pilot districts have been selected in different parts of the country to develop spatial databases on natural resources and collateral socio and agro-economic parameters. Decision support models are being developed in the sector of land, water and bio-resources management, which would demonstrate the utility of the databases in managing the local resources in a sustainable manner, Figure 3.4.

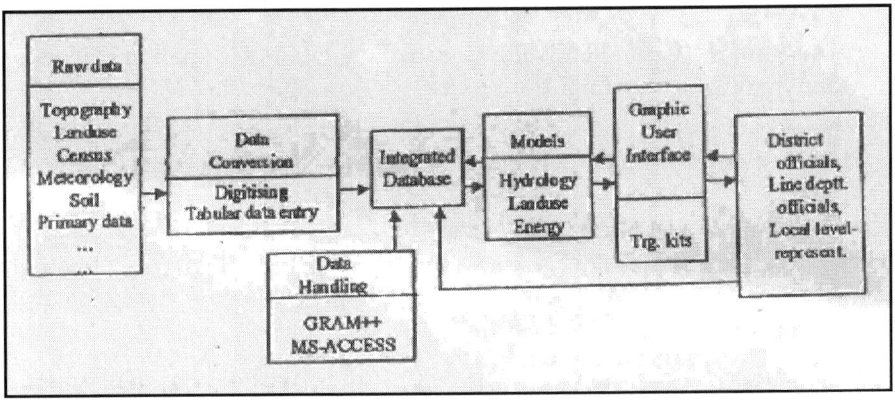

Figure 3.4: Components of Natural Resources Data Management System

14. Future Directions

Natural hazards caused by forces latent in the atmosphere, or inside the solid earth, need to be understood better before such occurrences can be predicted and diffused. The study of the causes of such occurrences and building up of their chronological record together with their impact on physiography of affected regions over the last 2000-5000 years calls for the application of different disciplines of earth system science and integration of the observations made. If the calamitous effects of the natural hazards are to be warded off or diffused in time, it is imperative that their causes are scientifically investigated and understood.

The initiatives, as described above, have laid a strong foundation for strengthening the science and knowledge base of natura1 disasters mitigation in the country. Through various other schemes, like National Council for Science and Technology Communication and State Councils for Science and Technology, DST is extending its reach to operational levels in States and districts. Considering the immensity of the task these efforts need to be fortified and enlarged in the future. Sharing of experiences and co-operation with the neighbouring countries will facilitate this process and help achieve the objectives of the International Decade for Natural Disasters Reduction.

15. Acknowledgements

Thanks are due to Secretary, Department of Science and Technology, for giving this opportunity to one of us (KRG) of participating in the Workshop and making the presentation. Thanks are also due to Dr.Vishwas Kale, Pune University for providing inputs related to flood studies in India and to Mr. M. Mohanty for help at various stages during the preparation of the manuscript and Mrs. Vandana for type setting the document.

16. References

1. Agarwal, A and Narain, S. (1991) Floods, flood plains and environmental myths. State of Indian's Environment–3. Center for Science and Environment, New Delhi.
2. Anbalagan, R. (1992). Landslide Hazard Evaluation & Zonation Mapping in Mountainous Terrain, Engineering Geology, Vol. 32, pp.269-277.
3. Arya, A. S. (1989). Earthquake Disaster Mitigation. Symposium on Preparedness, Mitigation & Management of Natural Disasters, Vol. 2, Central Water Commission, pp. 1-22.
4. Arya, A.S., Mandal, G.S., Thakur, V.C., Prem Krishna, Lakshamanan, N., Chaudhuri, S.K, Gupta, T.N., (1997). Vulnerability Atlas of India, Part 1, Building Material and Technology Promotion Council Ministry of Urban Affairs & Employment, New Delhi.
5. Arya, A.S., Mandal, G.S., Thakur, V.C., Prem Krishna, Lakshamanan, N., Chaudhuri, S.K., Gupta, T.N., (1998). Guidelines for Improving Hazard Resistance Construction of Buildings and Land Use Zoning 1998, Vulnerability Atlas of India, Part III, Building Material and Technology Promotion Council
6. Baker, V.R. (1998) Future prospects for post floods in India. In: Flood Studies in India. V.S. Kale (Editor). Geological Society of India, Memoir 41, pp. 219-228. .
7. Bhatnagar, A.K. (1999) Cyclone forecasting and warning systems. In: TCDC Workshop on Natural Disaster Reduction- Policy Issues and Strategies, Dec. 21-22, 1999, SERC Madras, India, pp. I. 10-1. 27.
8. Chandrasekaran, A.R., J.D. Das (1992). Strong Motion Arrays in Indian and Analysis of Data from Shillong Array, Current Science, Vol. 62, No. 1 & 2, pp. 233-250.
9. Chaudhuri, S.K. and Rajan, K.K. (1999), In: TCDC Workshop on Natural Disaster Reduction- Policy Issues and Strategies, Dec. 21-22, 1999, SERC Madras, India, pp. 1.28-1.37.
10. DST, (1986), Recommendations of Cyclone Review Committee, Vol. I, Govt. of India, New Delhi.
11. DST, (1994), Methodology for Landslide Hazard Zonation, Dept. of Science & Technology, pp. 1-32.
12. DST, (1996), The Indian climate Research Programme- Science Plan, Govt. of India, New Delhi
13. DST, (1998), Vision papers for R&D in Earth and Atmospheric Sciences. A publication of Earth System Science Division, Government of India, New Delhi.
14. Goswami, D.C. (1992a), Satellite monitoring of bank-line migration of the Brahmaputra River at Palasbari, Assam. Bulletin of NNRMS (B)-15, pp.26-27.
15. Goswami, D.C. (1992b), Zonal planning in water In: Planning for the Northeastern and Eastern zone. MS. Adisheshiah (Editor). Lancer Publishers, New Delhi, pp.9-22.

16. Goswami, D.C. (1998), Flurial Regime and Flood Hydrology of the Brahmaputra River, Assam. In: V.S. Kale Monsoon floods in India: A hydro-geomorphic perspective. In: Flood Studies in India. V. S. Kale (Editor). Geological Society of India, Memoir 41, pp. 53-75.

17. Gupta, G.D. (1992). Himalayan Seismicity. Geological Society of India, Memoir No. 23, pp. 1-21.

18. Gupta, H.K., Rastogi, B.K., Rao, M.N., C.V. Ramakrishna Rao. (1993). A Quick Look at Latur Earthquake of 30th September 1993, Current Science, Vol. 65, No.1 & 2, pp.517-520.

19. Kale, V. S. (1998), Monsoon floods in India: A hydro-geomorphic perspective. In: Flood Studies in India. V. S. Kale (Editor). Geological Society of India, Memoir 41, pp. 229-256.

20. Khattri, K.N. (1992). Seismic Hazards in Indian Region. Current Science, Vol. 62, No. 1&-2, pp. 109-116.

21. Khattri, K.N. (1998). A Seismic Hazard and Risk Scenario for Himalaya and Ganga Plains due to a Future Great Earthquake. National Academy Science Letters, National Academy of Sciences, India, Vol. 21, No.5 & 6 pp. 193-200.

22. Mahadevan, T.M. (1994). Deep Continental Structure of India: A Review. Geological Society of India, Memoir 28.

23. Mandal, G.S. (1992), Tropical Cyclones, their Forecasting and Warning System in India, Natural Disaster Reduction for Nineties: Perspectives, Aspects & Strategies. International Journal Services, pp. 327-329.

24. Midha, R.K. (1998), Natural Disaster Mitigation- Some initiatives of Department of Science & Technology. In: Proceedings of the Workshop on the Role of the R&D Institutions in Natural Disaster Mitigation, Colombo, Sri Lanka 10th–11th September, 1998, pp. 4-l to 4-8.

25. Midha, R.K. (1999), S&T initiatives for seismic and landslide disasters mitigation In: TCDC Workshop on Natural Disaster Reduction- Policy Issues and Strategies, Dec. 21-22, 1999, SERC Madras, India, pp. II-58 to III-68.

26. Mohan, J. (1982), Flood disaster in Ganga valley–Proceedings CBIP short-term course on flood control, Roorkee, Technical Report No. 31, pp.27-31.

27. Narula, P.L. and S.K. Shome, (1992), Macroseismic Studies of Recent Earthquakes in Northwest Himalaya–A Review. Seismology in India–An Overview, Current Science, Vo1.62, No. 1&2, pp.24-33.

28. Radhakrishna, B.P, (1993), Neogene Uplift and Geomorphic Rejuvenation of Indian Peninsula Current Science, Vol. 64, No. 11-12, pp. 787-793.

29. Ramaswamy, C. (1987), Meteorological Aspects of Severe Floods in India 1923-1979. India Meteorology Department, MMH 10, New Delhi.

30. Rao, D. P., Bhanumurthy, V., Rao, G. S. and Manjushri, P. 1998. Remote Sensing and GIS in Flood Management in India. In: Flood Studies in India. V. S. Kale (Editor). Geological Society of India, Memoir 41, pp. 195-218.

31. Rao, R P., Satpathi Rao, (1984), Historical Seismicity of Peninsular India. Bulletin of the Seismological Society of America. VoL 74, No.6, pp. 2519-2533.

32. RBA, (1980), Report of the Rashtriya Barh Ayog, Government of India, New Delhi, Volume I and II.

33. Sahai, A, Sinha, L.K. and Sharma, S. (1997). Flash flood prediction: A realistic approach. (Abstract). Conference on Geomatics in Disaster Management. Indian Institute of Remote Sensing, Dehradun, pp. 38-35.

34. Sarma, J. N. (1992). Flood flow characteristics of the Brahmaputra River. Jalvigyan Sameeksha, V. VII, pp. 62-73.

35. Seshagiri, N. (1992). NICNET based National Hazard Relief Management, Natural Disaster Reduction for Nineties: Perspectives, Aspects & Strategies. International Journal Services, pp.251-269.

36. Singh, I. B. (1996). Geological Evaluation of Ganga Plain–An Overview Journal of the Palaeontogical Society of India, Vol. 41, No. 96, pp.99-137.

37. Sinha, R. and Jain V.(1998), Flood Hazards of North Bihar Rivers, Indo-Gangetic Plains. In: Flood Studies in India. V. S. Kale (Editor). Geological Society of India, Memoir 41, pp. 27-52.

38. Starkel, L. (1972), The role of catastrophic rainfall in the shaping of the lower Himalaya (Darjeeling Hills). Geographia Polonica, V.21, pp. 103-160.

39. Sudhindra, C, (1992), Computerisation in Flood Forecasting. Natural Disaster Reduction for Nineties: Perspectives, Aspects & Strategies. International Journal Services, pp.277-287.

40. Wadia, D.N. (1975), Geology of India, Tata Mcgraw Hill, New Delhi.

4

Improved Understanding About Indian Earthquake Hazard

***G.D. Gupta and **H.N.Srivastava**
**Department of Science and Technology, New Delhi- 110016*
***128, Pocket A, Sarita Vihar, New Delhi- 110076*

1. Introduction

The Himalayan region, northeast India, Myanmar, Andaman and Nicobar Islands region is a part of the global seismic belt running from Mediterranean sea, Turkey, Iran, Afghanistan, Himalaya, Myanmar extending to Indonesia and thence to the Pacific Ocean. The occurrence of earthquakes in this belt is attributed to the north northeasterly movement of the Indian plate at the rate of about 5cm per year. This plate collides with the Eurasian plate, causing a wide zone of deformation and multiple fault systems along the Himalaya. The frequency of earthquakes as well as their magnitude is, in general much larger as compared to earthquakes within the Indian plate (intra plate region). The Main Central Thrust (MCT) and the Main Boundary Thrusts (MBT) have contributed to the high seismicity of the region.

The north north-easterly movement of the Indian plate and the continued convergence process along the Himalaya is also responsible for the transmission of stresses over large part of the Peninsular India causing east north-easterly oriented fault systems. The other tectonic features in the Peninsular India like the Narmada-Son rift zone, Godawari garden and other smaller fault systems could have formed due to local crustal adjustments. Their genesis has still been attracting the attention of Geoscientists.

The objective of this study is to discuss the significant contributions obtained through D.S.T. programes in the region as an efforts toward hazard mitigation.

2. Seismotectonic Study

Improved seismotectonic model for earthquake hazard assessment requires modern seismological network to understand the activity of faults and source mechanism of earthquakes. Close network of micro earthquake and other stations were established to monitor seismicity and aftershocks. The observations are supplemented by geomorphological GPS and other studies. Some of these results are briefly given below.

(a) Kangra Region

The Kangra Chamba region of Himachal Pradesh is one of the seismically active zones of the Himalaya where the great Kangra earthquake 1905 occurred. Seismological network of 8 short period analog stations was operated since 1989 with the objective of understanding the kinematics of the earthquake processes by the WIHG. A high level of earthquake activity was recorded in a narrow zone bordering the northern flanks of the Dhauladhar range. The depth of focus of these events lay in the upper 12 km of the crust. A composite focal mechanism solution obtained for a cluster of events occurring close to the Dhauladhar range showed thrust faulting along a steeply north dipping nodal plane. Gravity survey conducted in the Dharamsala–Palampur region revealed the presence of a gravity high structure trending NE-SW and transverse to the regional Himalayan trend.

This was corroborated by the focal mechanism of the earthquakes of magnitude 4 to 4.5 in 1968 and 1978. Other earthquakes in the region, however, showed northwest south- east trending thrust faults. (I.M.D)

From the gravity data, the crustal thickness in the Dharamsala-Palampur region was estimated to be about 45 Km. which was in conformity with the seismological observations from Beas local project monitoring network. The seismic gap between Kangra and Kinnaur regions continued to be well marked first identified by Srivastava and Chaudury (1978) which is considered to be of Geodynamical interest due to its location near plate boundary (I.M.D).

(b) Garhwal Himalaya, Uttaranchal

This is one of the most seismically active regions where recent Uttarkashi (1991) and Chamoli (1999) earthquakes occurred causing lot of damage and loss of life.

Composite fault plane solutions determined for two clusters of events in the region showed reverse type mechanism with strike-slip component which was also seen in earthquakes of intermediate magnitudes in this region. (IITR). The occurrence of low stress drop events intermixed with high stress drop events were observed. Attenuation relations for the region of the Garhwal Himalaya showed that the attenuation is frequency dependent in the region and decreases as frequency increases. Also, operation of digital telemetered seismic array (DTSA) in the Garhwal Himalaya for the purpose of monitoring local seismicity brought out seismic source zones, delineating active faults, estimation of source parameters and determination of attenuation characteristics of the region.

(i) Uttarkashi Earthquake (1991) (MB 6.6)

The focal mechanism solution suggested a thrust type mechanism along a fault trending WNW-ESE direction along the general trend of tectonic features in the region. This earthquake was followed by a number of aftershocks, more than 40 of them could be located using the data from the seismic stations over an area defined by 30.6^0 N to 30.9^0 and 78.5^0 to 78.9^0 E in about 30 km by 40 km area.

(ii) Chamoli Earthquake, 1999 (M_L 6.8)

The focal mechanism solution suggested a thrust type mechanism along a fault trending WNW-ESE direction.

The area defined by the aftershock activity through several field observatories was approximately 510 (30x17) km^2, with the longer axis tending parallel to the general trend of the tectonic features in the region.

(c) Gangetic Plains

Active Tectonics of the western Gangetic plains including the piedmont zone was studied by soil geomorphic approach. A recurrence interval of 1000-3500 years for major movements in the area was inferred.

(d) Andaman-Nicobar region

Generalised stress pattern and neotectonic activity was studied in Mayanmar Andaman region. Focal mechanism solutions of moderate earthquakes occurring in these regions during the period from 1981 to 1995 showed that due to the ongoing pushing of the Indian plate, the shearing stresses are quite predominant on Myanmar and Andaman-Sumatra regions. (ISM, IMD).

(e) Delhi

Delhi and adjoining regions have experienced earthquakes of magnitude 6.0 and above since historical times. Geologically, Delhi is located at the northern end of the ancient Aravalli mountain ranges and is surrounded by the Gangetic alluvium on almost all sides. Regular monitoring of the seismicity of Delhi and the surrounding region showed three clusters of events around Rohtak, Sonepat and near Delhi. Local tremors were correlated with the plausible faults in the region.

(f) Northeast India

The area comprises the north eastern part of Surma Basin (fore deep) in the west to a considerable portion of Indo Myanmar Ranges (IMR) characterized by a series of thrusts trending NNS-SSW to N-S. The seismological investigations during 1994-97 using microearthquake Data indicated a high seismicity zone particularly IMR with subduction zone.

(g) Madhya Pradesh

(i) Jabalpur Earthquake (1977)

Its focal mechanism showed a thrust fault. The area in which the aftershock activity was located, lay in a rectangular block bounded by 22.87^0 N, 80.18^0 E to 23.0^0 N to 79.97^0 E. The aftershock activity was concentrated along the fault delineated by DSS studies (IMD report).

(h) Kutch

This region has assumed importance due to recurrence of great earthquake 2001 only after a gap of about 183 year. A large number of programmes were sponsored by DST to study aftershocks, the source characteristics of the earthquake and seismic tomography. Spectral anaysis showed stress drop of 153 bars due to recent earthquake. The aftershocks and the focal mechanism studies showed association with Kutch main land fault. In terms of frequency content of S waves, it may be mentioned that considerable differences are reported from the aftershocks for larger magnitude earthquakes after the great Bhuj earthquake.

(i) Maharashtra

(i) Koyna Region

The Koyna-Warna area situated in the western part of the Deccan Volcanic Province (DV-P) of India showed that during 1993-98, over 4000 earthquakes of M>1.0 were located using seismic phase data from 19 stations (analog + digital), using a four-layered velocity model. The M>5 events of 1993-94 occurred after a lapse of 13 years, and were associated with a NW-SE trending fault in the vicinity of Warna reservoir and Koyna main fault. The event of 5 September 2000 (M 5.3) occurred at the junction of NW-SE fault in the vicinity of Warna reservoir and Koyna faults and suggested a normal faulting.

2. Palaeosismological Studies

Recent developments in palaeosismology have provided ample scope to scan a period of a few thousand years to search past earthquakes. The study provides constraints and checking earthquake recurrence models based on limited instrumental data.

The investigations were undertaken in the following regions.

(a) Himachal Pradesh Kaurik–Chango Fault Zone

In the Baspa Valley, a minimum recurrence interval of 148 to 1000 years for earthquakes of magnitude more than 7 was suggested on the basis of rate of sedimentation and TL technique. Based on the trenching excavation in the rupture zone of the great Kangra earthquake (1905), two earlier surface rupture events during the past 650 years and possibly a third one (still older) were inferred.

(b) Kumaun Himalaya

Two prominent structures formed by fluidization of gravels observed on the terrace of Kosi river, very close to the MBT gave some clues about a possible earthquake in its vicinity.

(c) Bihar Nepal Region

The radiocarbon dates characterized the paleosismic events dated as (i) 1934 event, (ii) 1833 or older than 1833 event, (iii) 1700-5300 r BP event and (iv) older than 25000 yr BP event.

(d) Northeast India

The palaeoseismic measurements, indicated, that the Shillong Plateau has been struck by large/major earthquakes around 500 ± 150, 1100 ± 150 and > 1500 ± 150 and > yr BP, in addition to the well- known great seismic event of 1897. This ^{14}C indicated a recurrence period of the order of 500 yr for large earthquakes in the Shillong Plateau.

(e) Kutch Region

It was surmised that a previous event of size comparable to 1819 earthquake occurred 800–1000 years ago in Kutch region.

Latur Maharashtra Region

It was suggested that earthquakes of similar size as Latur occurred at Killari as well as in other regions along the same or parallel structures. In this context, another earthquake about 1500 yr ago was surmised .

Strong ground motion results.

Central Himalaya

Analysis of Uttarkashi earthquake data indicated that maximum acceleration in a horizontal component was 304 cm/s*s and in vertical direction it was 289 cms/s*s. Attenuation of observed acceleration was almost comparable with the McGuire's relationship. The analysis of the records also brought out a rapid attenuation of (i) acceleration with respect to distance and (ii) response spectra with respect to low frequency of Chamoli Earthquake,1999. The pattern of decay showed that the peak ground acceleration for Uttarkanchi (1991) and Chamoli (1999) earthquakes was similar for increasing epicentral distance.

Delhi

Attenuation studies for Delhi region using strong motion data showed frequency dependent Qc value as ($Qc=252f^{0.82}$). (CBRI).

Northeast India

The characteristics of strong ground motion were found to be quite different in NE India as compared to northwest Himalaya. The vertical component showed the same trend as horizontal component in northeast India. Northeast India data showed that Mc Guire's relationship does not fit with the recorded data for all the events.

Kutch Region

An amplification of about 2 in the period between 0.2 to 0.7 seconds was reported from the accelerographs triggered at Ahmedabad.

Modeling of Accelerograms

Several techniques were used for simulation and estimation of strong ground motion namely:

- ❖ Auto regressive moving average (ARMA) methods (stochastic simulation of ground motion)
- ❖ Composite source model
- ❖ Empirical Green's function approach to synthesize the strong ground motions from sub-events of small earthquakes.

Using two finite source stochastic models, the strength factor is physically related to the maximum slip rate on the fault. It was found that the stress drop Ds that explains AMAX data for shield events may be a function of depth, increasing form ~50 bars at 10 km to ~400 bars at 36 km. Strong motion data generated during Chamoli earthquake (1999) showed that the maximum acceleration value at the "hard" sites are 3 to 4 times less than the "soft" sites while maximum velocity were roughly 2 to 3 times more at "soft" sites as compared to the "hard" sites.

Geotechnical Investigations

The process of soil liquefaction was investigated numerically based on modified discrete element method, coupled with designed laboratory testing of sand. The liquefaction process could be studied in detail in numerical 'experiments', to get a clear understanding of the microscopic behaviour affecting the liquefaction process.

Dynamic Properties of Soils and Liquefaction Behaviour of Sands

Soil being heterogeneous material, exhibits highly non-linear behaviour. Prediction of the ground response using non-linear models based on material non–linearity is essential because the dynamic soil properties such as shear modulus (G) and damping (D) are influenced by the factors like confining pressure, shearing strain amplitude, stress history and number of cycles of loading. Accordingly, the process of soil liquefaction and dynamic properties with designed laboratory testing of sand were studied. An experimental program was devised to evaluate the dynamic properties as well as the liquefaction behaviour of the soil samples collected exclusively from the sites close to epicenter of Bhuj earthquake (Sabarmati river belt in Ahmedabad) and meizoseismal region of Shillong Plateau, from the zone of liquefaction, using the state-of-the–art Cyclic triaxial testing facility.

Site Response Estimation

It is well known that each soil type responds differently when subjected to ground motion from earthquakes. A generalized inversion technique was used to compute site response by solving data of a number of recorded events for all source/path effects and site effects simultaneously. The receiver function analysis was also attempted. Site Response (SR) studies were undertaken at a few places in the country to prepare preliminary (first or second order) microzonation map. The Jabalpur urban domain has been classified into three hazard units of low, medium and high hazard. The high hazard areas are restricted to the Southern and south eastern margin of the alluvial fill, north eastern extension of the city on Mesozonic sediment.

Precurrsory Studies

With the growing network of modern seismological observations with broadband instruments, attempts were made to intensify earthquake-prediction research.

(a) Foreshocks in Koyna Region

The moderate size earthquakes in Koyna-Warna region occur at a shallow depth possibly due to water level fluctuation of the reservoir fault zone finally triggering the main shock at the base of seismogenic layer at a depth of 5-10 km. This result was based on the clustering of foreshocks for 8 moderate magnitude earthquakes in Koyna-Warna region.

(b) Precursory Swarms Over Peninsular India

Distinctive criteria between precursory and dissipating swarms were worked out. It was found that precursory swarms have deeper focal depth (^{3}2 km) as compared to dissipating swarms. This model fitted with Pandana swarms where focal depth decreased with time suggesting that the activity need not be related to a major earthquake.

(c) Seismic Quiescence

Seismic quiescence has been observed before Uttarkashi (1991) and Chamoli (1999) earthquake which has been considered as promising method for prediction of earthquakes.(I.M.D.)

(d) Crustal Deformation

Regional GPS networks designed mainly to monitor strain for earthquake research and forecasting have proved useful in detecting the crustal displacements. GPS measurements initiated in the Bhuj region were vital tool to monitor post seismic deformation resulting from crustal adjustment following the devastating 2001 earthquake. Observations were taken in February, September and November, 2001 to compute horizontal components of velocity vectors at 14 sites. (IIG) From a limited data set, a velocity of 62 mm per year in a direction of N47^0 E was inferred in Bhuj region. The estimated dilatational strain was about 0.4 micro strain per year. In this region, the N-S compression and E-W expansion was inferred. No co-seismic displacements was observed.

Remote Sensing Method

The digital remote sensing data prior (4 January 2001) and after (29 January 2001) the Bhuj earthquake showed significant changes in ocean parameters (chlorophyll and suspended sediment concentrations) after the earthquake.

Electromagnetic, geomagnetic, radon and SAR interferometery have also shown promise as multidisciplinary geophysical observations for precursory studies.

Post Earthquake Surveys

Each earthquake-affected region becomes a laboratory to study the impact on structures and devise remedial measures to mitigate risk. After the damaging earthquakes of Latur (1993), Jabalpur (1997), Chamoli (1999), Bhuj earthquakes (2001) and Andaman Islands (2002), DST has been deputing a team of experts to the affected regions to map the causative faults and study field effects. A number of mobile field parties were also sent for aftershock surveys with high gain digital seismographs to correlate the field observations with the instrumental data.

Education and Media

Mass awareness is the key for success of a disaster mitigation strategy. Mass awareness programmes were undertaken by DST for common man through lectures, T.V. film and distribution of literature and workshops.

Manpower Development

The coordinated seismicity programme provided a momentum to generate trained man power through 45 institutions in the country.

Training Programme

Several training programs were also organized through DST at different Institutions in the country on variety of subjects like Earthquake Resistant design for non Engineered structures, strong motion Instrumentation, Paleoseismology, Disaster Mitigation and awareness.

New Infrastructural Facilities

DST accelerated in generating several new capabilities in the field of seismology like UHF/VHF/V-SAT telemetry networks established for monitoring earthquakes and quicker data analysis. Facilities were established to handle such a large data for reception, analysis, dissemination and archiving at National Data Center (IMD), New Delhi and Seismological Computing and Data Center (NGRI), Hyderabad. Observational techniques were introduced like Global Positioning system (GPS), Synthetic Aperture Radar (SAR) and Remote sensing based geothermic technique. It also promoted indigenous design of instruments like 24 bit digital recorders and accelerometer. Shake table modernization (upgrading), Cyclic triaxial testing facilities and locating survivors through telemetry equipment were also taken up.

Future Thrusts

Mission Mode Project

This project has been undertaken to create substantial new research and infrastructure and appropriate human resources for mitigating the adverse impacts of earthquakes. It aims at developing/enhancing human resources equipped with the state–of-the-art knowledge and skills to profitably translate the massive set of data planned to be generated into meaningful information and understanding, and developing user friendly knowledge products that could form a credible basis for executive action by disaster managers, planners, policy makers, and for self help and creative responses by widely distributed groups and communities in the country,

Earthquake Risk Evaluation Centre

The Government of India recently notified the establishment of an Earthquake Risk Evaluation Centre (EREC) in India Meteorological Department, New Delhi, under Department of Science & Technology. The Center is in operation since then.

The objectives of Mission Mode Project and EREC are specific in terms of deliverables and considerable support of D.S.T is required to achieve the following:

Since there is a need of about 175 modern seismological stations in the country to reduce the detection threshold of earthquakes upto magnitude 3 in the country, the setting up of new stations should be accelerated further in order to supplement IMD efforts. A few such stations may also be started in project mode under the D.S.T. programs on seismicity.

Earthquake Early Warning system (EWS) may be started in project mode in selected regions. It may be mentioned that earthquake early warning is an emerging application of seismic monitoring technology that offers the automated capability to recognize when an earthquake is in progress and to provide seconds to tens of seconds of warning before the onset of strong shaking at a site, depending on its distance from the epicenter. Early warnings can enable individuals in vulnerable situations to protect themselves or others. School children could take cover to avoid injury from falling structural debris or nonstructural building components. Surgeons can suspend delicate operations. Businesses and industries can stop critical processes such as toxic substances and protect assets like databases. Utilities and transportation lifelines can take preventive action to avoid major service disruptions. With 15 to 20 seconds of warning, air traffic controllers can wave off inbound aircraft, factories can stop production lines, traffic can be prevented from entering freeways, gas pipelines can be shut off, and trains can be stopped. Depending upon time, people can also evacuate some buildings and schools.

Acknowledgements

The authors are grateful to Dr V.S. Ramamarthy, Secretary DST for his keen interest for the expansion of the activities as briefly projected in this report based on the D.S.T projects and other institutions.

5

R&D for Cyclone Disaster Mitigation

T.V.S.R. Appa Rao
Director, Structural Engineering Research Centre, Madras

1. Introduction

Cyclones, typhoons or hurricanes cause colossal loss including loss of life every year in different parts of the world. Developing countries such as Bangladesh, India, Philippines, Malaysia, Sri Lanka and also the developed countries such as Australia, Japan and the U.S.A. experience heavy losses due to cyclones or typhoons. Cyclones are considered to be most dangerous among all the natural hazards, if viewed in terms of intensity, duration and the extent of destruction. Around eighty tropical cyclones occur each year around the globe, of which about 5 to 6 on average occur over the north Indian Ocean. The Bay of Bengal is one of the six most vulnerable cyclone-prone regions of the world. When a cyclone hits a region, besides killing people it brings about large scale damage to crops, houses and buildings, roads, electrical transmission lines, communication facilities, water supply systems, etc. It is of concern to note that there has been an increase in the number of wind storms and the losses to the economy [1,2] over the years. The economic losses during the decade 1989-1998, was reported as US$ 137.7 billion, which implies a five times increase over the decade 1960-1969. Among the five continents of the world, Asia is the worst hit in respect of human deaths and economic loss suffered. Therefore, cyclone disaster management and mitigation assumes great importance both nationally and internationally.

Damage and losses due to natural hazards can be minimised if effective, timely and adequate measures are taken in pre-disaster planning/preparedness, management during disasters and post-disaster relief by providing safe drinking water, food, shelter, emergency medical aid and also taking the measures required to contain epidemics and rehabilitating the people. This requires a holistic approach and highly coordinated efforts by different Government departments, and public, private and voluntary organizations and cooperation of the people in the region. Disaster management/mitigation requires multi-disciplinary effort involving financial, scientific and technological inputs, managerial effectiveness, social understanding and above all dedicated efforts of all concerned agencies. Major activities and players in cyclone disaster mitigation and their role are shown in Figure 5.1.

It is well known that cyclone disaster can be reduced considerably if appropriate pre disaster measures are taken including effective and early communication of cyclone warnings and evacuation of people to safer places depending on the situation. There is a thumb rule that every dollar invested in disaster preparedness will save 20 times later on.

One of the major causes for loss of human life due to natural disasters is that people live in disaster-prone areas and that the houses, buildings and other structures are not disaster proof. While it is practically not possible and economically feasible for any society, to afford or build houses and structures that are absolutely safe against worst disasters, the main aim of the scientific and technological efforts is to develop rational methodologies for minimising the damage.

While it may be emphasized here that the scientific knowledge, techniques, and expertise developed till now have to be utilized effectively for disaster management/mitigation, it is necessary to continue research and developmental efforts to improve upon the knowledge/data base, methodologies and techniques for arriving at rational solutions/decisions. Imparting education and training to all those involved in disaster management/mitigation including the people in the cyclone-prone areas has to be given major emphasis in order to get full benefits from the S&T developments and to achieve success in disaster management. The major areas of research and development relating to engineering of structures that are of considerable importance for cyclone disaster mitigation are discussed in this paper. The R&D work being carried out at the Structural Engineering Research Centre (SERC), Madras and that relating to the Indian context have been presented in this paper after giving an overview of the cyclone hazard and the built environment.

2. Cyclone Hazard

Cyclones are formed due to atmospheric disturbances and they derive their energy from the latent heat released by the condensation of warm moisture picked up from the sea. Unlike tornadoes, which may occur almost anywhere, cyclones originate between 5° and 30° latitudes on either side of the Equator and affect islands and coastal regions. Cyclones are characterised by a revolving wind system with very high wind speeds covering a large area with a diameter of typically about 300 km

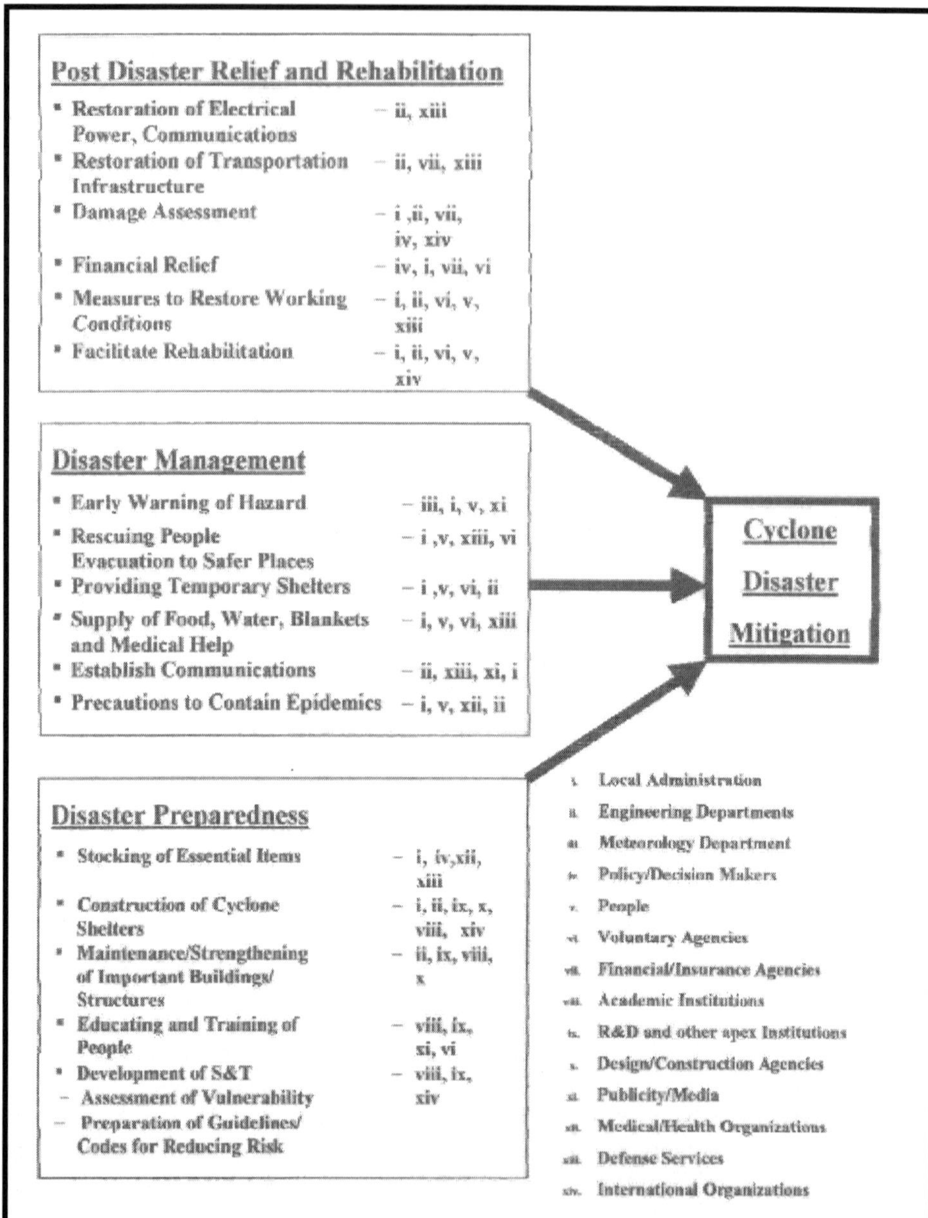

Figure 5.1: Major Activities and Players in Cyclone Disaster Mitigation

and height of 150 km. Cyclonic wind speeds ranging upto 270 kmph sustained over a period of one minute have been observed in the past in the coastal districts of India, and other parts of the world.

For example, the reported wind speed of the Super Cyclone, which hit Orissa during October 1999, was about 260 kmph. The new classification of cyclonic disturbances as per the India Meteorology Department (IMD) is as shown in Table 5.1.

Table 5.1: New Classification of Cyclonic Disturbances and Storms

IMD Classification	*Wind Speed, kmph*
Low pressure	31
Depression	31 to 51
Deep depression	52 to 62
Cyclonic storm	63 to 87
Severe cyclonic storm	88 to 117
Very severe cyclonic storm	118 to 221
Super cyclonic storm	222 and above

Characteristics of cyclonic winds are reported to be different from those of non-cyclonic winds, normally considered in the codes of practice. It is observed that cyclonic winds cause damage to the habitat lying in the central region (eye) of the cyclone due to the reversal of direction of strong gusts with the movement of the storm centre.

3. Built Environment: Present Scenario

There is considerable economic activity in most of the cyclone hazard-prone coastal districts of India and the population is also quite dense in the towns/cities of coastal districts. Besides houses, residential and public buildings, schools, and hospitals, a variety of structures exist in the coastal districts, such as storage sheds, power plant buildings/structures, electrical transmission line towers, radio and microwave towers, port and harbour structures. At one end of the spectrum there are non-engineered buildings built with locally available materials which are often found to be widely varying in quality. At the other end of the spectrum are engineered buildings that are well planned, designed and constructed. In between these extremes, are a wide variety of structures majority of which are partly engineered, using the 'rule of thumb approach' and conventional practices, and these may be termed as semi-engineered structures. These structures exhibit varied performance when they are subjected to natural hazards such as cyclones and earthquakes. The expert group set up by the Government of India under Ministry of Urban Affairs and Employment on Natural Disaster Prevention, Preparedness and Mitigation having a bearing on housing and related infrastructure has brought out the Vulnerability Atlas of India [3], which includes among other things distribution of houses, for each district of the country, and their classification based on the predominantly used materials for roofing and walling. The dominant building stocks fall under the category of non-engineered buildings. The percentage of fully engineered buildings is very less. A structure well built using quality bricks and tiles, for example, is quite safe under normal times, but vulnerable when exposed to earthquakes and cyclones, and may even collapse because the masonry walls cannot withstand high lateral forces due to cyclonic winds. The present day scenario of buildings and structures thus represents a wide range of structures having highly variable risk levels.

4. Lessons from Post-Disaster Damage Surveys

Analysis of data and information collected during damage surveys on buildings and structures, after any cyclone damage, will enable one to identify different improvements required in their design and construction, so as to reduce the loss. Damage or failure of structures during natural hazard may be considered as the outcome of full-scale experiments in the field. There are, of course, many unknowns in these experiments such as the loading on the structure, the state of health of the structure at the time of disaster, the first component that failed and the sequence of failure of structural elements. Yet, based on the knowledge and expertise of the person who undertakes the damage survey, patterns in failures and damage can be identified. SERC, Madras, has been conducting post-disaster damage surveys and analysing the damage and failure of structures due to cyclones since the Andhra Pradesh cyclone in 1977. Figures 5.2–5.4 shows typical damages suffered by some structures during cyclonic storms. In addition to the common observations such as flying off of roof tiles and asbestos roofing sheets, failures of compound walls and damage to non-engineered buildings, etc., there were a number of cases of damage or failure of engineered buildings and structures. To quote an example, the analysis of failure of an elevated water

Figure 5.2: Damage to an Industrial Building (Kavali Cyclone, 1989)

Figure 5.3: Damage to a Steel Lattice Tower (Orissa Cyclone, 1999)

Figure 5.4: Damage to Roof Cladding of a Building (Kavali Cyclone, 1989)

tank revealed the importance of taking into account the dynamic effects of wind gusts and soil-structure interaction, besides the influence of reinforcement detailing on the ultimate strength of the structure. Thus, the post-damage surveys and analysis can help in identification of: i) Vulnerable locations, orientations and geometries, ii) Vulnerable elements in structural systems, iii) Inadequacies in load path, iv) Weak links in joints and connections, v) Influence of structural detailing on connections of the structure, vi) Improvements needed in design and construction. Analysis of damage clearly points out that much of the damage or failures of engineered structures could be avoided by paying more attention for estimating the design wind loads, detailing of connections, and quality of construction and maintenance. Also, a detailed dynamic analysis, instead of an equivalent static analysis, is recommended for wind sensitive structures. Based on the research and development activities in the field of wind engineering and cyclone disaster mitigation conducted at SERC, Madras, over the years, guidelines for design and construction of buildings and structures in cyclone-prone areas have been brought out [4].

5. Determination of Normal and Cyclonic Wind Characteristics

Unlike dead and live loads, assessment of wind loads for design of buildings and structures poses challenging problems. Wind flow in the atmosphere is random both in time and space and wind is conceived to be a conglomeration of several eddies with varying sizes (wavelengths) and associated energies. Mean velocity profiles, describing the height variation of mean wind speeds, turbulence intensity profiles which describe the role of fluctuating wind speeds along the height and power spectrum of horizontal component of wind speed are the basic parameters which are important from the point of view of structural design of buildings and other structures. Measurement of wind characteristics leading to the evaluation of loads on structures and structural response can be done through carefully planned full-scale experiments. Only a limited number of full-scale investigations have been reported in the literature. Some of the full-scale bench mark studies on measurement of wind characteristics include the field investigations conducted by Duchene-Marullaz [5], the Aylesbury experiment [6] and experiments on Texas Tech University building [7]. The parameters of interest in such studies include measurements of wind speed, pressure, temperature, humidity, wind force and structural response characteristics. Very little reliable data is available on wind speeds measured in India beyond 200 kmph because of limited instrumentation and measurement facilities. However, such data are important for realistic evaluation of wind characteristics.

During the recent years, SERC, Madras, has developed methodologies, facilities and expertise for conducting field experiments on measurement of wind characteristics at different heights of an instrumented tower, as well as its structural response. The characteristics of wind and the response of a 101 m high lattice tower were studied by making measurements with cup anemometers and piezo-electric type accelerometers at various levels [8]. The experimental structure was located in a sub-urban area in Chennai very near to the seacoast. The mean values of power law coefficient, surface roughness length, shear friction velocity; surface drag coefficient, turbulence intensity and length scales have been calculated. Power spectrum of wind speeds at different levels were compared with recommended spectra of Davenport, Harris, Hino and Shiotani. Good agreement was noted between various experimental values with corresponding values given in the literature for a similar type of terrain.

Normal and tropical cyclonic wind characteristics are being studied by conducting full-scale experiments on a 52 m tall steel lattice tower [9] located in the campus of SERC, Madras. Data collected from the instrumented tower during tropical cyclones in June and December 1996, were analysed and compared with characteristics obtained during normal wind conditions. One of the significant conclusions of this study was that cyclonic spectral characteristics are significantly different from those corresponding to well-behaved normal winds. In the case of cyclonic wind speeds, gust energy can be noted even at frequencies beyond 1 Hz, as can be seen from Figure 5.5. This has significance for design of structures in tropical cyclone-prone regions. The damage suffered by some of the well-engineered lattice towers during cyclones may be explained by the above observation. The future R&D work will include further collection of cyclonic wind data to develop a modified spectrum of tropical cyclonic winds that may be used in the design of structures.

6. Risk Analysis of Cyclonic Wind Speeds

Estimation of cyclonic wind hazard intensities and specification of design wind speeds for cyclone-prone coastal regions are of considerable importance to designers as well as for other decision makers. Currently, as per the Indian Standard IS: 875 (part 3) 1987 [10], the country has been divided into six zones and the basic wind speeds for these zones vary between 33 m/sec to 55 m/sec. Even though the code specifies that cyclonic wind speed has been included in the estimation of basic wind speed, the measured/observed wind speeds during actual cyclones are found to be considerably higher. Risk analysis of wind speeds is a rational approach to estimate the risk, *viz.*, the exceedence probability of a wind speed of a given intensity during the life period of a structure. Such an analysis has been carried out by Simiu for estimation of design wind speeds in the USA [11]. For the coastal regions of India, SERC, Madras, carried out risk analysis of cyclonic wind speeds [12, 13]. In this study, using the concept of mean return period, T(x), of a characteristic wind speed, x,

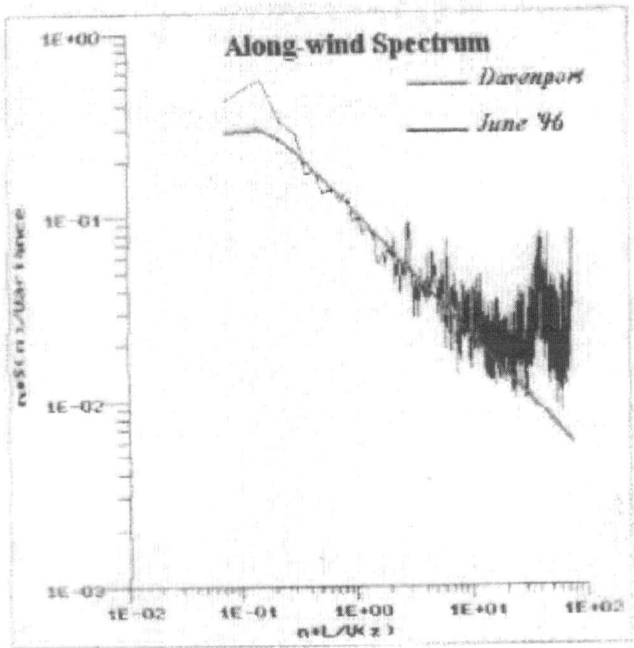

Figure 5.5: Power Spectrum of Cyclonic Winds

it can be shown that the probability of a future wind speed, X exceeding a given wind speed, x during the life period, N of the structure is given by:

$$P_N(X \geq x) = 1 - \left(1 - \frac{1}{T(x)}\right)^N \quad \text{.......................................(1)}$$

The available cyclonic wind speed data pertaining to different coastal regions were collected from the India Meteorological Department. These data, being limited in number, were augmented using the Monte Carlo simulation technique. Only wind speeds exceeding 115 kmph (33 m/sec.), which are known to cause damage to structures have been considered in this analysis. Different statistical distributions were tried to fit the data and Gumbel (Type-I) distribution was found to closely fit the data. From the above study, characteristic cyclonic wind speeds computed for different life periods of structures at 63 per cent risk level are given in Table 5.2.

Using the information on probability distribution of extreme wind speeds alone, it is not possible to predict directly the number of occurrences of winds of specified intensities within a given time interval. Such information is necessary to determine the collapse/fatigue reliability of a structure during its lifetime. A time homogeneous Poisson process model [14] can be used to determine the probability of occurrence of cyclones of different intensities (cyclones classified according to Saffir Simpson scale) for coastal regions of India.

Table 5.2: Characteristic Cyclonic Wind Speeds (63 per cent risk) for the Coastal Regions of India

Life Period of Structure (years)	Characteristic Cyclonic Wind Speed (kmph)				
	Tamil Nadu	Andhra Pradesh	Orissa	West Bengal	West Coast
5	180.80	188.74	183.90	165.21	165.50
25	233.17	241.11	238.49	200.76	206.52
50	254.85	262.79	259.00	215.48	223.51
100	276.39	284.32	279.32	230.09	240.37
200	297.83	305.77	299.60	244.65	257.18

7. Microzonation

Risk estimation of a structure in a given region exposed to the cyclone hazard depends on extent of spatial distribution of wind speed data considered in the preparation of vulnerability maps. Smaller the grid size considered in vulnerability maps, more accurate will be the estimation of the risk. Microzonation, by definition is an exercise carried out for hazard or risk estimation on smaller spatial scales. In the Vulnerability Atlas of India 1997, mentioned in an earlier section, the Cyclone Hazard Map is prepared based on district-wise data and on macro-scale definition of wind speeds. Future work may include generation of additional data base up to the level of villages and modification of the risk estimation suitably. In order to estimate the risk in a more scientific and reliable way it is necessary to carry out microzonation of the regions based on additional data and detailed risk analysis.

8. Dynamic Response Analysis and Design of Structures

Assessment of wind loads on structures and their dynamic response is a very complex problem, because of the random nature of wind speeds both spatially and temporally and also due to the presence of turbulence in the wind flow and its aerodynamic interaction with the structure. The problem is more complex when the structure is subjected to cyclonic wind conditions. It is necessary to use advanced methods of dynamic response analysis to ensure safety of structures. Over the years, considerable advances have been made in developing analytical models for dynamic response of structures using numerical methods such as the finite element method. The gust response factor approach after Davenport [15] is a rational method for prediction of line-like structures subjected to buffeting. The method proposed by Vickery and Basu [16] is currently regarded as the most reliable method for studying across-wind response of structures due to vortex shedding. The well recognized method of boundary layer wind tunnel testing proves highly useful for studying (i) dynamic pressure fluctuations and critical pressure distributions on buildings and other wind sensitive structures, (ii) dynamic response of structures, and (iii) group effects. However, it may be mentioned that the current state of knowledge and expertise using these above methods are still limited to well behaved wind climate. Because of this, even some of the well-engineered structures have failed during cyclones/

hurricanes in different parts of the world. Therefore, it is necessary to carry out further R&D investigations to understand better the characteristics of cyclonic winds, behaviour of structures during cyclones by conducting both analytical arid experimental studies (including model and field studies). Towards this, Structural Engineering Research Centre (SERC), Madras, set up a state-of-the-art boundary layer wind tunnel facility for carrying out investigations on models of wind-sensitive structures and also to study group effects. A model of a 220m tall reinforced concrete chimney under test *in* the wind tunnel is shown in Figure 5.6. As mentioned earlier, SERC has also developed reliable instrumentation for measuring wind speeds and dynamic response of structures in the field. A number of R&D studies have been carried out to measure wind data and to determine the structural responses at different levels of tall steel lattice towers.

Further R&D studies in this area are needed to develop improved methodologies and guidelines for optimal design of structures in cyclone-prone areas and to mitigate failures of structures.

9. Damage Assessments and Vulnerability Analysis

Post-disaster assessment of damage of structures would be required for making decisions about whether the structure is to be repaired or demolished and rebuilt based on technical as well as financial or other considerations. Presently damage assessment is based on field observations followed by analysis and engineering judgement by experts including qualitative estimation of structural damage and

Figure 5.6: Structural Model of a Chimney under Wind Tunnel Testing

qualitative estimation of consequences of damage. Reports from field observations may have different types of uncertainties such as vagueness of linguistic description of the state of damage, incompleteness and inconsistencies of information. Therefore damage assessment is a complex problem.

Another important area of interest to decision makers is the estimation of vulnerability of a region or a structure likely to be exposed to cyclonic storms. This again is a complex problem involving imprecise data and engineering judgement. The basic uncertainties involved in cyclone vulnerability analysis relate to occurrence of cyclones of specific speed in a particular region, and uncertainties in structural performance and other equally important socio-economic aspects. Very little work has been reported in the literature on vulnerability analysis of structures subjected to cyclones.

There is considerable scope to improve upon the methodologies for damage assessment and vulnerability analysis by making use of scientific/rational methodologies such as probability and fuzzy set theories to deal with uncertainties. A knowledge-based expert system was developed by Murlidharan *et al.* [17] for damage assessment and vulnerability analysis of structures. Cyclone hazard, structural damage and building importance including economic consequences are the three major factors that are considered in damage assessment. On the other hand, for vulnerability analysis, cyclone hazard, structural features, building importance and cost are the major factors. The complex and nonlinear interaction among various factors has been dealt with by using inference mechanism based on fuzzy sets. The hierarchical representation of knowledge/data associated with each one of the major factors enables the inference mechanism to traverse the hierarchy to estimate vulnerability or to assess the damage. Based on vulnerability analysis, buildings in a region can be ranked and priorities assigned for strengthening the buildings. Such knowledge-based systems can serve as useful tools for decision making for resource allocation by Government Departments, Finance/Insurance organisations and other agencies involved in natural disaster mitigation.

10. Design/Construction/Maintenance Guidelines and Standards

The main purpose of scientific research and development in engineering of structures is to develop/improve guidelines/standards for design, construction and maintenance of structures besides improving the methodologies for assessing and understanding of the behavior of structures subjected to different loads due to in-service and environmental conditions including natural hazards such as cyclones. The R&D findings can be beneficially used to bring out guidelines and standards which when implemented by building and other regulatory authorities would contribute towards reducing damage/failures of structures. It can be inferred from post-disaster damage surveys that some of the failure can be attributed to deficiencies in design, quality of construction and/or in maintenance of structures. Therefore, adopting proper methodologies in design, exercising good quality control during construction and periodic maintenance of structures according to the guidelines/standards laid down would contribute towards disaster mitigation.

11. Information Technology (IT) for Disaster Mitigation

Large volumes of data and information concerning different aspects is necessary to be compiled, analysed and shared on a continuing basis among the organisations or individuals involved in disaster management and mitigation. Developments in computers and Information Technology (IT) can be advantageously utilised in building up data bases and sharing/dissemination of information speedily, among all the parties concerned. Presently, application of IT for disaster management and mitigation in India is very much limited. Methodologies and strategies have to be developed for taking the best advantage of developments in computer and Information Technologies. One of the ways is that all the major organisations involved in disaster management and mitigation may create a web site with data and information that they can share. Geographic Information System (GIS) can also be effectively used in creating necessary data bases required for analysis.

12. Conclusion

Natural disaster management/mitigation requires a multidisciplinary approach involving administrators, financiers, engineers, scientists, volunteers and above all the affected people. A well-planned, coordinated work only will yield the best results. It is important to realise that pre-disaster planning and preparedness is of paramount importance besides management during the disaster and post-disaster rehabilitation works. Effective use of developments in Science and Technology and pursuing R&D efforts to improve upon the present knowledge and techniques can contribute significantly towards disaster preparedness besides helping in management during disasters and post-disaster rehabilitation. An overview of R&D in important areas relating to engineering of structures for cyclone disaster mitigation has been presented in this paper. It can be seen that guidelines and standards for wind–or cyclone-resistant designs of structures, risk and vulnerability analysis of regions and structures can help in cyclone disaster mitigation. It has also been pointed out that software tools (such as knowledge-based expert systems) can be developed based on rational methodologies for use by Government authorities, Finance/Insurance organisations and others for making important decisions on resource allocation for disaster management/mitigation. The potential of Information Technology is still to be fully exploited for disaster management/mitigation.

13. Acknowledgement

The author is grateful to Shri S. Arunachalam, Assistant Director, SERC, Madras, for his help in compiling this paper.

14. References

1. Proceedings of the TCDC Workshop on "Natural Disaster Reduction: Policy Issues and Strategies", December 21-22, 1999, SERC, Madras, India.
2. Davenport, AG., "What can Civil Engineers do to Reduce Natural Hazards?", Earthquake, Hurricane and Flood Hazard Forum–Seminar, Key note Lecture, Institution of Civil Engineers, London, U.K Jan 1999.

3. Vulnerability Atlas in India, Expert Group on Natural Disaster Prevention, Preparedness and Mitigation having a Bearing on Housing and Related Infrastructure, BMTPC, Ministry of Urban Affairs and Employment, Government of India, 1998.
4. Lakshmanan, N., and Shanmugasundaram, J., "Guidelines for Design and Construction of Buildings and Structures in Cyclone-prone Areas", Publication of SERC, Madras, December 1997.
5. Duchene-Marullaz, Ph, "Effect of High Roughness on the Characteristics of Turbulence in Cases of Strong Winds", Wind Engineering, Edited by J. E. Cermak, Vol. 2, 1980.
6. Eaton, K. J., and Mayne, J.R., "The Measurement of Wind Pressures on Two-Storey Houses at Aylesbury, Building Environment", Journal of Industrial Aerodynamics, Vol. 1, 1975.
7. Levitan, M.L., and Mehta, K.C., "Texas Tech Field Experiments for Wind Loads", Parts 1 and 2, Journal of Wind engineering and Industrial Aerodynamics, Vol. 43, 1992.
8. Shanmugasundaram, J., Gomathinayagam, S., Harikrishna, P., Arumugam, M., and Venkateswarlu, B., "Full-scale Field Measurements of a 101 m High Lattice Tower", Poc. of 9th International Conference on Wind Engineering, New Delhi, 1995, Vol.1.
9. Shanmugasundaram, J., Harikrishna, P. Gomathinayagam, S., and Lakhsmanan, N., "Wind, Terrain and Structural Damping Characteristics under Tropical Cyclonic Conditions", Journal of Engineering Structures, 21 (1999).
10. Indian Standards, "IS: 875 (part 3)–1987, Indian Standard Code of Practice for Design Loads for Buildings and Structures, Part–3, Wind Loads, Bureau of Indian Standards, New Delhi, 1989.
11. Simiu, E., Changery, M.E., and Fillibin, J.T., "Extreme Wind Speeds at 129 Stations in the Contiguous United States", BSS 118, National Bureau of Standards, Washington, DC, 1978.
12. Venkateswarlu, B., Arumugam, M., and Arunachalam, S., "Risk Analysis of Cyclonic Wind Data", Proceedings of the National Seminar on Tall Reinforced Concrete Chimneys", New Delhi, 1985.
13. Shanmugasundaram, J., Annamalai, G., and Venkateswarlu, B., "Probabilistic Methods for Cyclonic Wind Speeds in India", Proc. Second Asia Pacific Symposium on Wind Engineering, Beijing, China, June 1989.
14. Balaji Rao, K., Thomas, K. C., and Appa Rao, T.V.S.R, "Stochastic Modelling of Cyclones", Proc. Third Asia-Pacific Symposium on Wind Engineering, December 13-15, 1993, pp: 543-548.
15. Davenport, A.G., "Gust Loading Factors", Journal of Structural Division, ASCE, Vo1. 93, No.ST6, June 1967.

16. Vickery, B. J., and Basu, R.I., "Across-wind Vibrations of Structures of Circular Cross-section", Parts 1 and 2, Journal of Wind Engineering and Industrial Aerodynamics, 12 (1983).

17. Murlidharan, T. L., Durgaprasad, J., and Appa Rao, T.V.S.R., "Knowledge-Based Expert System for Damage Assessment and Vulnerability Analysis of Structures Subjected to Cyclones", Journal of Wind Engineering and Industrial Aerodynamics, Vo1. 72, 1997.

6

Natural Disaster and its Mitigation

Wisyanto
Researcher,
Directorate of Technology for Land Resources and Area Management,
Agency for the Assessment and Application of Technology, Indonesia

1. Introduction

Indonesia is an archipelago which consist of more than thirteen thousands of islands. There are five big islands in it, that are Sumatera, Java, Kalimantan, Sulawesi and Irian Jaya (see Figure 6.1). Indonesia is located approximately at 95°E-140°E and 7°N-10°S with two seasons, dry season and rainy season.

As other countries, Indonesia is not free from threatening of disaster. Disaster can be divided into two groups *i.e.* natural disaster and man-made disaster. The natural disaster which usually threats human lives in Indonesia are earthquake, tsunami, volcanic activities, drought, landslide, flood and fire. In other hand, man-made disaster usually appear as a side effect of the rapid development growth and land and forest mismanagement, that finally can cause the following disaster, pollution (air, water and environment), poor environmental dwelling and casualties of traffic accident (air, water and land traffic).

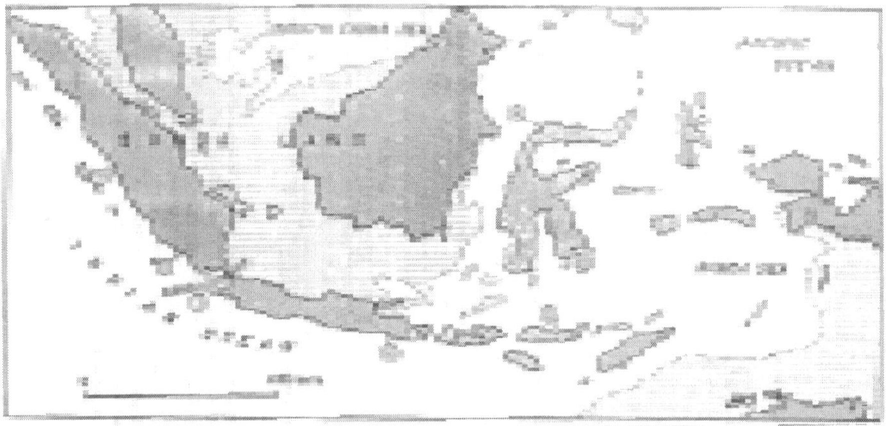

Figure 6.1: The Global Map of Indonesian Region

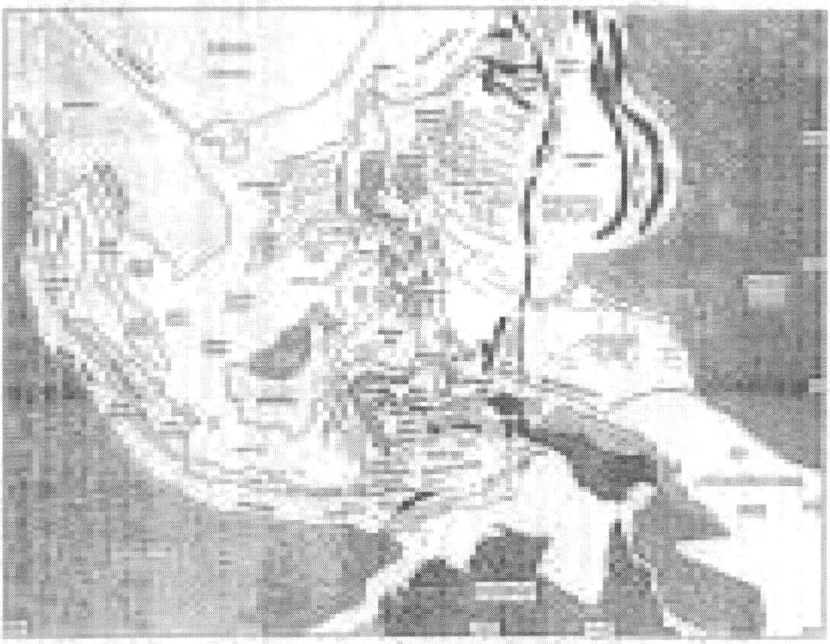

Figure 6.2: The Map Showing the Existence of Three Mega Plates (Indian Australia Plate, Eurasia Plate and Pacific Plate), where they interact forming unstable region (cited from Hall, 1995)

Indonesia is a suture of three mega plates (and many smaller plates) (Figure 6.2) forming subduction zones. The diverse subduction system of the Indonesian region record the interactions mainly between stable northwestern Eurasia Plate, Northward Indian-Australia Plate and west-northwestward Pacific Plate (Hamilton, 1988). The plate configuration lead to Indonesian become an unstable region, especially in

Sumatera, Java, Sulawesi and Irian Jaya. Among the four unstable islands, Sumatera is the one which have been studied intensively. The oblique plates convergence between Eurasia Plate and Indian Plate have resulted. In Active Semangko Fault where earthquake occurred frequently. A shock of earthquake could be a trigger to generate other natural disaster, such as tsunami and landslide. Besides earthquake, the subduction zone also have generated a chain of volcanoes, namely Sunda Arc (Figure 6.3), where the Mount Krakatau (Anak Krakatau) is apart of it.

A Natural disaster and man-made disaster could devastate and destruct human lives and their economic assets anytime. Concerning those phenomenon, government in cooperation with many institutions make disaster mitigation programs to decrease the risk of disaster.

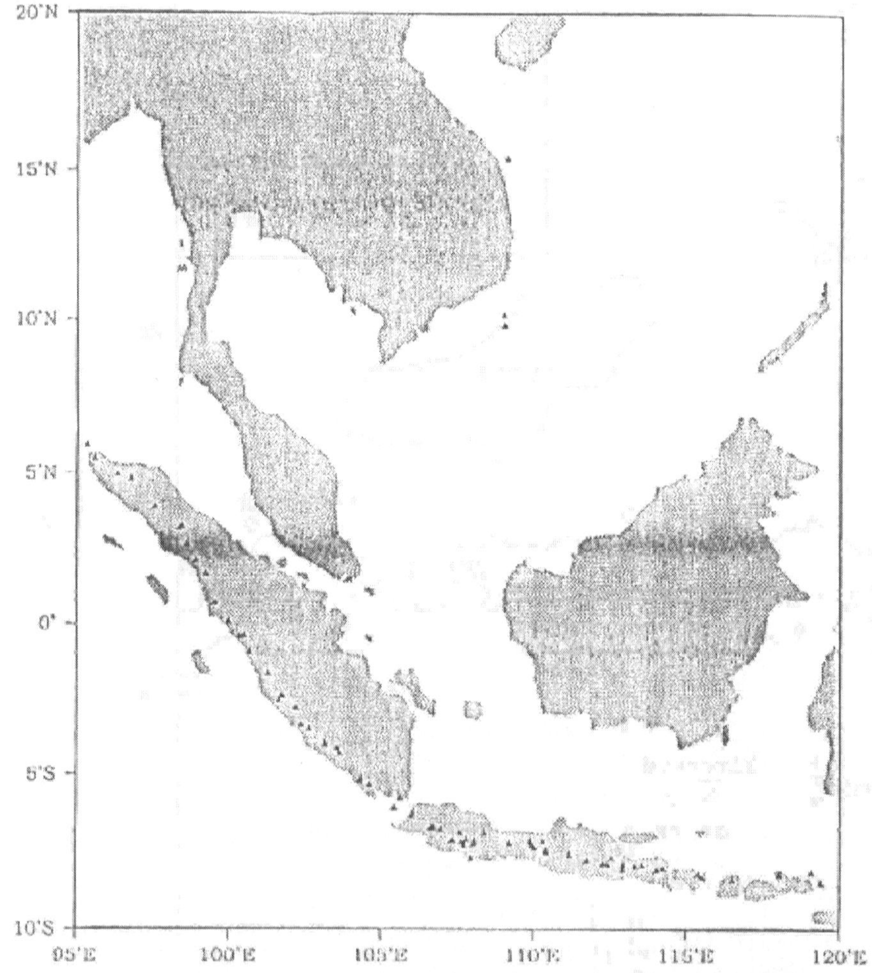

Figure 6.3: A Chain of Volcanoes (Sunda Arc) as a Result of Converging Between Indian Plate and Eurasia Plate (cited from Nagao, 1995)

This report is stressed on natural disaster, especially the natural disaster which have occurred along 1999 as well as the efforts of disaster mitigation which have been done by Indonesian Government. As an addition, it is also presented some destructive natural disaster that would never be forgotten.

2. Natural Disaster In Indonesia

(a) Natural Disaster Before 1999

The Eruption of Mount Krakatau In 1883 (loc. 1)

It is recorded in the Indonesian National Story, that Mount Krakatau has erupted for many times and the most destructive one is the eruption which occurred on August 27, 1883. The eruption have poured 18 Km^3 of material and its dust have been blown upto 80 km. The eruption also generated tsunami with the height of wave 30-40m and invaded Merak–Banten Beach and South Lampung, destroyed 295 city and killed more than 36,000 peoples (Naryanto, 1999).

The Mount Krakatau (Anak Krakatau) is still active. Anak Krakatau which located in Sunda Strait are a threatening to many facilities and human lives, because The Sunda strait have been a centre place of factories growth and occupied by dense population. The Sunda Strait is the main connector between Sumatera and Java.

Flores Earthquake in 1992 (loc.2)

A destructive earthquake have struck Flores on December 12, 1992 at 05 29 25 GMT. The magnitude of the main shock is 6.8 Mb, located at 122° 5′ 6″ E and -8° 24 ′0′ S with a focal depth of 36 Km. Most of the shocks were located North of Flores Island or just off shore. Only 10 shocks were located South of Flores or slightly off South of Flores Island (Figures 6.4 and 6.5) (Zen, *et al.*, 1993).

The earthquakes have generated tsunami, subsidence, uplift and landslides (Figure 6.6). The height of tsunami wave is different from place to place depending on their morphology. The highest wave reached 26.2m in North of Tangahdai (Figure 6.7). The shock which generated the tsunami devasting the North Coast of the Island was caused by the main shock. Eyewitnesses reported the tsunami came as a train of 5 tidal waves. The losses of the Flores Earthquake are 2000 people killed and thousands of buildings destroyed.

Liwa Earthquake (loc.3)

Liwa Earthquake occurred on February 17, 1994 at 24.10.00 (AM). The magnitude of the earthquake is 6 RS (Richter Scale). The highest intensity was VIII MMI (Modified Mercalli Intensity) which is located in Liwa City (Wisyanto, 1994). The earthquake devasted more than 190 peoples and destroyed nine thousands of buildings. The earthquake generated landslides in many places and isolated Liwa from the other city. The disconnection road have disturbed the relief and rescue operations.

Tsunami of Banyuwangi (loc.4)

Tsunami of Banyuwangi occurred in 1995. The tsunami was generated by earthquake, where the epicenter located South of Banyuwangi (in Indian Ocean). The tsunami destroyed more than ten of villages which located along the South Coast of

Figure 6.4: The Map Location of Flores Island

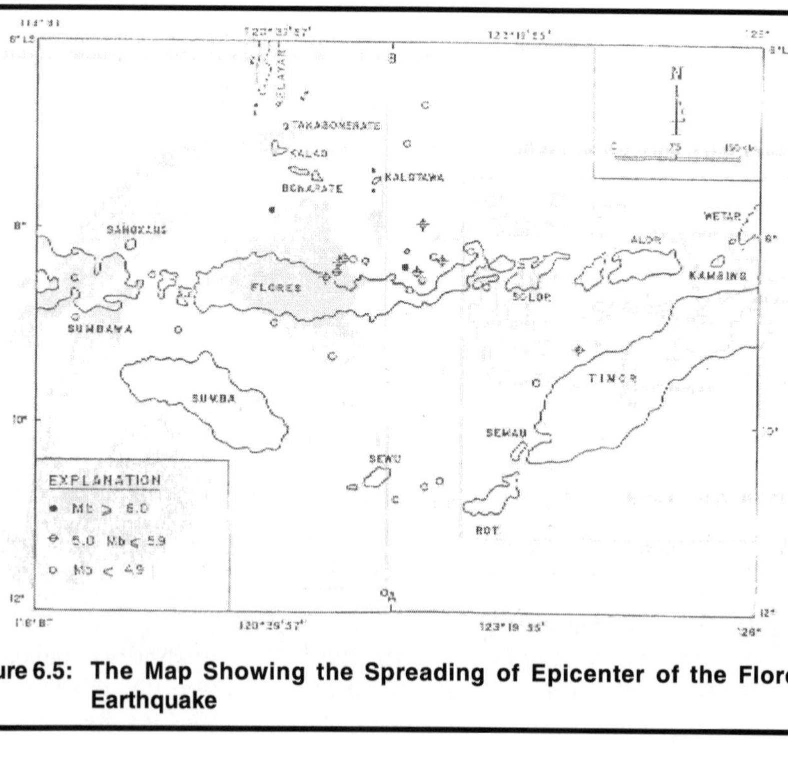

Figure 6.5: The Map Showing the Spreading of Epicenter of the Flores Earthquake

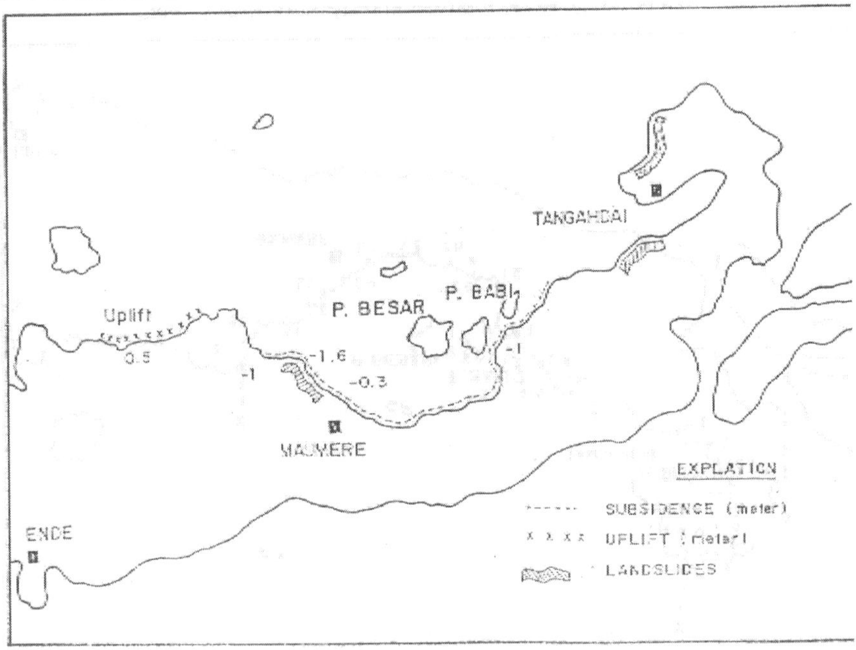

Figure 6.6: The Map Showing the Location of Landslides, Subsidence and Uplift as a Result of the Flores Earthquake

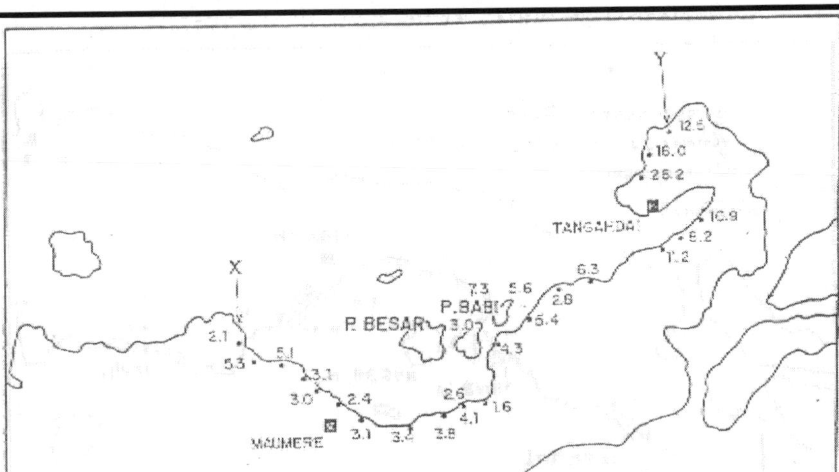

Figure 6.7: Tsunami Wave Height Data (in meter) Along the Coast of Norther Flores

Eastern Java. Bande AIit was the most damaged village due to the tsunami. It is recorded that the tsunamic wave invaded land up to 300 m from its shore line, 73 buildings made of bamboo damaged. The wave height was 5-7m and 5 people killed.

Kerinci Earthquake (loc. 5)

Kerinci Earthquake occurred on October 7, 1995 at 01.09.00 (AM), with the epicenter located just South of Sungai Penuh City. The earthquake destroyed more than 1000 buildings, 737 people injured seriously and 79 peoples died. (Media Indonesia, 1995). Besides generating landslides, the earthquake cracked many roads in the centre of the city.

Tsunami in Buol Tolitoli (loc.6)

Tsunami of Buol Tolitoli was generated by earthquake that occurred on January 1, 1996 on 7RS, located at 0.6°N and 119.92°E with focal depth of 33 km. The tsunami invaded land until 200m from its shore line and swept all villages which located along East Coast of Buol Tolitoli Regency, Middle Sulawesi. The tsunami damaged more than 400 of buildings and killed 8 peoples in Tonggaladidi village (Media Indonesia, 1996). The similar tsunami had happened in Balaesang approximately 26 years ago. The tsunami of Balaesang that occurred in 1968 destroyed many thousands of buildings and killed hundreds of peoples.

(b) Natural Disaster Along 1999

Flood

Flood in Sinjai, South Sulawesi

Flood that occurred on July 3, 1999 is the biggest flood on twenty years latest. The flood which is caused by pouring-rain for some days inundated approximately 600 ha of a shrimp dam (Kompas, 1999, op cit. Tejakusuma, 1999).

Flood In Jayapura, Irian Jaya

Flood that occurred on *Juni* 1999 inundated a part of Abepura District and killed 1 people, 540 buildings were inundated and about 3.413 peoples had to be evacuated to other places.

Flood in Ujung Pandang, South Sulawesi

The flood was caused by pouring-rain for a week continuously. The height of water achieved 1.5 m in Biringkanaya, Tamalate and Panakkukang District causing 4000 people to be evacuated.

Flood in Maros Regency, South Sulawesi

The flood inundated 6000 ha of wet rice-field and killed one people. The flood is an effect of overflowing of Maros River.

Flood in Semarang, Central Java

The flood inundated a part of Semarang City, Kendal and Grobogan. The flood was caused by rain that occurred since afternoon until Saturday night on February 1999. The roads which connect Semarang to Kendal, beginning from waleri, Ketapang,

Pasar Sore Kaliwungu until Pasar Mangkang were inundated and couldn't be passed.

Flood in Karawang, West Java

The flood was the effect of overflowing of rivers which surround the northern beach. The overflowing was caused by the occurrence of rain with height tide in the same time. The highest water level occurred in Muara Village (Cilamaya) causing 60 buildings were inundated and 70ha of rice-field in threating of harvest failure.

Flood in Serang Regency, West Java

The flood that was caused by overflowing of Ciujung River is an annual phenomenon. Since Friday (January 1,1999) The flood inundated some villages, such as villages in Cikande District, Walantaka District and Kragilan District. There were thousands of people moved and erected temporary camp along Jakarta- Merak highway.

Flood in South Sulawesi

Pouring-rain that had occurred for a week inundated Ujung Pandang, Maros, Pangkep and Gowa. The water level achieved more than 1 m. Hundreds of people were evacuated, thousands of rice-field and dam also inundated. The rivers which overflowed are Pampang River in Ujung Pandang and Jeneberang in Gowa. The flood destroyed Panciro Dam, killed 4 people and disconnected road from Ujung pandang to eastern places.

Flood in Pontianak, West Kalimantan

Pouring-rain that occurred on January 2, 1999 together with a high tide caused overflowing of Landak and Kapuas River. A shopping center and a market whose distance of 20-150m from the rivers were inundated. The flood didn't damage any building but disturbed traffic in the city.

Flood in Samarinda, East Kalimantan

The flood which occurred on January inundated 175 ha of rice field in Lempake and 75 ha of rice field in Sempaja. The flood also inundated some dwelling places in Lempake, Temindung Permai, Semaja and Samarinda Ulu Village.

Flood in Surabaya, East Java

Until January 2, 1999, the flood had inundated Surabaya Municipality. The height of the flood reached 1m, with rain intensity of 125 mm a day. The area which suffered from the inundation seriously was in the eastern Surabaya, where Kali Rungkut Street could not be passed.

Flood in Sukarno-Hatta Highway, Jakarta

Pouring-rain caused a flood and inundated Sukamo-Hatta Highway on 26th km. The flood reached 110 cm from its road surface. The flood disturbed passengers who were going to Sukarno-Hatta Airport and caused changing of many flight schedules.

Flood Tide and Hurricane

Karawang, West Java

A flood tide inundated Karawang Regency on the last December 1999. The flood tide which reached 2 caused 5017 ha of dam and rice field inundated, 51 of buildings damaged and hundreds of buildings inundated.

Batam, Riau

Flood tide and hurricane struck many building that made of wood in Batu Merah Village. At least 2000 people lost their dwelling places. Besides Batu Merah Village, the hurricane also ruined 30 buildings in Nongsa Village and 10 buildings in Batu Besar Village.

Earthquake

A destructive earthquake that occurred in 1999 was on December 21, 1999 at 21.14.59. The epicenter located at 105.64E and 7.21S 83 km SE of Panaitan Island or 200 km SW of Jakarta) with a focal depth of 33 km. Magnitude of the earthquake was recorded 6 RS. The shock struck Pandeglang Regency with the intensity of IV-V MMI, destroyed 3521 buildings and killed 5 peoples.

According to BMG's record (Meteorology and Geophysical Agency), besides this earthquake two more destructive earthquakes occurred on December 18, 1999 at 17.44.56, magnitude of 6 RS, epicenter at 139.76E and 2.68N(108 km SW of Jayapura) with a focal depth of 12 km and December 13, 1999 at 09:30:41, magnitude of 5.59 RS, epicenter at 127.04E and 1.84 (208 km E of Bitung) with a focal depth of 33 km.

3. Disaster Impact To Human Activities

Natural disaster can be met througout Indonesian Region. Usually, giving attention just only to the places that have developed intensively and had occupied by high concentration of population. The impact caused by natural disaster can appear in many forms depending on the local situation, such as the type of disaster, lithology, local morphology, the state of preparedness, the type of building etc.

Earthquake, Tsunami and Landslide have made many type of losses, such as destroying of building (house, school and other public facilities), cultivated land, telecommunication net, electrical net, road and human lives. All of that would have lead to disturbing on the role of economy. A hard situation was going to increase the crime ratio. In other side, flood disaster that occurred in Indonesia frequently also have made many losses, moreover appearing epidemic problems when the flood strike. Flood in Sukarno-Hatta Highway also disturbed many schedule of flight.

The last five years, Forest fire occurred in Indonesia frequently. The disaster also have caused disturbance of many flight schedule. Cloud and gas that were produced by the fire have disturbed the health of people that stayed near the burned forest and also have disturbed on relationship between Indonesia with neighbouring country.

Impacts of the natural disaster are going to influence many factor and create a multiplying effect, started from the society occupying place which is near to the source of disaster then spread to a wider society.

4. Natural Disaster Mitigation Efforts In Indonesia

(a) The Application of Technology for Disaster Mitigation

Earthquake and Tsunami Monitoring

For monitoring earthquake, Meteorology and Geophysical Agency operates 28 non-telemetered stations installed throughout Indonesia. There are also 27 seismic telemetered stations that were grouped into five regional networks, *i.e.* North Sumatera, West Java, Bali, South Sulawesi and Irian Jaya. Every regional network is equipped with processing facilities (Ibrahim, 1995).

A broad band station is being installed at Treter equipped with software to predict seismic moment of a strong earthquake that could be recorded by the mentioned station. If the seismic moment value is stronger than a certain value and be compared with other parameter earthquake sources, those earthquakes are predicted as tsunamigenic. This instrument is connected to alarm and facsimile that could indicate the occurrence of tsunami.

GIS For Fire And Flood Mitigation

Agency for "The Assessment and Application of Technology (BPPT)" is in cooperation with Jakarta local government and applying GIS (Geographic Information System) for fire and flood mitigation. For this moment, Directorate of Technology for Land Resources and Area Management (TPSLK) under BPPT mapped Jakarta on many aspects. Every theme of the map separated into layers, such as layers for elevation contour, drainage pattern, road net, electrical net, spreading of hydrant, water sources, buildings, etc. Every layer could be overlain according to the need.

As an example, occurring a fire in a place, we can use the database above to identify where is the fire occurred exactly (Figure 6.8), then we could determine the fire office that located nearest from the fire and the shortest road that could be passed (Figure 6.9), even a detailed information also could be met directly, in which it would be useful information for fire officials. Such as; the number of people who stay in the building, the number of windows or doors that would be able to be passed for extinguishing operations, location of hydrant (Figure 6.10) and also the situation inside etc. Finally, we will be able to rescue and give a relief effectively and fast.

Volcanological Disaster Monitoring

BPPT in cooperation with faculty of Geophysics of Gadjah Mada University installed a telemetered monitoring tools to monitor Merapi activities. The tools are used to monitor amount of gas that produced by Mount Merapi and also to monitor seismicity of Merapi. The gas content and seismicity could be red in the monitoring station. Increasing seismicity and gas content that is higher than the limit value will be reported to the chief of Sleman Regency. The report will be passed to the chief of Pakem District and then the official of District are giving a dangerous signal to society which live in surround of Mount Merapi.

Figure 6.8: Identification of the Location of Fire Using GIS

Figure 6.9: Determining the Nearest Road for Fire Disaster Mitigation

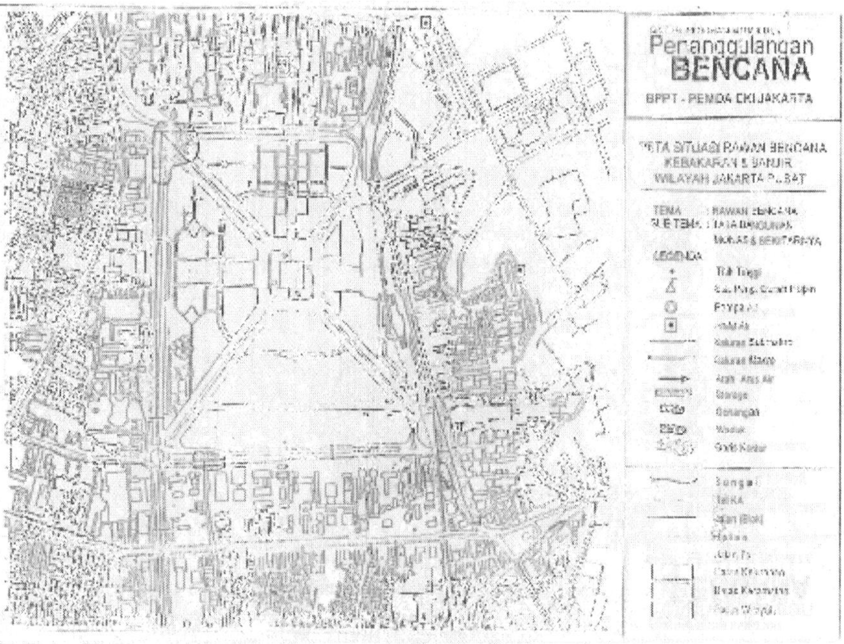

Figure 6.10: The Map Showing the Existence of Hydrant

Disaster Risk Assessment

BPPT in cooperation with local government of Lampung Province are making a risk assessment for disaster mitigation of Lampung Area. As we know that Lampung that transected by The Active Semangko Fault is a vulnerable area of natural disaster, especially of earthquake; moreover the existence of Mount Anak Krakatau are adding a threatening to Lampung. In that way, the local government should have a special attention to mitigate the area.

Disaster risk assessment will be done by three groups of works, that are hazard identification, vulnerability assessment and finally a risk analysis. The results of the assessment will be presented in a natural hazard zoning map which will be used as a guidance by decision maker (Rofiq, 1997).

5. Non Technological Efforts for Disaster Mitigation

Disaster mitigation, by application of technology also could be done by managerial efforts. BPPT in cooperation with many institutions held workshop, socialize disaster mitigation procedures to society and take part in conducting a field exercise for mitigation.

(a) Workshop

- BPPT cooperated with Bakornas PB (National Coordinating Agency for Disaster Mitigation) and Hanns Seidel Foundation (NGO from German) held workshop on Disaster Mitigation For Sunda Strait 1st on April 11-12, 1995 in Jakarta

- BPPT cooperated with Bakornas PB and Hanns Seidel Foundation held Workshop on Disaster Mitigation For Sunda Strait 2nd on April 1-3, 1997 in Jakarta.
- BPPT in cooperation with local government of Lampung Province and Hanns Seidel Foundation held Workshop on Disaster Mitigation For Lampung Area on October 27, 1999 in Bandar Lampung. In this event, we invited other government institution, local NGO and universities.

(b) Socialization of Disaster Mitigation

Socialization of Disaster Mitigation have been done by teaching of disaster mitigation procedures to public society, in order to increase awareness of the public society to natural disaster.

(c) Field Exercise for Disaster Mitigation

Field Exercise for Disaster Mitigation have been conducted by Bakomas PB (National Coordinating Agency For Disaster Mitigation) on November 1995 in Mount Merapi, Yogyakarta Province). On the field exercise, we used Military Civil Defence Assets that consist of Indonesian National Army, Civil Defence, organization from high school and university, Indonesian Red Cross, local government and also local society, where the total amount who have took apart in the event were 500 people.

6. Conclusion

- Natural disaster occurred in almost throughout Indonesian Region, especially earthquake, tsunami, landslide and flood.
- The Sunda Strait occupied by many factories with dense of population should get a special attention to be mitigated.
- Workshop, application of technology and socialization of disaster mitigation procedures must be increased, since losses from natural disaster are increasing.

7. References

1. Hadi, A.R., 1997, Mikrozoning Untuk Pengkajian Resiko Dan Mitigasi Bencana, Pros. Lokakarya Mitigasi Bencana Selat Sunda II, 95 hal.
2. Hall, R., 1995, Plate Tectonic Reconstruction of The Indonesian Region, Proc. Indonesian Petroleum Association, 24th Annual Convention, pp.71-84.
3. Ibrahim, G., 1995, Earthquake and Its Monitoring System In Indonesia, Proc. Workshop on Tsunami, BPPT, di Jakarta.
4. Nagao, T., 1995, Compilation of Heat Flow In Southeast Asia and Estimation of Underground Temperature Regime Including The Effect of Volcanic Heat, CCOP technical Bull., pp. 5-21.

5. Media Indonesia, Giliran Aceh Diguncang, Gempa Ancam Sumatera, harian Media Indonesia, terbitan 10 October 1995.

6. Media Indonesia, Delapan Orang Tewas Akibat Bencana Gempa Di Sulteng, harian Media Indonesia, terbitan 3 January 1996.

7. Naryanto, H.S., 1997, Kajian Aspek Bencana Dalam Pembanguna Kawasan Selat Sunda, Proc. Mitigasi Bencana Selat Sunda II, Dit. TPSLK, BPPT, hal. 51-60.

8. Naryanto, H.S., 1999, Bencana Alam Di Kawasan Selat Sunda dan Bandar Lampung Serta Upaya Mitigasinya, Proc. Lokakarya Mitigasi Bencana Di Wilayah Propinsi Lampung, 107 hal.

9. Tejakusuma, I.G.,1999, Bencana Di Indonesia Di Akhir Millenium ke Dua, Tahun 1999, (in progress).

10. Wisyanto, B. Marwanta dan A. Kuncahyo, 1995, Gempabumi Dan Tsunami Banyuwangi, BPPT internal report (unpublished).

11. Wisyanto dan Y. Sudiyanto, 1994, Intensitas Gempa Liwa Dan Faktor Pendukungnya, Proc. BPPT.

12. Zen, M. T., B. Massinon, Wisyanto, J.Surahman and Karyoto, 1993, Source Parameters of The 1992 Flores Earthquake, Proc. 18th Annual Convention of The Indonesian Geophysical Society.

7

The ESCAP-IDNDR Regional Survey on Assessment of Achievements during the International Decade for Natural Disaster Reduction (IDNDR)

Le Huu Ti

Economic Affairs Officer, Water and Mineral Resources Section
Environment and Natural Resources Development Division
Economic and Social Commission for Asia and the Pacific (ESCAP), Thailand

1. Introduction

In resolution A/RES/51/185 adopted at its fifty-first session, the General Assembly called upon the secretariat of the Decade to continue to facilitate a concerted international approach to improvements in early warning capacities for natural disasters and similar disasters with adverse impact on the environment within the process leading towards the closing event of the Decade. It reaffirmed that the secretariat of the Decade will continue to serve as the substantive secretariat for the preparation of the closing event of the Decade, working with the full support of relevant bodies of the United Nations Secretariat and drawing on the contributions of the organizations of the United Nations system concerned, other international organizations and Governments.

To prepare for the Closing Event of the Decade scheduled for July 1999, the IDNDR Secretariat started the process of data collection, with reference to contributions and accomplishments achieved during the Decade in the Fall of 1997. The Event will consist of the review by the Economic and Social Council of the United Nations of the achievements of the Decade and of the need for further institutional support to disaster reduction by the United Nations. The second part of the Event will consist of a Programme Forum, to be organized in Geneva in cooperation with agencies of the United Nations System, which will propose a platform for the future activities in relation to disaster reduction in the 21st century.

Within the context of the above direction and in line with the existing close cooperation between the IDNDR Secretariat and ESCAP, a detailed programme of collaboration for the preparation of the Closing Event of the Decade was established at the beginning of 1998. The programme includes a regional survey for Asia and organization of a regional meeting. In July 1998, ESCAP in cooperation with the IDNDR Secretariat started the regional survey. The questionnaire, which was prepared by the IDNDR Secretariat in consultation with ESCAP for its global study on achievements, was adopted for the survey.

Table 7.1: Memberships of the Typhoon Committee, the Panel on Tropical Cyclones and the Mekong River Commission

Name of Organization	*Members*
Typhoon Committee	Cambodia, China, D.P.R. of Korea, Hong Kong, China, Japan, Macau, Malaysia, Lao P.D.R., Philippines, Republic of Korea, Singapore, Thailand, United States, Vietnam
Panel on Tropical Cyclones	Bangladesh, India, Maldives, Myanmar, Oman, Pakistan, Sri Lanka, Thailand
Mekong River Commission	Cambodia, Lao P.D.R., Thailand, Vietnam

As part of the survey, the questionnaire was sent at the end of July 1998 to all the 16 focal points of IDNDR recommended by the IDNDR Secretariat and to all the focal points for water-related and geology-related disasters of the ESCAP networks. As of the end of 1998, 18[1] completed questionnaires were returned to ESCAP as listed in the Summary Table. The active participation of various national agencies and experts in the survey is reflected by the details provided in the completed questionnaires and attachments and the way the questionnaires were transmitted to ESCAP. In several cases, the questionnaires were sent to ESCAP directly by fax together with a copy by airmail and through the IDNDR Secretariat.

This report presents a summary of the main features of the information provided by the returned questionnaires as an introduction to the detailed analysis on water-related and geology-related disasters to be conducted separately by ESCAP consultants for discussion during the IDNDR-ESCAP Regional Meeting for Asia.

2. Context and Design of the Survey

(a) Geographical context

The part of the Asian region designated by the IDNDR Secretariat for the survey covers the North-East, South and South-East Asian sub regions with a total population of 3 billion people and the total land area of more 20 million km^2. Many countries of these three sub regions of ESCAP are severely affected by various types of annual disasters, most importantly tropical cyclones, floods, drought and earthquakes. Most of the countries in these sub regions are developing countries, including seven least developed countries. The impacts of natural disasters in these countries are therefore important not only in terms of economic aspects but also because of severe social implications.

(b) Other related ESCAP's ongoing efforts

Natural resources reduction activities of ESCAP started 50 years ago, when the Bureau for Flood Control (now the Water and Mineral Resources Section) was established in 1949 to advise and assist member governments with regard to flood control and related river problems. 1999 thus marks the fiftieth year of ESCAP's contributions to flood control and management in the region in particular and to water resources management in general. With the long experience in regional activities on natural disaster reduction, ESCAP has extended its technical assistance to cover various types of water-related and geology-related disaster reduction activities in Asia and the Pacific. ESCAP has also played major roles in strengthening sub regional networks on this area, such as the Typhoon Committee, the Panel on Tropical Cyclones and the Mekong River Commission.

As the survey aims to assess achievements of the Decade at the national and regional levels, a brief summary of achievements through the work of ESCAP is given below for reference. In terms of water-related disaster reduction, the scope of the main activities of ESCAP was extended to address water-related disaster reduction, especially flood control, within the framework of basin development, then the economic and social development process and finally as part of an integrated water resources management programme. Many workshops and seminars were conducted. In collaboration with the IDNDR Secretariat, then UNDRO, ESCAP organized a regional meeting on launching the IDNDR in February 1991. From this joint effort, ESCAP published a two-volume publication on water-related and geology-related natural disasters. ESCAP organized annually the IDNDR Day in collaboration with all United Nations organizations, international and national agencies working on the subject in the region. ESCAP also prepared and presented a Mid-Decade Report on natural disasters in Asia at the Yokohama World Conference in 1995.

A score of publications on this area of work have been produced by ESCAP in its efforts to assist the developing countries in the region to reduce natural disasters, especially by floods. These efforts culminated into detailed guidelines and manuals to facilitate application of regional experiences and transfer of know how. The latest

ESCAP publications of this category dealing with detailed guidelines for flood control planning are (1) *Manual and Guidelines for comprehensive flood loss prevention and management* in 1991 and (2) *Guidelines and Manual on Land-Use Planning and Practices in Watershed Management and Disaster Reduction* in 1997. In addition, ESCAP devoted the June issue of the Water Resources Journal to present its annual survey of water-related disasters for the preceding year in its members and associate members. Also in this June issue, assessments of disaster impacts and achievements in disaster reduction discussed at the annual meetings of the Typhoon Committee and the Panel for Tropical Cyclones are presented. Such a review and assessment of past major activities was made in order to identify past strategies of ESCAP in response to the common and/or priority needs on water-related disaster reduction, particularly for flood control and management. Activities of ESCAP in the area of water resources management reflect not only the needs of the member countries but also their priority in regional cooperation, on the basis of the commonality and urgency of these needs.

In its Geology for Planning programme, ESCAP has been working towards inducing decision makers to take geological factors into account, to improve the quality of land-use planning and reduce the effects of natural hazards posed by earthquakes, volcanism, ground subsidence and flooding. This is particularly urgent for the coastal lowlands of the region, habitat to an estimated 1.7 billion people, and even more so for the urban centres, most of which are located in the coastal zone. The programme strives to guide geologists to present their data in a user-friendly manner, such as thematic maps including hazard zoning, readily understandable to the decision makers. In this connection, the Forum on Urban Geology in Asia and the Pacific (FUGAP), initiated and established by ESCAP in 1995, has consistently served as a vehicle for creating awareness, sharing experience and arranging for specific training to enhance both technical and communication skills among geoscientists and planners.

Having long involved in water-related and geology-related disaster reduction activities, ESCAP took an active part in the implementation of various Resolutions of the United Nations General Assembly relating to the IDNDR from the conception of the Decade. The Water and Mineral Resources Section of the Environment and Natural Resources Development Division is the focal point for the coordination of the natural disaster reduction activities of ESCAP. The current Regional Meeting marks another collaborative activity of the IDNDR Secretariat and ESCAP that aims to review the achievements during the past decade and to make projections into the future.

(c) Main elements of the survey

The survey aimed to collect information and data on the following points:

- Progress which has been made, since the inception of the Decade, in the field of disaster reduction as a component of planning and risk management;
- Structures which are in place (institutional and legal structures), in relation to the noted accomplishments including, where applicable, the relative position of the IDNDR National Committees or Focal Points; and
- Future requirements foreseen to formulate and implement the relevant disaster reduction policies effectively in terms of protecting national assets

and population and creating those institutional arrangements required to deal with disaster reduction as a part of national policy.

The information and data collected were classified into five categories:

1. Experience and recent disasters including impacts, responses and success story,
2. Progress made on various aspects of disaster management planning;
3. Regional/subregional achievements based on national perspectives;
4. Infrastructures in place including legislative framework, training institutions and networking;
5. Future requirements for successful implementation of disaster reduction activities in the 21st century at the national and international levels.

3. Summary of Findings

In order to provide the readers an overall picture of the survey, the following statistics are extracted from the 18 returned questionnaires:

- 18 completed questionnaires along with additional information were received from 13 members and one associate member of ESCAP. These responses covered all the three targeted sub regions of ESCAP: North-East Asia (4), South Asia (4) and South-East Asia (6).
- 15 responses were from national government agencies, one from a provincial government agency and two from non-governmental organizations. Five responses indicated that their agencies were the focal points of the national IDNDR programmes dealing with disaster prevention, reduction and management Nine responses from national agencies responsible for activities related to disaster preparedness. Two agencies were responsible for disaster prevention, preparedness and reduction.

The information provided in the completed questionnaires was compiled in the Summary Table. The main findings are summarized below:

(a) Experience and recent disasters

Disasters identified by the responses included floods, cyclones, earthquakes, drought, tornado, debris flow including landslide and mudflow, hailstorms, surge, tsunami and regional haze. The most common disaster experienced practically in all the responding countries was floods. These disasters resulted in loss of lives, serious economic damages and severe impacts on the social conditions. The critical years listed in the responses included all the years from 1992 to 1998 (up to the time of the survey). Although the severity of these events, floods or earthquakes or drought and others, is different from one country to another, the most critical year appeared to be 1998, followed by 1997 and 1995. In 1998 alone, the economic damage in these countries was estimated to be over US$23 billion (US$20 billion in China, $1 billion in Bangladesh, $1 billion in Republic of Korea, several hundred millions in India and Vietnam.)

Various measures were adopted by the respective authorities in all the countries and areas to reduce impacts of disasters and to prevent future disasters. They were structural and non-structural measures, short-term and long-term plans or strategies, legislative measures, institutional development and publicity programmes. The non-structural measures included land-use guidelines and zoning, disaster-prone and risk mapping, disaster proofing measures and warning systems. The wide spectrum of measures taken by the members and associate members of ESCAP indicates a diversity in the experiences and offers good opportunities for information exchange. All the responses believed that further improvement in disaster preparedness and prevention is possible, particularly with respect to warning systems, public awareness in risk management, institutional capacity building, disaster management planning and coordination, construction of structures, application of advance technology, better land-use planning and enforcement of zoning, and most importantly political commitment

Almost all the responses indicated that the IDNDR had helped their respective countries to give greater attention to disaster reduction. Few responses indicated lack of direct contact with the respective national IDNDR activities. Examples of the importance of IDNDR's contribution are given below:

- "IDNDR has in fact helped our government in taking into consideration the criteria of sustainable development through effective disaster reduction in the planning and implementation of development projects with regard to infrastructure development" (Malaysia)
- "The Decade has laid down model frameworks which may be adopted by governments in fortifying its disaster management systems." (Philippines National Red Cross)
- "IDNDR has aroused public awareness and enhanced international cooperation on disaster reduction." (Hong Kong, China)
- "A national programme in line with IDNDR objectives and resolution is being implemented to minimize the adverse impacts of disaster on population and environment of Bangladesh" (Bangladesh Dhaka Metropolitan Development Planning)
- IDNDR led to the establishment of China National Committee on IDNDR (CNCIDNDR), IDNDR action in China, National Report, China National Plan for Disaster Reduction, China Centre for Disaster Reduction (CCDR), many projects and programs for disaster reduction, etc. China Modem Setup of Disaster Prevention and Reduction is to be established. (CNCIDNDR, China)
- "Because of IDNDR, it has been possible to get greater commitments of the Government in disaster management and as such project for comprehensive disaster management in Bangladesh with UNDP, UNICEF sponsorship has been taken up by Government for implementation. To build up public awareness at all levels, Government takes up every year elaborate programme for the observance of IDNDR Day and has also introduced

'National Disaster Preparedness Day' for observance on last working day of March every year." (Bangladesh Disaster Management Bureau)

- "The World Conference on Natural Disaster Reduction in Yokohama 1994 helped us realize the critical situation over the world, in particular in developing countries affected by natural disasters and necessities of international cooperation in the field of disaster mitigation." (Japan)
- "IDNDR has certainly helped to give greater attention to disaster reduction particularly in the field of activity of the scientific community but there exists wide gaps between planning and its execution due to various reasons." (India)

The above information illustrates a general picture of achievements of the Decade from different angles of disaster management planning and implementation as well as disaster preparedness and risk reduction.

Several examples of "success story" were indicated in the responses from Bangladesh, Malaysia, Myanmar, Republic of Korea, Turkey, and Hong Kong, China. Among these, the most distinguished example from Bangladesh indicated that "Early warning and timely action limited the number of deaths to about one hundred in May 1997. The cyclone of the same intensity of 1988 took 138,000 lives."

(b) National achievements

All the responses confirmed accessibility to national and local warning systems and some indicated their established link with regional and international mechanisms, such as the Typhoon Committee, the Panel on Tropical Cyclones and WMO programmes. Many countries confirmed availability of various components for risk management but only two indicated existence of comprehensive risk assessment at the national level, one at selected localities. Various stages of preparation of structured mitigation plans were indicated in the responses and six countries indicated availability of national structured mitigation plans and one with provincial and local plans.

Various reasons were identified as obstacles by the countries or areas in their efforts to implement the Decade targets. Among these, the lack of financial resources was the prevailing reason, followed by the lack of technical capacities, particularly advance technology and modern equipment, and weakness in coordination and institutional arrangements. Other reasons included that the Decade targets were too ambitious and prioritization would be necessary; lack of strong political commitments; vigorous international efforts would be required.

In order to generate public awareness, various programmes have been adopted at the national, provincial and local levels. Media and publications are widely accepted. Short-term programmes in the form of workshops or seminars and formal education curriculums have been adopted for training purposes. Involvement of decision makers and major groups to ensure their support and participation in disaster reduction programme was achieved through various established mechanisms and procedures as indicated in almost all the responses. These mechanisms included those responsible for information dissemination, for disaster management planning, policy formulation, strategy implementation and legislative bodies. Collaboration with other sectors was indicated through the established guidelines and mechanisms (Malaysia), information dissemination (Thailand, Hong Kong, China), development plan (Bangladesh), and projects (China, Singapore, Turkey). Seven responses indicated the benefits of the international arena provided by the IDNDR for information exchange. Others did not get direct access to the arena.

(c) Regional/sub-regional Achievements

Important achievements from sub regional cooperation were identified in several responses in the field of tropical cyclones, floods, tsunami forecasting as well as training in disaster preparedness and management. Reference was made to the work undertaken within the framework of the Typhoon Committee, the ESCAP/WMO Panel on Tropical Cyclones, UNESCO Tsunami Warning System, Eastern Asia Natural Hazards Mapping Project, the Asian Disaster Preparedness Centre, Asian Centre for Disaster Reduction in Tokyo and lately the ASEAN Regional Haze Task Force (1998). It was believed that regional mechanisms are needed to continue promoting exchange of information and experience. Regional cooperation was also expected to make important contribution to disaster reduction in general and enhancement of resource mobilization, communication networks, warning systems, improvement in forecasting techniques and training.

(d) Infrastructures and legislation established

All the responses confirmed commitment of the respective Governments to disaster reduction and also the existence of a designated government authority for coordination. However, there were significant difference among the government institutional arrangements for the designated authority. In some cases, the authority was chaired by the Government Head, others chaired by the Minister concerned and one was a parliamentary commission. Budgetary resources were indicated to be available for the purposes. Firm legislative frameworks have been set up as indicated in most of the responses, for disaster management in general or particular disasters such as floods, forest fires, tropical cyclones, earthquakes or development planning. In one response, it was indicated that the comprehensive Act was being drafted.

With respect to education and training on disaster reduction, most of the responses indicated various measures adopted in the respective members and associate members of ESCAP. However, most of the responses indicated the field of training in their respective areas of work. On the perspectives and experience of the respective agencies participating in the survey, the responses indicated a wide diversity in the established networks to aid in the transfer and application of knowledge and technology, information dissemination and international collaboration. The networks referred to included the existing mechanisms such as the Typhoon Committee, the South Asia Association for Regional Cooperation (SAARC), WMO and Japan Meteorological Agency; newly established bilateral project (Malaysia-France, Pakistan-USA and Japan). In one response, it was indicated that the networks were first established for sectoral disasters and developed into multi-sectoral coordination (China.)

(e) Future Requirements and Priority Areas of Cooperation

Most responses indicated their agreement to the importance of the criteria identified in the questionnaire as requirements for successful implementation of disaster reduction activities in the 21st century. However, the order of priority of the elements of requirements was different among the responses. Policy and budgetary commitment and public awareness together with strong linkage to economic and social development programmes were commonly accepted as top priority. Other priority included international cooperation, information dissemination, strengthening of local authorities, and network building. Several responses provided additional criteria as necessary conditions for the future operations:

- Proper land-use planning and to apply integrated approach in management of resources.
- Establishment of programmes to promote awareness on disaster prevention and reduction. Cooperation can be made on specific tasks, projects, information dissemination and warning systems, and post disaster management assessment.
- Latest technology be used.
- Improvement of sophisticated numerical models to predict local heavy rainfalls; to simulate tsunamic generation and propagation; to improve seismic observation network.
- To support science and technology transfer. Establish central data and information systems in the region. Cross-sectoral coordination.
- A strong bonding mechanism among the IDNDR related international programs and national projects is required.
- Build up effective networking at national, regional and global levels.
- TCDC be improved; lack of financial resources; common policy needed in the region; regional network and communication be upgraded.
- More budget resources; strengthening legal system.

All the responses reaffirmed the needs and importance of international cooperation for future disaster reduction activities. Among the top priorities identified by most of the responses were technical assistance, financial support and technology transfer. With regards to technical cooperation, most of the responses attached priority to sub regional cooperation on early warning systems, communication networks and disaster preparedness.

With regard to future programmes and measures, several responses identified the need to put in place national disaster reduction programmes (or plans or strategies) with political commitment, proper institutional framework for coordination and resources availability. Several responses confirmed the need to establish or strengthen regional/sub regional mechanisms for better interaction, information exchange, forecasting systems, enhanced public awareness and technology transfer. One country suggested that "IDNDR be changed to International Committee on Natural Disaster Reduction (ICNDR) to keep up the momentum at international and national levels."

Table 7.2: Summary of Regional Survey on Assessment of Achievements during the IDNDR Decade

Sl.No.	*Country*	*Recent Disasters*	*Progress*	*Regional Results*	*Structures in Place*	*Future Requirements*
1.	Singapore Meteorological Service	Transboundary haze pollution. No direct impacts on health and assets, but on tourism and transportation.	Structured plans well coordinated. Formation of local haze taskforce for mitigation. Plans well coordinated. Good linkage with neighbouring countries. Study funded by ADB will be conducted as follow up action.	Member of ASEAN Regional Haze Taskforce.	Singapore Police Force, Singapore Civil Defense Force and Ministry of Environment.	International mechanism and policy commitment. Early warning systems and communications. A well-coordinated natural disaster mitigation program for each country.
2.	Pakistan Federal Flood Commission (FCC), Ministry of Water and Power	Catastrophic floods in 1994 and 1995. Damage to infra-structure, including education and health facilities.	Substantial protection been provided to 250 flood-prone sites. Flood forecasting and warning systems been provided. Assessment made for projects. National Disaster Management Plan made. Comprehensive Flood Warning Manual being prepared.	Since 1990, flood forecasting. Work-shops on community participation.	Embodied in Government structure, priorities, budget and legislation.	Financial resources, technical assistance, technology transfer, directory, establishment of regional warning systems, disaster preparedness and awareness for public. Better regional and sub-regional interaction; state-of-the-art manuals on disaster management facilities; more effective use of space information and technology (real-time); establishment of disaster mitigation directory at national, sub-regional and regional levels.

Contd...

Table 7.2–Contd...

Sl.No.	Country	Recent Disasters	Progress	Regional Results	Structures in Place	Future Requirements
3.	Malaysia Geological Survey Department	Landslide in 1993, debris flow in 1995 and 1996. Loss of lives and damage to properties.	National Disaster Management & Relief Committee (NDMRC) set up at the federal, state and local levels; early warnings issued by Department of Meteorology. Close cooperation with related agencies. A pamphlet on earthquake disaster has been prepared. Geo hazards incorporated into Town and Country Planning and EIAs.	Not much improvement in preparedness and reduction of geologic disasters. More information on climate and rainfalls is required.	The NDMRC is chaired by a Cabinet Minister. Training on geological hazards being offered by Department of Geology at the local universities.	Proper land-use planning and application of integrated approach in management of resources are needed. Need (1) technical assistance, (2) financial resources, and (3) technology transfer. A mechanism and strategy on disaster management should be in place.
4.	Malaysia Crisis and Disaster Management Unit, National Security Division, Prime Minister Department	Landslides (93,95), mudslide (96), typhoon Greg (96), peat/forest fire (98). 361 lives lost, RM200 million damaged, 2,000 ha burnt and haze affected health.	Formulation of National Hazard Action Plan, Special Malaysia Disaster Assistance and Rescue Team (SMART), Policy and Mechanism of National Disaster Management Relief (Directive No. 20), Warnings provided by the Malaysian Meteorological Servi-ces. Malaysia has a good networking	ASEAN Expert Group on Disaster Management in April 98, Signing of MOU between Malaysia and Indonesia in Dec 97. Holding of joint exercises of disaster assistance and rescue teams with Singapore, An ASEAN Ministerial Meeting on Haze was held and the Sub-regional Fire Fighting	No specific authority, Each agency has its own regulation. RM800 million allocated in the 7th Malaysia Plan (1996-2000) for flood mitigation projects, Environmental Quality Act (74), Land Government Act (76) and Uniform Building By Laws (84). Five Professional Associa-tions Malaysian Institute of Public Works, Malaysian Architects	Establishment of programmes to promote awareness on disaster prevention and reduction. Non-structure: strengthen disaster management system, training activities, promote public awareness, improve forecasting and warning systems and improve hazard mapping. Structure: mitigation measures against landslide and embankments

Contd...

Table 7.2–Contd...

Sl.No.	Country	Recent Disasters	Progress	Regional Results	Structures in Place	Future Requirements
			relationship with other countries in exchange information and experiences.	Arrangement (RFAs) for Borneo and Sumatra was established in April 98. World Conference in Yokohama in Japan in 1994, Natural Disaster Reduction, Confe-rence in Australia in 1996, High-level seminar on MCDA in Indonesia in 1997, and ASEAN Expert Group Meeting in Singapore in April 1998.	Association, Petroleum National Berhad (Petronas), University Putra Malaysia, National Institute of Public Administration (INTAN) have contributed to disaster reduction, MoU signed with the French Government on training of personnel on disaster management	improvement. International cooperation for the transfer of expert knowledge in disaster reduction, to increase awareness and relief services.
5.	Hong Kong, China Hong Kong Observatory	Floods and landslips caused by Typhoons Dot (93), Helen (95), Victor (97) and heavy rain in July 94, June and July 97 resulted in severe damage to property, farmland, fish ponds, 10 deaths, disrupt in traffic and social activities.	Global QRA of pre-1978 slopes, results published; Hong Kong contingency Plan for Natural Disasters with operation instructions for each government department; under WMO framework, warning services provided. Special and general education and information programs in place for the public. Legislative authority, policy bureau, depart-	More accurate weather prediction products have become available from the regional meteoro-logical centres; Operational exchange of cyclone and rainstorm warnings started since 1996 in the Pearl River Estuary. Participated in the World Conference in Yokohama in 1994.	The Security Bureau oversees the Contingency Plan for natural Disasters.	Need policy and budgetary commitment; public education; multi-media dissemination of information; continue international cooperation. To enhance information communication networks; research in short-range rainfall forecasting and development of human resources through education and training. Application of innovative information technology for weather services; state-of-

Contd...

Table 7.2–Contd...

Sl.No.	Country	Recent Disasters	Progress	Regional Results	Structures in Place	Future Requirements
			ments, organization and media are closely liaised. Regular press conferences, briefings provided. Talks, meetings and education programs carried out. Hong Kong is linked to Beijing, Tokyo and Bangkok to contribute to early warning systems.			the-art technology to short-range weather forecasting; promotion of international cooperation.
6.	Bangladesh Dhaka Metropolitan Development Planning Project (DMDPP)	Cyclone in May 97; Floods in July-Sep 98. Flood of 1998 inundated ¾ of the country, killed 1,000 people, damaged infrastructure and changed socio-economic scenario. Early warning and timely action taken limited the number of death in 1997 to 100 (as compared with 138,000 deaths in 1991 from the same intensity).	Comprehensive national assessment of risks (CNAR) under process; National Disaster Management Plan being prepared. Disaster management committees formed at national and local levels. Standing orders issued by Government, legislation being processed. Weather forecasts and early warnings issued through media. Maps and documents published and dissemination through media, seminars and workshops.	Information on cyclone and floods for early warning received from the neighbouring countries. Especially for flood mitigation.	Ministry of Relief, Rehabilitation and Disaster Management. Effective inter-disciplinary approach is yet to be developed.	Upgrade dissemination of information and strengthen local authorities. Updated technology, financial resources. Humanitarian approach of development policies.

Contd...

Table 7.2–Contd...

Sl.No.	Country	Recent Disasters	Progress	Regional Results	Structures in Place	Future Requirements
7.	India Geological Survey of India, Kolkata	Earthquakes: Killari (93), Jabalpur (97); Landslide (98); Flood in July-Sep 98. Loss of lives (10,000), severe damage.				Policy commitment; budgetary commitment; responsible local authorities; links to social development programs. Disaster preparedness regional warning system; financial resources. Future disaster reduction programs for floods, cyclones, earthquakes and landslides. Scientific knowledge needs to be applied and provided to local authorities. Enhancement of public awareness. International cooperation required.
8.	Turkey General Directorate of Disaster Affairs (GDDA), Ministry of Public Works and settlement.	Earthquakes Erzincan in 92, Dinar in 95, Ceyhan-Misis in 98; floods in Izmir in 95 and Black Sea Region in 98. Nearly 1,000 deaths, US$ 4 billion loss and structures damaged.	Comprehensive national assessment of risk (CNAR) is being studied under a UNDP project. Structured disaster response plans exist at provincial and local levels. Early warning systems for floods and landslides being developed. Public awareness made through TV spots	Cooperation made for the Black Sea and Mediterranean region. Needs to enhance scientific and technical cooperation or reduce political tension.	GDDA is the authority under the comprehensive Disaster Law. Legal frameworks enacted by national authorities. Enforcement lies with local governments who often lack manpower. The GDDA and the European Natural Disasters Training Centre, the Turkish Earthquake	Link with social and economic development programs. Public awareness. Regional early warning systems, information networks and technology transfer are necessary. Active participation of agencies and communities is essential. Six principles were recommended as guidelines for disaster

Contd...

Table 7.2–Contd...

Sl.No.	Country	Recent Disasters	Progress	Regional Results	Structures in Place	Future Requirements
			and pamphlets. GDDA serves a parliamentary investigation commission for impacts of disasters and makes recommendations. Information exchange in the Balken Region and cooperation with other international agencies.		Foundation and the Turkish National Committee for Earthquake Engineering are key organizations on technology transfer. The Middle East Technical University established a centre to deal with this.	reduction in the 21st century.
9.	Philippines Philippines Red Cross, Manila	Drought caused by El Nino in 97/98, typhoons: Gloring, 96, Angela, 95, Kadiang, 93; Mindoro earthquake, 93 and lahar avalanches in Central Luzon (92-96). Loss of lives, impacts on health, displacement of the poor, economic slow down due to destruction of infrastructure and agriculture production; rephasing of development.	A tool for Comprehensive National Assessment of Risks (**CNAR**) being developed. National disaster management plans exist. Training programs developed and interactive learning strategies adopted for public awareness programs. Work contributed more on health and emergency responses. Coordination with other sectors worked well.		Response not proactive.	

Contd...

Table 7.2–Contd...

Sl.No.	Country	Recent Disasters	Progress	Regional Results	Structures in Place	Future Requirements
10.	China China National Committee on IDNDR	Rainstorm-flood, drought, typhoon-surge, earthquake, hailstorm, snowstorm, landslide, mudflow, forest fire, insects, pests, etc. Impacts Ranked as above.	CNAR was published in the National Report. Needs financial support. Media is used. Annual meetings with those concerned. Cooperation with UNDP, World Bank. ADB assistance.		CNCIDNDR is the national authority. Budgets allocated to Line Ministries. Legislatives exist for floods, earthquake, forest fire, etc. Disaster reduction concept incorporated in training under the auspices of the Chinese Academy of Sciences. Networks first developed for sectoral disasters then extended to multisectoral ones (CCDR). Interdisciplinary approach through CCDR.	IDNDR be changed to International Committee on Natural Disaster Reduction (ICNDR) to keep up the momentum at international and national levels. Information dissemination be continued and strengthened. International assistance be provided to China and the Third World.
11.	Pakistan Pakistan Meteorological Department	Flood of 97 and earthquake on 28 Feb 97. Many people killed, heavy loss of animals and damage to properties.	CNAR not available. Early warnings with weather data received from India and Bangladesh. Public awareness made through media.	Data exchange and early warning systems be improved.	Emergency Relief Cell (ERC) in Cabinet Division. Budget allocated with concerned agencies. Legislatives available. Collaboration with USA and Japan.	Latest technology be used. Technology transfer, technical assistance and financial resources. International seminars and workshops be organized.
12.	Thailand Environmental Geology Section, Department of Mineral Resources	Floods, cyclones, land subsidence, karst collapse, coastal erosion and earthquake. Floods and cyclones are	CNAR not yet available. Improve flood-forecasting network. Implementation of modern techniques for monitoring and	Eastern Asia Natural Hazards Mapping Project to compile natural hazard maps.	Ministry of Interior. Legislative available. Enhance awareness on importance of geoscience in coastal zone management and	To support science and technology transfer. Establish central data and information systems in the region, Cross-sectoral coordination. Technology

Contd...

Table 7.2–Contd...

Sl.No.	*Country*	*Recent Disasters*	*Progress*	*Regional Results*	*Structures in Place*	*Future Requirements*
		main disasters with loss of lives and damage to assets. Earthquake is seldom.	warning. Public awareness through poster and paper presentation. GIS for policy makers, planners and local governments. Provided geo-hazard data to agencies and private sector.		natural hazards. Works mainly with geologists.	transfer and disaster preparedness. Warning system and protection measures and monitoring.
13.	Bangladesh Bangladesh Nari Pragoti Sangha, BNPS, Dhaka	Floods and cyclones. Massive damage, food shortage, threat to health, environmental hazards and non-availability of drinking water.	Government has established a disaster management plan in 1996. It has a network for early warning system. Recently, India has agreed to provide early warning on natural calamities like flood or cyclone to Bangladesh. The Flood Action Plan was considered to have caused serious threats to the environment. Government has increasingly involved NGOs in its programs. Government and NGOs have developed good information base.	Took part in World Conference In 1994. Regional cooperation may help reduce disasters such as floods in 1998.	Yes, but not well equipped. Budget not enough. Government agencies looked disintegrated in this respect. Not many educational institutions involved. South Asia Association for Regional Cooperation (SAARC) has a small unit on disaster reduction. BNPS has a network of 19,000 women members in rural areas.	Network building, information dissemination and budgetary commitment. Regional or sub-regional warning system and financial resources followed by technology transfer and technical assistance. Formulation of comprehensive policy is required.

Contd...

Table 7.2–Contd...

Sl.No.	*Country*	*Recent Disasters*	*Progress*	*Regional Results*	*Structures in Place*	*Future Requirements*
14.	Japan Japan Meteorological Agency	Warnings issued against storm, snowstorm, heavy rain, heavy snow, storm surge, high waves, and flood.	Comprehensive National Assessment of Risks (CNAR) not available. Holding seminars, "Weather Festivals" and provide information to the general public. JMA established communication systems to disseminate information as stipulated in the Meteorological Service Law.	JMA provided numerical prediction data through Regional Specialized Meteorological Centre (RSMC) and meteorological products, satellite imagery and typhoon tract forecasts to the members of the Typhoon Committee since 1995. Assisted Fiji and Bangladesh to strengthen their warning systems. JMA held regional seminars and training courses on typhoon disaster prevention. To improve accuracy of typhoon track forecasts.	Disaster Countermeasures Act designates agencies to be responsible at national and local levels. Disaster Countermeasures Basic Act and Large-scale Earthquake Countermeasures Act. Disaster Prevention Research Institute of Research made by Universities. RSMC Data Serving System provides East Asia with prediction and data through the Internet.	JMA continues to improve sophisticated numerical models to predict local heavy rainfalls; to simulate tsunami generation and propagation; to improve seismic observation network.
15.	Republic of Korea Korea Meteorological Administration (KMA)	Drought, typhoon, flood, severe storm and gale. Loss of lives, heavy damage. Regular inspection of disaster-prone areas; construction of disaster prevention facilities, allocation of resources.	CNAR published; yes; to provide warnings and advices on prevention and mitigation of natural disasters. Earthquake monitoring and tsunami warnings. Public awareness through Mass-media and internet.	KMA is a competent authority of the International Coordination Group for the Tsunami Warning System (TSU) of UNESCO. KMA proposed to establish a regional tsunami-warning centre for the Far East Seas. Gained knowledge and experience through information exchange.	US$78 million allocated to 15 cities and 230 counties. Funds can be used only for disaster reduction. Legislatives available. Disaster prevention education and drills and practice emergencies. A Website is operated by KMA.	A strong bonding mechanism among the IDNDR related international programs and national projects is required. Regional/sub-regional warning systems be adopted for regional/sub-regional events. Political commitment is required. Substantive measures at the regional/sub-regional level are required

Contd...

Table 7.2–Contd...

Sl.No.	*Country*	*Recent Disasters*	*Progress*	*Regional Results*	*Structures in Place*	*Future Requirements*
16.	Bangladesh Disaster Management Bureau	Cyclone, flood, drought, tornado, earthquake. Property and infrastructure damage. Cholera outbreak. Reduction of impacts of May 97 cyclone.	CNAR study made but not published yet. Disaster Management Plan to be published in 1999. Early cyclone warnings issued in real time through national broadcasting network. A system of two-hour lectures has been introduced at all training institutes. In curricula of class V to XII. Training modules prepared. Four committees established for policy makers, local authorities, NGOs and media to meet regularly.	Regional cooperation helped reduce damage in 1997 flood. Member of WMO/ESCAP Panel on Tropical Cyclones. Regional mechanism is needed to promote exchange of information and experience.	Ministry of Disaster Management and Relief with its Disaster Management Bureau (DMB). Draft Act being prepared. Existing Directives and curricula development.	Build up effective networking at national, regional and global levels. Technology transfer, financial support and technical assistance and balanced institutional development. Political and financial commitments at national and international levels are required.
17.	Myanmar Department of Meteorology and Hydrology (DMH)	Floods in July/Sep 97. Loss of lives, property and agricultural production.	CNAR not available, but only for sub plans being prepared. Flood risk done for some areas. A map of earthquake prone areas has been made. Early warning system on weather and climate available to public with early flood warnings. Training courses	Disaster management training programme was organized in 1994 with high-level participation. Myanmar participates in regional events on disaster reduction. Exchange of data and information be improved and through computer network. Technology transfer.	National Disaster Management Committee, headed by Minister of Social Welfare. Budget allocated to related Departments. Legal framework exists for land-use planning, water and forest management, building codes, etc. Curricula with Yangon Institute of Technology	TCDC be improved; lack of financial resources; common policy needed in the region; regional network and communication be upgraded; disaster reduction be integrated into economic and social development and environmental protection. Financial and technical assistance required and

Contd...

Table 7.2–Contd...

Sl.No.	*Country*	*Recent Disasters*	*Progress*	*Regional Results*	*Structures in Place*	*Future Requirements*
			organized in townships. Committees of all agencies formed to deal with disasters. Fire insurance adopted and relief donations mobilized. Myanmar is a member of ASNET-RESED Project of ASEAN on seismology.		and Department of Geology. DMH computer is linked with the neighbouring countries.	technology transfer. National Action Plan be formulated and revised regularly.
18.	Vietnam Standing Office of the Central Committee for Flood and Storm Control (CCFSC)	Flood, storm, drought, flash flood, landslide & mud-flows, hailstorms, tornadoes. Annual severe damage.	CNAR not yet available, but being prepared. Strategy & action plan documented and disseminated in 1994. Early warning well practiced. Public awareness campaign is made through training of local officials, NGOs and mass media.	Improvement in disaster management from better flow of related information Associated with ADPC, Asian Centre for Disaster Reduction in Tokyo	The CCFSC with its annual budget is a commitment at the top-level to disaster reduction. A firm legal framework has been established. Disaster-reduction curricula yet to be developed.	More budget resources. Disaster reduction must be integrated in economic and social development process. Strengthening legal system; Capacity building; Better information dissemination; and Better mechanism for international coordination. Financial resources; quicker information exchange; regional network; technology transfer and technical assistance.

(f) Remarks

The responses provided an overwhelming amount of information, including important developments in the legal and institutional frameworks of the respective members and associate members of ESCAP related to disaster reduction. The information provided in the completed questionnaire together with attachments is expected to be analyzed in more detail in two separate papers on the water-related and geology-related disasters. However, various gaps of information could also be identified during this initial analysis and it is hoped that additional information could be further provided during the Regional Seminar by the respective delegations, particularly from those countries, which have not participated in this survey yet.

4. Conclusions

During the past decade, the region was severely affected by various types of natural disasters, particularly during the past few years. To cope with these disasters, a variety of measures have been adopted and the diversity in the experiences in the region offers good opportunities for effective regional cooperation among the developing countries in the related fields. Most of the responses noted a significant increase in the awareness on the importance of disaster preparedness and in the commitments by the Governments to disaster reduction. In several countries, these commitments were translated into institutional infrastructures to ensure effective mobilization of resources and sustained public participation in the national efforts, such as creation of national disaster reduction coordinating committees, establishment of disaster management systems, formulation of national strategies and action plans, and preparation of disaster management programmes. Apart from the national achievements, the responses also noted achievements of regional efforts in sharing information and experiences as well as in coordination of activities. Examples included the sharing of meteorological data for better flood warnings by Bangladesh, India and Pakistan realized through the Panel on Tropical Cyclones; the achievements of the members of the Typhoon Committee in typhoon tracking and flood forecasting; and the establishment of the Regional Haze Action Plan by ASEAN countries. In this context, space technology applications were highlighted as an important tool for monitoring of natural hazards and related communications. With respect to future requirements, most of the responses endorsed the need to integrate disaster preparedness and mitigation activities into the economic and social development process, to increase public awareness and participation, to strengthen regional networking and transfer of technologies.

In order to have a more complete picture of regional achievements, additional information is necessary, particularly from those countries which have not participated in the survey. The participants to the IDNDR-ESCAP Regional Meeting for Asia: Risk Reduction & Society in the 21st Century are therefore urged to provide the information so as to fill up the gaps.

8

Overview of Experiences and Responses to Recent Disasters

Cengiz Ertuna

Chief, Water and Mineral Resources Section,
Environment and Natural Resource Development Division,
Economic and Social Commission for Asia and the Pacific (ESCAP),
Thailand

1. Introduction

The Asian and Pacific region covers a total area of about 35 million square kilometres or 26 per cent of the world's land area and nearly 60 per cent of the world's population. It was estimated that nearly 50 per cent of the world's major disasters have occurred in Asia and the Pacific in the past two decades. During this period, natural disasters were estimated to have claimed about 3 million lives around the world as well as severely affecting the livelihood of about 1 billion people. Floods, droughts, cyclones, storm surges, earthquakes, landslides and volcanic eruptions were the frequent hazards affecting a large number of countries in the region, causing great loss of life and extensive damage to property and infrastructure.

Over the past two years the region has suffered exceptionally heavy losses from natural disasters. With respect to floods alone, in 1997 the total damage was estimated at about US$7 billion in seven countries, according to an annual ESCAP survey on water-related disasters[1]. In 1998, the most extreme floods in several decades have devastated some countries in the region, particularly Bangladesh, China, India, Republic of Korea and Vietnam, resulting in a total damage estimated over US$ 23 billion, while EI Niño Southern Oscillation (ENSO)-related droughts caused water shortages and forest fires in Indonesia and the Philippines and affected neighbouring countries as well. In July 1998, the 10-metre tsunami that hit Papua New Guinea took more than 2,000 lives in several coastal villages. The Kobe earthquake of January 1995, which killed over 5,000 people in addition to tremendous damage it caused, is still fresh in people's memories. In terms of desertification, the region is among the world's worst affected areas with 35 per cent of the region's productive land considered to be desertified, including 70 million ha in rainfed areas and 16 million ha in irrigated croplands. Impacts of natural disasters in the region may reach catastrophic levels; for example in Bangladesh the damage due to recent floods reached above 5 per cent of GDP. According to some estimates, the Kobe earthquake in Japan requires rehabilitation costs of over US$ 100 billion.

In the above context, I will present, in this keynote statement, an overview of the experiences and responses to recent disasters in Asia as an introduction to the three presentations that will be made by my colleagues on their analysis of past experiences on water-related and geologic disasters. They are (1) Report of the IDNDR Asian Survey of Accomplishments, (2) Water Hazards, Resources and Management for Disaster Prevention: A Review of the Asian Conditions, and (3) Geological Hazards, Resources and Management for Disaster Prevention: A Review of the Asian Conditions. These are given below:

2. Regional Experiences on Water-related Disasters Reduction

ESCAP has some 50 years of experience in water-related disaster reduction since ESCAP (formerly ECAFE) established the Bureau for Flood Control in 1949. This long experience highlights the long-standing spirit of regional cooperation for natural disaster reduction and also underlines the importance of the threat to the economic and social development process in the region posed by water related hazards. The occurrence of water-related natural hazards is common in the ESCAP region. The impact of these disasters is becoming more devastating, as increasing populations and denser occupation of hazard-prone areas contribute to the growing costs of damage and disruption of activities. Tropical cyclones occur more frequently in the region than in any other part of the world, and are usually accompanied by severe flooding. As reported in a publication of the Department of Humanitarian Affairs of the United Nations, among 5,370 natural disasters that occurred between 1986 and 1995, floods caused 55 per cent of total loss of lives amounting to 367,000 people of which 92 per cent was in Asia and 31 per cent of total economic loss of which 54 per cent was in Asia. The total value of damage by floods in Asia during 1987-1996 was estimated at US$136 billion. (If the damages caused by floods of 1997 and 1998 are included the total damage would exceed US$ 160 billion.)

Despite the strenuous national efforts in disaster reduction as reported in detail later, the extreme floods of 1998 caused nearly 7,400 deaths, more than 6 million houses damaged and nearly 25 million hectares of crops destroyed in only five countries, Bangladesh, China, India, Republic of Korea and Vietnam. In China alone, it was estimated that 223 million people–one fifth of China's population were affected, 3,004 people died and 15 million were made homeless. 15 million farmers lost their crops. The floods caused severe damage to critical facilities such as health clinics, schools, water supply, and other infrastructure such as roads, bridges and irrigation systems as well as industrial facilities. At the end of August 1998, direct economic damage was estimated at over US$ 20 billion. Elsewhere, the drought events associated with the El Niño phenomenon, which occurred from May 1997 to June 1998, were reported to be the strongest experienced in this century, resulting in severe shortages of water in several countries, including Malaysia and the Philippines. EI Niño is expected to be followed by La Niña phenomena, with opposite effects of El Nino, in some parts of the region. These extreme events have generated awareness for creation of a new dimension in water resources planning and management.

(a) National Experiences in Water-related Disaster Reduction

Significant progress has been achieved in the region on water-related disaster reduction during the past decade regarding improvements in the planning, management, prevention and preparedness works. Experiences indicate that success depends on how effectively disaster reduction activities are integrated into the national development processes. Progress on such integration has been achieved in three following aspects: (i) as an integral part of the national development process; (ii) as a social component such as in the Bangladesh case, and (iii) as a major requirement for sustainable development. The first aspect includes examples from Brantas and Citarum River Basins in Indonesia, Klang River Basin in Malaysia and Chao Phraya River Basin in Thailand. The second aspect highlighted work already undertaken for the Ganges and Bramaputra Delta. Examples for the third aspect included the amendment of the River Law of Japan in 1997 to incorporate environmental dimensions into the flood control programmes, and the implementation of "the Klang River Basin Environmental Improvement and Flood Mitigation Project" in 1998 in Malaysia.

(b) Experiences in Regional Cooperation for Water-related Natural Disaster Reduction

A two-pronged approach has long been adopted by ESCAP to promote regional cooperation: (a) promotion of technical cooperation, and (b) regional network building with reinforced sub-regional elements. With respect to technical aspects of regional cooperation in flood control and management, ESCAP have, over the past 50 years, advised and assisted member governments with regard to flood control and related river problems. The main activities of ESCAP during the first few years of its work were concentrated to flood control. Subsequently, the scope of work was extended to address flood control within the framework of basin development, then the economic and social development process and finally as part of an integrated water resources management programme. Numerous workshops and seminars have been organized and scores of publications on this area of work have been produced by ESCAP in its efforts, during the past five decades, to assist the developing countries in the region to reduce natural disasters, especially by floods. Recent efforts culminated into detailed guidelines and manuals to facilitate application of regional experiences and transfer of know how. The latest ESCAP publications of this category dealing with detailed guidelines for flood control planning are (1) *Manual and Guidelines for comprehensive flood loss prevention and management* in 1991 and (2) *Guidelines and Manual on Land Use*

Planning and Practices in Watershed Management and Disaster Reduction in 1997. Other publications include Urban Flood Loss Prevention and Mitigation (1990), Natural Hazards and Disaster Reduction in Asia and the Pacific (1995). Another special publication on regional cooperation in flood control and management is under preparation. Every year June issue of the Water Resources Journal presents a survey of the water-related natural disasters experienced during the previous year and their consequences.

On the basis of the above ESCAP's experiences, the following conclusions can be drawn. Flood control cooperation has evolved from mainly a single subject into a multidisciplinary area. Cooperation in natural disaster reduction has become more sophisticated involving modern and latest technologies. Cooperation has expanded from limited activities to projects, programmes and institutions. While the modality adopted by ESCAP continues to be relevant, its limited resources available for promoting regional cooperation call for more active participation of the members and stronger support of the donor community. Finally, prioritization of ESCAP's activities is required to meet the increasing needs of its members.

In terms of network building, ESCAP's experiences in supporting the three sub-regional networks, namely the Mekong River Commission, Typhoon Committee and Panel on Tropical Cyclones in cooperation with the World Meteorological Organization, over the past decades, have indicated the following conclusions. Firstly, success in cooperation for flood mitigation depends on how the related measures are integrated into sub-regional development and annual disaster preparedness plans. Secondly, external assistance is essential to gradually build up national capacities into an effective and sustainable system of cooperation, in addition to firm commitment of the governments. Thirdly, effective sub-regional cooperation can create an environment conducive to foreign investment in the respective sub-regions. I should like to take this opportunity to highlight some of the major achievements of these sub-regional networks from their coordinated efforts to reduce water-related disasters.

(i) The Typhoon Committee covers a wide range of activities on typhoon-related disaster reduction for which several important initiatives were launched and completed under its framework with regard to meteorology, hydrology and disaster reduction. Over the years, this sub-regional cooperation programme continues to strengthen its work and among major achievements, the following can be cited in the field of flood control:

(a) A good network of modern facilities has been established with investments by the members and assistance from donors. With these facilities, several good data sets of typhoons are now available for research on the sub-regional scale, particularly for flood forecasting and warning.

(b) From the experience of joint experiment programmes related to designing flood warning systems and developing proper techniques of warnings, a good guide has been established to improve existing forecasting systems and designing new ones in the sub-region.

(c) Past joint activities, particularly in terms of intensive mobilization of facilities over a short period of time, have provided good lessons and modalities for the maintenance of facilities and training of personnel. These lessons were considered to be instrumental to the smooth operations of the existing systems and the Typhoon Committee's cooperation programme.

(d) Good achievements were made by the member countries in installation of new flood forecasting and warning systems and in upgrading existing systems. As a result of the close cooperation, forecasting systems were successfully established for several pilot river basins in some members. New standards for the forecasting operations were established and modern equipment was introduced, including telemetry systems.

(ii) In parallel to the operations of the Typhoon Committee, the Panel on Tropical Cyclones directed their common endeavours towards successful implementation of a comprehensive cyclone operational plan to facilitate the most effective tropical cyclone warning system for the region with existing facilities. The plan also aims at the development and improvement of the cyclone warning system of the sub-region. The plan includes a hydrological programme comprising two main components: (i) hydrological network and flood forecasting systems, and (ii) storm surge project. Cooperation among the members continues to be strengthened with the implementation of these components in addition to work on meteorology. An important point to note in this respect is that through the implementation of the plan, the exchange of hydrological data among the member countries for flood warnings has been greatly improved.

(iii) The Mekong River Commission continues to undertake its annual flood forecasting operations, since 1971 to provide information and forecasts to the riparian countries in the Lower Mekong Basin. It has also conducted annual low flow forecasting operations since 1978 and salinity intrusion forecasting since late 1980s. Apart from the benefits from disaster prevention and reduction, these annual operations also enable the member countries to enhance their cooperation in the transfer of technology and improvement of water resources management.

3. Regional Experiences on Geology-related Disasters

Geology-related disasters are generally one of the most destructive in terms of human lives lost. In a global survey covering the period 1970-1997 prepared by the Swiss Reassurance Company, published in 1998, of the 40 worst catastrophes in terms of fatalities listed, having caused over a million deaths, 48 per cent were caused by earthquakes. The fact that 30 of the 40 above-mentioned catastrophes had occurred in the ESCAP region (and 87 per cent of the casualties) highlights the importance of this issue for the countries of Asia and the Pacific. The continued population growth in the already heavily populated parts of the region will increase the number and size of large cities, placing more and more people and assets at risk due to potential natural disasters. In this context, it becomes more important to particularly prevent geology-related hazards, such as earthquakes, volcanic eruptions, landslides, etc., from developing into natural disasters. In this connection, the ESCAP secretariat continues to promote integration of geological information into urban planning and decision making. To date, a number of member countries have established their own "geology for planning" programmes, supported either by national funding or from bilateral sources. Notable examples are the initiatives taken by the Ministry of Land and Resources of China and the Geological Surveys of India and Vietnam. Not surprisingly, the rationale followed in these cases is to keep the people and assets away from hazard-prone areas, an approach most effective in areas of newly planned urbanization.

It should be noted that the past Decade or even a period of several decennia is too small a "window" to obtain a reliable estimate of earthquake hazard, due to the often very long return times of high-amplitude, and therefore very destructive tremors. New methods such as probabilistic seismic hazard analysis, as developed in New Zealand, make use of both the historic record and the geological evidence of preceding events, thus producing more realistic hazard maps that may prove to be very useful in many other vulnerable countries of the ESCAP region. Such techniques and other relevant experiences are being shared periodically at the Forum on Urban Geology in Asia and the Pacific organized annually by ESCAP, which serves as a framework for regional cooperation for the integration of geology in planning and decision making.

A geology-related aspect often not realized is the phenomenon of slow or "creeping disasters". Examples of this can be found in ground subsidence due to neglecting geological conditions in groundwater exploitation, giving rise to "geology-related flooding". But other phenomena also qualify, such as widespread arsenic poisoning, resulting from geochemical, *i.e.*, geology-related natural conditions of the subsurface, as evident in India, Bangladesh and China. These and other under-reported disasters also deserve the attention of the international community in order to be addressed effectively in the not too distant future.

4. Regional Experiences on Other Disasters

Land degradation and desertification are other major disasters, which pose serious threat in the region in the wake of growing population and enhanced food demand. The countries most affected by desertification are China, Islamic Republic of Iran, Afghanistan, Mongolia, Pakistan, India and the Central Asian States. A comparison of desertification among the continents indicates that Asia is most severely affected in terms of loss of land productivity and agricultural output, whereas Africa has the highest percentage of desertified dry land. Although desertification process can be seen as a complex interaction of natural and socio-economic forces, in fact human-induced factors such as deforestation, faulty land use practices, mismanagement of irrigation systems and overgrazing, are responsible for accelerating the process. In order to assist the countries in combating desertification, a Desertification Control Network in Asia and the Pacific was established by the ESCAP secretariat to promote exchange of experiences and provide training on desertification control methodologies and to assist in the development of an Asian annex to the United Nations Convention to Combat Desertification (CCD).

Forest and bush fires have always been a hazard in the region but recently they reached catastrophic dimensions. During 1997-1998, massive fires in Southeast Asia destroyed millions of hectares of forest, caused more than $4.5 billion in damage. The fires were caused by the combination of drought, slash and burn agriculture, and exploitation of forests and created a thick, choking haze that covered the sub-region, creating serious health problems; causing accidents on land, at sea, and in the air; disrupting transportation systems and resulting in a steep drop in tourism in parts of the region where declining economies could hardly afford it. In order to prevent, and/or effectively deal with future forest and bush fires, ASEAN Secretariat has developed a fire prevention and suppression strategy in the form of a Regional Haze Action Plan to provide training in fire fighting and haze management, improve meteorological services, launch air and ground surveillance, strengthen early-warning systems, and provide technical assistance for coal and peat fire suppression, which was endorsed by ASEAN Ministers in December 1997. A number of United Nations agencies, donors and others assisted in this endeavour of ASEAN. In this regard, ESCAP has initiated a project, funded by the Government of Australia, to create awareness on prevention and promote monitoring of forest fires, which is being implemented in close collaboration with ASEAN Secretariat and other organizations involved in the implementation of this Action Plan.

5. Conclusion

In concluding my keynote statement today, I should like to present our perception of achievements and emerging regional concerns as inputs to your deliberation on "Risk reduction and Society in the 21st Century".

Significant progress has been achieved in disaster preparedness and reduction in the region over the past decade, in terms of improvements in planning, institutional strengthening and use of advance technology including space technology applications. Important benefits have been realized from these disaster reduction and preparedness efforts by various countries in the region. However, the increase in the intensity of natural disasters requires continuing and more intensive efforts at local, national and regional levels. In this respect, pertinent geological and hydrological information, such as thematic hazard maps, have a very high potential for reducing fatality rates and losses due to natural disasters.

Regional cooperation for better natural disaster prevention, reduction and management becomes even more important in view of such driving forces as: the rapid urbanization process, increasing rates of economic and social development, and other global factors that would increase the severity of disasters, such as EI Niño and potential global climate changes. Within this context, prioritization of regional activities for effective planning, management and development of disaster reduction measures and for applications of space technology to meet the urgent needs, requires wide application of strategic approaches to natural disaster reduction and management. These activities need to be effectively integrated into the national economic and social development process. Such integration and regional cooperation need to be formulated in a well-conceived framework and well-developed regional strategy. Development and updating such a framework and regional strategy is a priority emerging issue for cooperation in the 21st century.

Such a regional strategy may need to address the following five priority areas: (a) realistic integrated planning for disaster prevention and mitigation; (b) enhancement of disaster preparedness including real-time information exchange; (c) community participation throughout the natural disaster reduction and management process; (d) more effective transfer of disaster reduction and management technology; and (e) exchange of experiences and information on institutional arrangements for disaster reduction and management.

In order to culminate regional efforts to realistic targets in the development of a regional strategy for better disaster reduction, the following common objectives may be adopted: (a) realistic reduction of damage, (b) increased disaster awareness, and (c) improvement of forecasting systems. It may be noted that specific targets of these common objectives depend on the economic and social conditions of the respective countries. Formulation of strategies and programmes towards meeting these objectives is therefore of high priority.

9

Accomplishments, Current Activities and Future Requirements for Disaster Reduction

Kamal Bin Hussain

Crisis and Disaster Management Unit,
Division for National Security, Prime Ministers Department,
Putrajaya, Malaysia

1. Introduction

Although Malaysia is geographically outside the APacific Rim of Fire@ and is relatively free from any severe ravages and destruction caused by natural disasters such as earthquake, typhoons and volcanic eruptions, nevertheless the country is subjected to monsoonal floods, and slides and severe haze episodes. The country also from time to time experiences some man-made disasters which causes considerable damages to property and loss of lives. To mention a few, Malaysia had experienced disasters (natural and man-made) during the last five years as follows:

- Fire and explosions at Bright Sparklers factory in Sungai Buloh in 1991 which claimed 22 lives.
- Fire and explosions at South Port Klang in 1992 which claimed 10 lives.

- ❖ Collapse of Highland Towers Condominium at Hulu Kelang in 1993 which claimed 48 lives.
- ❖ Landslide at Genting Highlands in 1995 which claimed 20 lives.
- ❖ Mudslide at the Aborigines village at Pos Dipang, Perak on 29 August 1996 which claimed 44 lives and the damage of 30 houses.
- ❖ Tropical Storm > Greg which struck Keningau, Sabah in December 1996 which claimed 238 lives.
- ❖ Severe haze episodes in July–November 1997 caused by forest fires which had adverse health effects on the people and on the economy of the nation.
- ❖ Landslide at Sandakan, Sabah on 7 February 1999 due to heavy downpour which claimed 17 lives and damaged 4 houses.

Experience from the above mentioned disasters indicated that there is a need to address disaster mitigation problems efficiently and effectively to alleviate the suffering of the people and reduce the loss of lives and damage to properties.

This paper outlines the disaster management and relief mechanisms and summarises some of the accomplishments, current activities and future requirements for Disaster Reduction in Malaysia.

2. Mechanisms of Disaster Management and Relief

(a) The National Security Division

The National Security Division (NSD) in the Prime Ministers Department is responsible for coordination of all activities related to disaster. The National Security Council (NSC) Directive No. 20 was issued to provide guidelines on the management of disasters including the responsibilities and functions of the various agencies under an integrated emergency management system.

(b) Disaster Management and Relief Committee

To carry out the responsibilities of the NSC of coordinating all the activities related to disaster, *i.e.* the various aspect of preparation, prevention, response, recovery and rehabilitation. The Disaster Management and Relief Committee was established at three different levels, *i.e.* at the Federal, State and District levels, whereby the NSD is the Secretariat. The main functions of the Disaster Management and Relief Committee (DMRC) are as follows:

- ❖ At Federal level, DMRC is responsible in the formulation of national polices and strategies regarding the alertness and the preparation of various agencies involved in the handling of disasters. The DMRCs at the State and District levels are required to implement and carry out such policies and strategies.
- ❖ To ensure sound coordination among the agencies involved in the handling of disasters and determine the roles of the principal emergency services (Police, Medical and Fire Department) and other supporting services.
- ❖ To activate the Disaster Operation Control Centre at District, State or Federal Level whenever required.

- To coordinate and mobilise whatever resources and logistics available from Government agencies and if necessary also from the private sector.
- To coordinate assistance and rehabilitation to disaster victims.
- To carry out a post mortem and report upon completion of the disaster operations for the purpose of recording and performance evaluation for future reference and planning.

(c) Composition of Disaster Management and Relief Committee

The members of the Disaster Management and Relief Committee are as follows:

Federal Level

- Chairman: Deputy Prime Minister
- Members: Minister of National Unity and Community Development.
- Minister of Finance.
- Chief Secretary to the Government.
- Chief of Armed Forces.
- Inspector General of Police.
- Director General of Health.
- Director General of National Security Division.
- Director General of Fire and Rescue Department.
- Director General of Atomic and Energy Licensing Board.
- Director General of Road and Transport Department.
- Director General of Public Work and Utilities Department.
- Director General of Department of Environment.
- Director General of Meteorological Department.
- Director General of Drainage and Irrigation Department.
- Representatives from Ministry of Finance and Attorney General Office.
- Director General of Department of Occupational Safety and Health.
- Secretary: Director, Crisis and Disaster Management Unit National Security Division
- Prime Ministers Department.

State Level

- Chairman: State Secretary.
- Members: State Chief Police Officer
- Brigade Commander of Armed Forces
- State Director of Fire and Rescue Department
- State Director of Health Other Directors of various relevant government agencies/departments at State Level.
- Secretary: Director of State NSD.

District Level

- Chairman: District Officer
- Members: Officer in charge of Police District (OCPD)
- District Fire Officer
- Medical and Health Officer
- Representatives from various relevant departments and agencies at District Level
- Secretary: Assistant Director for District NSD.

(d) On-Scene Control Post (OSCP)

An On-Scene Control Post (OSCP) will be opened immediately as soon as disaster has occurred. The On-Scene Commander will be either the OCPD, CPO, or the Director, Internal Security and Public Order Royal Malaysia Police, depending on the level of disaster. The main functions of the On-Scene Commander are as follows:

- To make an early assessment at the scene of potential or actual disaster and immediately activate OSCP if deemed necessary.
- To identify the equipment and logistic requirement in handling the disaster.
- To coordinate the functions of various agencies involved in search and rescue operation.
- To report and advise the Disaster Management and Relief Committee at their respective level.

(e) Special Malaysia Disaster Assistance and Rescue Team (SMART)

SMART was established in 1995 as directed by the NSC Directive No. 19. SMART is directly responsible to the Director, Crisis and Disaster Management Unit, NSD. SMART comprises of 85 officers and personnel from the Fire and Rescue Department, Royal Malaysia Police and The Armed Forces. The Team is equipped with specialised skills and equipment's to respond to any search and rescue operation in any major disaster on land which is beyond the capabilities of the existing principal emergency services Search and Rescue (SAR) teams. The team members were trained in SAR training institutions abroad such as the USA, Sweden, Australia and Singapore. The decision on the mobilisation and. the deployment of the SMART team is made by the Director, General of the NSD or the Director, Crisis and Disaster Management Unit.

(f) The Role of the Malaysian Meteorological Service in Disaster Management

The Malaysian Meteorological Service (MMS) is the agency responsible to provide information and warning occurrences adverse weather phenomena to the general public through the mass media or to other government agencies directly involved in disaster mitigation. A Central Forecasting Office has been established in the Meteorological. Headquarters to monitor closely the weather and sea conditions over the Malaysian region. Special emphasis was given to the following:

Heavy Rainfall

Prolonged widespread heavy rainfall are often experienced in the east coast of Peninsular Malaysia, Sabah and Sarawak during the Northeast Monsoon season from November to January causing floods in low lying area. The MMS monitors the weather and issues advisories and warnings regarding impending occurrence of heavy rain spells to the Department of Irrigation and Drainage, the National Security Council as well as the State Operations Rooms.

Strong Wind and Heavy Rainfall Associated with Tropical Storms

Although Malaysia is not directly affected by the destructive forces of typhoons, however the northern part of the country especially Sabah experience the strong wind associated with tail effect of typhoons and tropical storms in the West Pacific Ocean and South China Sea areas. On very rare occasions, the northern part of the country is directly hit by tropical storms. Tropical storm > Greg which hit Sabah on Christmas eve of 1996 brought heavy rain and strong wind which claimed 238 lives. Hence, the MMS monitors the formation of tropical storms in the Malaysian region very closely to ensure that adequate warning can be given to potential victims so as to reduce the adverse impact of these devastating storms.

Strong Wind And High Waves

The MMS also continuously monitors the sea conditions and issues warnings of strong wind and high waves over Malaysian territorial waters to vessels and oilrigs operating in the area.

Intense Haze Episodes

The MMS works very closely with ASEAN specialised Meteorological Centre in Singapore to monitor and issue long range forecast for the ASEAN region, with special emphasis on the drought condition affecting the region by the EI Nino phenomena. MMS also monitors the occurrences of local and cross-boundary haze in the country and provides meteorological information, including satellite pictures depicting locations of forest fires, to the various government agencies involved in the prevention, monitoring and remedial measures to combat haze caused by open burning, forest fires and other sources of smoke.

Drought

The 1997/98 EI Nino had caused very significant reduction in rainfall from January to April in Sabah, northern Sarawak and Peninsular Malaysia. Besides monitoring the drought conditions, the MMS also conducts cloud seeding as an attempt to induce rains and to increase the water levels in dams in the affected area.

3. Roles and Functions of the Drainage and Irrigation Department of Malaysia (DID)

(a) Flood

Flood is the most severe natural disaster in Malaysia from the perspective of area extent, population affected and economic impact. The National Water Resources Study (1982) estimated that some 29,000 sq. Km (9 per cent *of* the total land area) were flood prone and more than 2.7 million people (18 per cent) were affected. The average flood damage was estimated at RM100 million at 1995 price.

(b) Flood Control Measures

After the disastrous flood *of* 1971 which affected many areas in Malaysia, various strategies and measures have been implemented by the Government to mitigate flood impacts. Such strategies include:

- Establishment of the Permanent Flood Control Commission in December 1971 to implement flood control measures in order to reduce flood occurrence and to minimise flood damages in the events of flood.
- Establishment of the Natural Disaster Relief Committee in 1972 with the task to coordinate flood relief operations at federal, state and district levels. (The Committee was replaced by the National Disaster Management and Relief Committee in 1997).
- Implementation of structural flood mitigation measures.
- Provision of flood forecasting and warning services to river basins experiencing frequent floods.

Since 1971, the Drainage and Irrigation Department of Malaysia (DID) has been designated with task to implement structural flood mitigation works. Flood mitigation plans have been developed for 17 major river basins and 27 towns. Based on these plans, various structural and non-structural measures have been proposed and partially implemented. Such measures include improving river channel sections, building of flood bunds, levees, ring bunds, by-pass flood ways, use of mining pools for flood attenuation and construction of flood retention dams to regulate flood flows and minimise flood occurrence.

4. Flood Forecasting and Warning Services (FFW)

(a) Telemetry System

DID is directly involved in the collection and analysis of real-time river water level and rainfall data for flood forecasting and warning operation during the flood season. To date, a total of 72 rainfall and 89 water level telemetric stations have been installed by the DID in river basins for FFW purpose. The telemetry data are transmitted through VHF Radio, telephone or satellite. Similar systems are being implemented for another 10 river basins under the Seventh Malaysia Plan (1966–2000). Presently real time flood forecast are issued for 7 river basins by the DID state offices during the flood season. The forecast river levels have greatly enhanced relief operations and evacuation during flood period.

(b) Manual Flood Level Monitoring

In addition to the telemetric stations, a total of 137 manual flood level monitoring stations have been set up at strategic locations in the country to monitor the river level on a real-time basis during the flood period. Whenever a river level exceeds a predetermined critical level, the local observer shall transmit continuously real-time water level information to the DID state office via telephone or VHF radio equipment.

These information are further transmitted to the flood operation rooms at the district, state or federal level for flood relief operation.

(c) Flood Warning Sirens

In river basins, which are subject to flash flood, little lead-time is available for effective warning. Therefore, a total of 60 flood warning sirens, which automatically trigger once the flood level reaches a critical point, have been installed at strategic locations along such rivers. These warning sirens are especially useful when flash floods occur at night.

(d) Flood Warning Boards

A total of 60 flood warning boards have been installed in flood prone areas in the major river basins. Levels marked on these warning boards are correlated to the levels at the observation points upstream. The residents of the villages are able to assess for themselves the impending flood situation in their areas based on real-time upstream river and the forecast levels shown at the warning boards.

5. Drought

Hydrology and irrigation are two the main functions of DID. During a drought situation, a task force will be set up by the DID to monitor and evaluate the drought situation at padi growing areas in the country.

Based on analysis of rainfall, river levels and discharge data, various measures have been implemented to reduce the impact of water deficit on padi production.

6. Role and Functions of the Social Welfare Department in Disaster Management

Under the NSC Directive No. 20 on Policy and Mechanism of Disaster Management and Relief, the Social Welfare Department has four main functions. These functions, which are related to Relief and Rehabilitation activities, are as follows:

- The provision and management of relief/evacuation centres and forward supply base.
  - In Malaysia, there are a total of 3,417 designated relief/evacuation centres, which can accommodate 943,000 evacuees, and a total of 348 forward supply bases.
- The provision and distribution of relief assistance, which includes food, clothing and other essential items to the affected victims.
- The registration of disaster victims for purposes of rehabilitation.
- To provision of Apost-trauma@ counselling services to the affected victims.
- In practice, the Social Welfare Department, being a member of the National Disaster Management and Relief Committee, will play its role before, during and after the occurrence of disasters.
- Preparedness Stage
  - To identify the locations of Relief/Evacuation Centres and Forward Supply Bases especially in the flood prone areas.

- To update the list of names of officials, who need to be contacted and mobilised in the event of any disaster (their addresses and telephone numbers).
- To identify the names of Suppliers/Agencies who will supply relief assistance, namely food stuffs (dry and wet rations) and other necessities.
- To update the Operation Rooms.
- To set up the Corp of Volunteers/Task Force, comprising members of the Premier Welfare Brigade and other voluntary organization.
- To prepare duty lists for the officials and volunteers.
- To provide training courses for the officials and volunteers in disaster management work.
- To send dry rations to forward-supply bases, prior to the event of a disaster.

❖ Response Stage

- To register the affected victims/evacuees.
- To manage the relief/evacuation centres and forward-supply bases.
- To distribute food supplies and other necessities.
- To mobilize the volunteers/task force to help in registration and food distribution works.
- To organize suitable activities for the evacuees in the relief/ evacuation centres.
- To provide Apost-trauma@counselling services to victims suffering from stress, depressions, etc.

❖ Recover/Restoration Stage

- To evaluate the damage involved, including the damage of houses, crops and livestock.
- To propose and draw up appropriate rehabilitation programmes/plan.
- To provide Ashort-term@ and Along-term@ relief/aid from the existing financial aid schemes.

7. Relief Assistance Schemes

Relief assistance schemes include the following:

Short-Term Schemes

- ❖ To provide food and temporary shelter.
- ❖ To give compensation to victims, either to repair or rebuild their houses.

Long-Term Schemes

- ❖ To provide monthly financial assistance.
- ❖ To give launching grants.
- ❖ To give compensation for the loss of crops and livestock.

8. Landslides

Besides flooding, Malaysia is occasionally subjected to landslides. Just as flooding, landslides inflict a heavy toll on human life and property. Described as an abrupt and short-lived geomorphic erosion process, landslides can be attributed to the internal properties of earth materials, the geomorphic setting, and independent external factors that influence the stability of slopes. In addition, excessive precipitation and human activities have contributed to slope instability and set the stage for land sliding.

Of late, Malaysia had experienced two major landslides. Farming activities involving indiscriminate clearing of land, coupled with continuous downpours, were partly blamed for landslides in Cameron Highlands over four days from 4th–7th December 1994 resulting in the death of 7 people. Another landslide on 30th June 1995, took place about 39 km from the capital city of Kuala Lumpur. The site of the tragic incident was a slip road leading to the Genting Highlands resorts. Part of the hill came crashing down as flood waters washed tons of earth and fallen trees down the hilly slope. About a dozen or so vehicles including cars, buses and vans which were on their way to Genting Highlands, were swept down. 21 people loss their lives, while 22 other were injured. The exact cause of the landslide has not been fully determined yet.

9. Landslide Reduction Measures

In spite of the growing geologic understanding of the landslide processes and a rapidly improving engineering capability for landslide control, losses and casualties caused by landslides are on the increase. This is partly a consequence of residential and commercial development activities that are carried out on steep sloping terrain that is prone to landslip. In order to control and reduce the impact of landslides, the Government has undertaken legislative and non-legislative measures such as:

- Identification and mapping of landslides prone areas;
- Adaptation of land use regulation in landslip-prone areas;
- Development of design and building codes that will ensure the construction practices appropriate to the maintenance or enhancement of slope stability;
- Amendments to Land Conservation Act 1960 to enable the government to have a comprehensive monitoring of development activities on hill slopes; and
- Amendments to Environmental Impact Assessment (EIA) Rules 1987. This is to enable the government to have a closer monitoring and enforcement over development projects on hilly areas for the construction of roads, buildings and recreational facilities.

10. Public Education and Awareness on Disaster Reduction

In order to enhance disaster preparedness, the Malaysian Government has continuously carried out public education on disaster prevention to the people living in flood prone areas with the ultimate objective of protecting of human lives and property, as well as avoiding or minimising social disruption and economic losses. Public education and awareness programmes are carried out through the various media including TV and radio broadcast, aimed at enhancing public awareness of the dangers of natural disasters. Civic education and practical training in life saving techniques are also conducted in the natural disaster prone areas. In addition, presentations on life-saving during floods have been made and pamphlets on disaster prevention targeted at children in flood prone areas during the monsoon season were also circulated.

Agencies such the Malaysian Red Crescent Society and Civil Defence Department have also played their part in educating the public especially children on how to protect themselves against floods. Therefore, public education and awareness on disaster reduction in Malaysia is aimed at creating a higher level of community awareness including the ability of putting into place appropriate emergency measures, so that they could withstand the impact of natural disasters and prepare for and survive disasters.

11. Forest Fire and Severe Haze

The northern region of Sarawak and the western part of Sabah in Malaysia have been experiencing severe drought since late December 1997 that has been brought about by the EI Nino phenomenon. The drought has brought about incidences of bush fires, mainly within the vicinity of Miri, Lawas, Limbang and Marudi in Sarawak and Sipitang in Sabah. In Miri, bush fire occurred in the dry peat areas during the first week of February 1998. The fires spread over a total area of more than 3,000 hectares. In Lawas, bush fire occurred in peat areas covering a total area of 1,000 hectares. A few incidences of bush fires covering approximately 70 hectares were also detected during March–April period in the State of Pahang in Peninsular Malaysia. The smoke from these peat and forest fires had resulted in severe haze episodes, especially in northern Sarawak, western Sabah, Peninsular Malaysia, Singapore, Brunei and to some event, southern Thailand.

12. Actions to Combat Forest Fire and Haze

To combat the forest fire and haze problem, the Malaysia Government implemented the following measures:

- Activate the National Haze Action Plan.
- Activate an operation centre to coordinate the activities to combat haze and forest fires.
- Mobilize fire-fighting personnel from the Fire Services and Rescue Department to fight fires on ground, equipped with specialized fire-fighting equipment.
- Mobilize the Army, Police and Local Authorities personnel to assist the Fire Services and Rescue Department in the fire fighting.
- Undertake aerial water bombing of area of forest fire.
- Institute legal action against offenders of open burning in plantations.
- Carry out air surveillance to detect bush fires.

13. International Cooperation

(a) Memorandum of Understanding between Malaysia and Indonesia

Malaysia and Indonesia signed a Memorandum of Understanding (MoU) on Disaster Cooperation and Assistance on 11 December 1997 allowing the two countries to work together to manage and handle any forms of disaster that may occur. The MoU on Disaster Cooperation and Assistance was signed by H.E. Datuk Seri Mohamed bin Rahmat, who is the National Disaster Management and Relief Committee Chairman as well as the Minister of Information, on behalf of the Malaysian Government and H.E. Dato Seri Utama Ir. Azwar Anas, Coordinating Minister for Peoples Welfare and also Chairman of the Indonesia National Disaster Management Coordinating Board (BAKORNAS-PB) on behalf of the Indonesian Government.

The initial objective of the MoU was for Malaysia and Indonesia to jointly tackle the haze problem, but the two countries had decided to include other areas of disaster management and assistance.

Under the MoU, both countries had agreed to the followings:

- Exchange of expertise and information on the latest technology related to disaster prevention, risk reduction, response, mitigation, recovery and rehabilitation including tele-detection. This also includes technology on detection by satellites, data interpretation and rescue operations in collapsed buildings or structures.
- Training of officers and personnel in disaster management, the concept of aeromobility emergency services (including the use of heliborne technique) and search and rescue techniques both on land and sea.
- Sharing of experience through seminars, conferences and publications on disaster management.
- Collaboration on public health studies related to the effects of particular disasters.

(b) Agreement Between the Government of Malaysia and the Government of the French Republic on Co-Operation for Disaster Prevention and Management and Public Safety

The agreement was signed on May 25, 1998 in Paris, France by H. E. Datuk Seri Mohamed bin Rahmat, Chairman of National Disaster Management and Relief Committee on behalf of Malaysia and H.E. Mr. Jean-Pierre Chevenement, Minister of Interior, France on behalf of the French Government.

For Malaysia, this is the first time that such an agreement between the Government of Malaysia and the French Government is ever held on disaster management and cooperation. The agreement would be the basis for bilateral cooperation which could pave the way for closer and wider scope in disaster management including prevention, mitigation, assistance, expertise, training and exercises. In extending the cooperation, the French Government has assisted Malaysia in training five (5) Malaysian officers in late 1998 in France. The training covered management of forest fire as well as technique of forest fire fighting.

The parties agree to develop co-operation in the fields of forecasting, prevention, assessment and management of natural, man-made and technological disaster situations by:

- ❖ Exchanging experts and specialists in the field of application of advanced technologies relating to natural, man-made and technological disasters or major incidents, including the use of satellite remote sensing, Geographic Information Systems (GIS), Satellite Based Positioning (SBP) Technology, spatial data analysis and modelling, and risk assessment;
- ❖ Initiating training activities for personnel involved in emergency response and disaster or major incidents, management, calculation of risk index and satellite data processing and interpretation and development of disasters early warning system through satellite remote sensing technology. This includes the deployment of transportable satellite data reception facility to enable effective monitoring of disasters such as forest fires, oil spills and waste discharge;
- ❖ Sharing their public health experiences, especially with regard to chemical, industrial and environmental hazards;
- ❖ Exchanging information on each country's laws and regulations pertaining to environment pollution and hazards;
- ❖ Exchanging technology and scientific information relating to natural, manmade and technological disasters or major incidents through electronic media, forum and publications; and
- ❖ Participation of specialists of one party in the relevant national technical training programmes of the other party.

(c) "DISTRESS 1/97"–Joint SMART and DART Rescue Exercise

The first joint rescue exercise involving two elite rescue teams, the Special Malaysia Disaster Assistance and Rescue Team (SMART) and Disaster Assistance and Rescue Team (DART) of Singapore Civil Defence Force (SCDF), was held in Genting Highlands, Malaysia on 25-26 November 1997. The joint exercise code name ADISTRESS 1/97 was based on the scenario of a collapse of an apartment at the hill slope of Genting Highlands due to a landslide, resulting in about 40 occupants being trapped. SMART and DART were given the task of handling complicated rescue problems in this major simulated disaster. The district disaster management elements and the local rescue and emergency relief agencies such as Royal Malaysia Police, Fire and Rescue Department, The Malaysian Armed Forces, Medical Emergency Response Team, Civil Defence Department and The Malaysian Red Crescent Society were involved at a minimal level. 35 DART and 26 SMART rescuers were involved in the joint exercise.

The joint exercise was to promote better teamwork, proficiency and exchange of experience among SMART and DART members. The exercise also helped to verify and evaluate the preparedness of SMART and DART in conducting specialized search and rescue operations and promote a better understanding of each others operational concepts. The joint exercise was officially opened on 25 November 1997 by H.E. Datuk Seri Mohamed bin Rahmat, Malaysia Minister of Information and also the Chairman of the Malaysia National Disaster Management and Relief Committee.

In order to further strengthen the existing close cooperation and goodwill between the two elite rescue teams of Malaysia and Singapore, both countries agreed in principle to have a Memorandum of Understanding (MoU) on Disaster Management and Assistance. Perhaps the joint exercise and the proposed MoU could be used as a basis to pave the way for similar cooperation in disaster management among ASEAN members countries in the future.

(d) Cooperation between Malaysia and Brunei on Forest Fire Fighting

Malaysia and Brunei have agreed on 1 April 1998 to cooperate and help each other in fighting the forest fires at the Sarawak–Brunei border. Both countries have pledged to cooperate and exchange experience in fire fighting technique at the border areas.

In principle, both countries have agreed to cooperate in conducting cloud seeding and water bombing operations on areas affected by drought, haze and forest fires, particularly at the border areas of both countries. In addition, exchange of information of weather and air quality indices will be intensified. Malaysia also allows Brunei fire fighters to use water from the Limbang River in Sarawak for forest fire fighting operation. Thus this cooperation between the two countries is a positive step towards addressing effectively future haze problems prevailing in the border areas of Sarawak and Brunei.

Sub-Regional Fire Fighting Arrangements (SRFAs)

During the Third ASEAN Environment Ministerial Meeting on Haze held on 4 April 1998 in Bandar Seri Begawan, Brunei Darussalam, it was agreed that Sub-Regional Fire Fighting Arrangements (SRFAs) are to be established for Kalimantan and Sumatera/Riau provinces. The SRFAs would ensure at all cost that fires are prevented from becoming an economic and environmental threat in Sumatera and Riau provinces, and that fires in East Kalimantan must be contained and not allowed to spread to Central and West Kalimantan. The SRFAs will incorporate mechanisms to rapidly activate and mobilise efforts to put out fires before they get out of control, and to manage additional and complementary resources from within and outside the region. In this regard, Malaysia was given the task of fire-fighting coordination. Malaysia is to work out procedures to activate, mobilise and channel fire-fighting resources to target sites.

14. Future Requirements for Disaster Reduction

(a) Risk and Vulnerability Analysis

Such analysis should be mandatory in the appraisal of all development projects. Pilot risk mapping projects and hazard and vulnerability analysis should be conducted at the micro-level using where appropriate, Geographic Information System (GIS) and Remote Sensing (RS) technology.

(b) Non-Structural Mitigation Measures

Disaster Management System

The need to strengthen national disaster management organisational structures and support them with sound administrative, financial arrangements and assets mobilisation.

Training

To increase in training activities in the country through international support and cooperation by multilateral and bilateral organisation, NGOs and others. Also to undertake training programmes for core disasters management personnel as well as supporting personnel in order to enhance disaster coordination and response.

Public Awareness

The need for more sustained public awareness programs directed at local communities in disaster prone areas through international cooperation and assistance.

Forecasting and Warning Systems

The need to improve in the methods and technology of warning system for flood, landslides and forest fire.

Hazard Mapping

The need to improve hazard mapping at macro and micro level.

15. Structural Mitigation Measures

The need to implement structural mitigation measures in both engineered and non-engineered structures, such as landslide control measure, river embankments and etc. International cooperation in the transfer of knowledge and expertise in the structural measures could greatly improve disaster reduction system in the country.

International assistance in improving disaster reduction system by integrating disaster reduction measures in disaster prone areas could reduce, the loss, damage and economic disruption caused by natural disasters in the country.

16. Conclusion

Policy makers as well as disaster and development experts recognise that each nations ability to achieve sustainable economic development can be increased by reducing the impact of disasters. Therefore, Malaysia is integrating disaster reduction in its international cooperation through enhancing regional cooperation in all aspects of disaster management, including, prevention, mitigation, preparedness, response and recovery, through more effective mutual assistance activities, in order to minimise the adverse consequences of disasters on the economic and social development internally.

Much has been accomplished within Malaysia in terms of disaster reduction since the onset of the International Decade For The Natural Disaster Reduction (IDNDR). In the spirit of IDNDR, which seeks to support sustainable economic development, natural hazard risk assessment, mitigation and warnings must be embedded in Malaysia's development plans and process.

Except for flooding and occasional occurrences of landslides, Malaysia is relatively not affected by other major natural disasters. However, our involvement in IDNDR is significant through our participation in a concerted international action aimed at reducing the impact of natural disasters in the Asian region. As a member of the UN, Malaysia fully supports and participates in the UNs efforts in the reduction of natural disaster by observing the UN sponsored International Day for Natural Disaster Reduction on October 13, aimed at enhancing public awareness on the effect of natural disasters and undertaking various activities towards reducing natural disasters. In this respect, Malaysia is advancing its mission in national disaster management through effective coordination and integrated approach in the building of a Culture of Prevention and Civil Protection/Public Safety in the community. Thus, Malaysia hopes to create a safe environment for the community through Disaster Management, sustainable development and risk reduction in the 21st century.

10

Management of Natural Disasters

Veersingh Boodhna
Assistant Secretary,
Prime Minister Office, New Government Centre,
Level 4, Port Louis, Mauritius

1. Background Information on Mauritius

Mauritius is found in the Indian Ocean at about 1800 to 2000 km on the East Coast of Africa in longitude 57° E and Latitude 20° S.

- Area of Mauritius: 1864.8 km^2
- Area of Rodrigues: 104.0 km^2
- Other Islands: 71 .2 km^2
- Total 2040.0 km^2
- Population: 1 .2 million

2. Major Sectors of the Economy

- Industry (manufacturing)
- Sugar
- Tourism
- Financial Services

3. Introduction

The major natural disaster affecting Mauritius is cyclone.

The official cyclone season in Mauritius covers the period between 1st November and 15th of May.

There is a Central Cyclone Committee under the aegis of the Prime Minister's Office (PMO).

There is a high degree of decentralisation–at regional level, (*i.e.* each town and district), Local Cyclone Committees are set up.

The management of cyclones in Mauritius is constituted of four stages:

(a) Preparedness

There is continuous need to make the public aware of the nature of cyclones, the need of precautionary activities before the cyclone season, the form of the cyclone warning system and protective action which should be taken during the storm.

There is a risk that some sections of the population will become aware of the necessity for protective action only after they have suffered damage. It is, therefore, necessary to remind the public of cyclone dangers before such cyclone season and more particularly after periods when the island has not suffered any damage as a result of cyclones. Moreover, people tend to forget the dangers to life and property inherent in such things as badly secured roofs, old electrical wiring, and overgrown or rotting trees.

The public needs reminders of the building practices required to withstand cyclones and of the necessity for annual overhaul of roofing and the removal of rotting or overgrown trees, of weak constructions and of all loose materials likely to be blown about to cause damage to better installations.

The Government Information Service, after consultation with the Meteorological Services, would distribute during the first fortnight of September an illustrated poster summarising general preparedness, describing the warning system and advising protective action to be taken before and during a cyclone.

Cyclone damage can be minimised if care is taken to ensure that installations are in a good state of maintenance. Heads of Ministries/Departments and occupants of government property are responsible for ensuring that satisfactory state of general maintenance is attained before the cyclone season and that fittings of doors, windows and shutters are secure.

All emergency lighting and power at Government institutions are checked at regular intervals and adequate stocks of fuel maintained.

The Secretary of the Local Cyclone Committee usually convenes a meeting in late August or early September and suggests any amendment to be made to the list of refugee centres to the Central Cyclone Committee, and also to lay down the specific responsibilities of each member of the Committee before, during and after cyclones.

(b) Mitigation

As soon as it appears that a cyclone is approaching the vicinity of Mauritius or Rodrigues and that gusts may be expected to exceed 120 km p.h the warning system is put into effect by the Meteorological Services. It consists essentially of a numbered series of Cyclone Bulletins and of a summary statement of the class of warning designed to keep the public informed of the progress of the cyclone.

The following terminology has been adopted in the South West Indian Ocean Region for classifying cyclonic disturbances and will be used in Cyclone Bulletins:

Sl. No.	Terminology	Speed of Gusts (Km. P.h.)
1.	Tropical Depression	Under 90
2.	Moderate Tropical Depression	90 to 134
3.	Severe Tropical Depression	135 to 179
4.	Tropical Cyclone	180 to 250
5.	Intense Tropical Cyclone	251 to 335
6.	Very Intense Tropical Cyclone	Above 335

Bulletins numbering from a few to a dozen or more for each cyclone, are issued at about 6-hourly intervals or more often (except when unnecessary during the middle of the night). Each bulletin is labeled first, second, third, etc, and dated and timed.

A bulletin gives the position, intensity and movement of the cyclone with a forecast of the expected changes in the conditions of the wind and sea, and the expected time of commencement of specified wind speeds and gust conditions. Advice about precautions is given in general terms but all recipients must necessarily apply the facts of the forecast to his own situation because, for instance, a householder may be able to close his shutters in a few minutes during the night whereas the proper protection of fishing boats require a considerable period of daylight hours.

Precautions cost money and effort and must be regarded as an insurance against the risk of loss and not as prevention of a certainty. It has been decided that the Class System of Warnings should be based primarily on the extent of the risk and secondly on the time factor. The coded Class System by itself can in no way indicate the intensity or size of the cyclone not the extent to which gusts will exceed 120 km p.h.

The warning system must take into consideration the degree of risk and the time factor. It is not yet possible to forecast the direction and speed of movement of a cyclone with certainty.

Cyclone Warnings

Class 1

To be issued 36 to 48 hours before Mauritius or Rodrigues is likely to be affected. There is a risk that gusts exceeding 120 km p.h will occur. The public is advised to take preliminary precautions.

Class II

To be issued so as to allow, as far as practicable, 12 hours of daylight before gusts of 120 km p.h. will occur at Mauritius/Rodrigues. The risk of gusts exceeding 120 km.p.h. at Mauritius/Rodrigues has increased. The public is advised to take precautions.

Class III

To be issued, as far as practicable in time to allow 6 hours of daylight before the advent of 120 km.p.h. gusts. It is now highly probable that the Cyclone will cause gusts exceeding 120 km.p.h. at Mauritius/Rodrigues. The public is urged to complete all precautions.

Class IV

Gusts over 120 km.p.h. have occurred and are expected to continue.

Cyclone information is distributed through the MBC, the Press, the telephone system and the Police. Code flags are flown on certain buildings.

The Mauritius Broadcasting Corporation should give top priority to broadcasting of cyclone warning bulletins at all times.

As soon as a Class II Warning is issued, the Government Information Service will also issue a communiqué to inform responsible parties that schools are being closed and that they must arrange to take their children/wards home.

All Authorities will arrange for proper distribution within their organisations of all Cyclone Bulletins and Warnings received.

Cyclone Flags will be flown at Town Halls, Village Halls, Police Stations and Fisheries Posts as well as any other suitable buildings according to the following code:

One red flag	Warning Class I
Two red flags	Warning Class II
Three red flags	Warning Class III
Four red flags	Warning Class IV
One blue flag	Termination

The CEB may cut off light and electric power at any time if it considers that circumstances render this necessary. The CEB will inform the MBC as soon as power is to be cut off and when a decision has been made that power should be restored.

If a Class II Warning is in force at the beginning of a school day, schools would not be open for school children. If a Class II warning is issued during school hours, classes will be dismissed without delay. Schools which are not used as Refugee Centres are closed when classes are dismissed.

(c) Response

During a cyclone, movement outside and the maintenance of services may become very difficult but officers employed on essential cyclone duties will do their utmost to maintain communications and services.

All possible warning will be given to the public by mobile police cars and other available means to ensure that the calm period during the passing of the eye of the cyclone is not mistaken for end of the hurricane winds.

When a Class III warning is issued the Mauritius Broadcasting Corporation will warn the public not to attempt to remove or dismantle or play around their television aerials.

(d) Recovery

Immediately after a cyclone, emergency relief operation will be directed from Government House, Port Louis by a standing Cabinet Cyclone Committee composed of the Prime Minister and other concerned Ministers.

The Committee will meet at Government House, Port Louis, at the first opportunity after the termination of cyclone conditions.

The Standing Ministerial Cyclone Committee will be supported by an organisation which will ensure that adequate information is at the Committee's disposal, that immediate executive action is taken to carry out the decisions of the Committee, and that there is a flow of information and instructions to Heads of Ministries/Departments primarily concerned with the work of relief and reconstruction.

The main functions of the Committee will be :

- ❖ To collect and present to the Cabinet Committee information on:
  - the general situation throughout the island (obtained mainly from the police);
  - the condition of Government Departments (obtained from Permanent Secretaries and other Heads of Ministries/Departments); and,
  - damage to non-government property (obtained mainly from local Cyclone Committees);
- ❖ To make recommendations on any relief immediately required;
- ❖ To ensure that immediate executive action is taken on the decisions of the Cabinet Committee; and
- ❖ To provide an accessible centre reporting point for Heads of Ministries/ Departments primarily concerned in the work of relief and reconstruction.

The Commissioner of Police should submit to the Secretary for Home Affairs, Prime Minister's Office, a general assessment of the damage and casualties and of the situation throughout the island based on information supplied by Police Stations/ Posts and helicopter surveys.

The Secretary, Local Cyclone Committees will submit to the Committee of Officials prompt and accurate information on casualties, damage to non-government property and the extent of immediate relief measures required in their respective areas.

Immediate steps will be taken by the Heads Ministries/Departments concerned to:

- ❖ Re-open roads
- ❖ Restore water supplies
- ❖ Restore essential telephones

- ❖ Restore power and lighting
- ❖ Re-open the Port
- ❖ Re-open the Airport
- ❖ Assess damage to load stocks
- ❖ Obtain and provide funds for scavenging in the Local Cyclone Committee areas
- ❖ Provide and maintain sanitary arrangements at Refugee Centres and clean and disinfect these latter.

All other Heads of Ministries/Departments will take steps to salvage damaged property and restore their Ministry/Department to full operational efficiency.

All requests for international aid should be channeled through the Secretary for Home Affairs, Prime Minister's Office.

After receiving complete information about damage caused by any cyclone in Mauritius, Rodrigues or the Outer Islands, the Secretary for Home Affairs, Prime Minister's Office will arrange for such information to be forwarded to the Secretary-General of the World Meteorological Organisation on agreed format.

11

Management of Natural Disasters

Krishna Prasad Parajuli
Under Secretary,
Ministry of Science and Technology,
Singha Darbar, Kathmandu, Nepal

1. Introduction

Nepal is a landlocked country. It is located between two large countries: China and India It covers an area of 147181 sq. km. Overall population density is about 135/km^2 Nepal lies between 26°22′ to 30°27′ north latitude and 80°4′ to 88°12′ east longitude. It is a mountainous country. Only 17 percent of its land is plain of Terai. There are different geographical features because of which climate, vegetation and way of life of the people are different from one part to another.

More than 42 per cent of the total 21 million peoples live in absolute poverty. The poor are rural farmers. Like other developing countries, Nepal is predominantly an agricultural country. About 90 percent of the total population derives its lively-hood from agriculture. The main crops are paddy, maize, barley, wheat, potatoes and jute etc.

Nepal has a multi-party democratic constitution, monarchial system of government. Sovereignty, rests with the people who exercise power in keeping with the principles separation of powers. The executive power is exercised through the cabinet headed by the Prime Minister. The Supreme Court is the highest court in the kingdom. In addition, there are a number of constitutional bodies in Nepal responsible for some important specific functions which they carry out independently, *e.g.*, Auditor General, Public Service Commission, and Election Commission.

For general administrative purpose, the government of Nepal is divided into two levels: Central and Local. A third, intermediate level in the regional level has been created by development purposes.

The country is divided into 14 zones and 75 districts. At the very foundation of the local level government are local government There are 75 District Development Committees (DDCs), 58 municipalities and 3913 Village Development Committees (VDCs). The relationship between the various levels are asymmetrical, the lower level is subordinate to the higher level. The central govt. is empowered to exercise supervision and control over both local authority levels. DDCs are empowered to exercise some supervision and control within that framework over the VDCs, in particular.

2. Background of National Disaster in Nepal

Nepal is characterized by a rugged topography, variable climatic conditions and. complex geological structure. The country faces high levels of earthquake hazard, the hilly and mountainous regions are characterized by variable water-shed conditions and are vulnerable to landslide and Debris Flow hazards. Lakes of glacial origin in the northern part of the country have created the possibility of Glacier Lakes Outburst Flood (GLOF). The flat plains of Terai and the low valleys in the mountains are susceptible to floods. Besides these, almost every year smaller or larger part of the country is struck by one or several forms of other disaster such as Drought, Hailstorms, Epidemic Fire etc. The country has many times suffered from these disasters in the past resulting in huge losses in terms of lost human lives and damaged public properties and infrastructure. The earthquake of 1934, 1980, 1988 and the floods of July 1993 are some of the examples of natural disaster events, which caused considerable, set back to the development efforts of the country.

The impacts of all disasters can surely be reduced significantly with the help of proper methods of disaster management focusing on pre-disaster preparedness activities. Nepal has accumulated considerable experiences in disaster management by facing with the problems of past disaster.

3. Organization for Natural Disaster Management

His Majesty's Government of Nepal has constituted the Nepal National Disaster Committee for the International Decade for Natural Disaster Reduction (IDNDR). Honorable Home Minister is the chairman of Nepal National Committee for IDNDR. Special Secretary, Ministry of Home is the member secretary of this body. While the IDNDR Nepal Committee is responsible for policy matters regarding the disaster management, the Disaster Response Committee is responsible for the day-to-day management of all routine works of disaster management works under the Home Ministry.

His Majesty's Government has constituted the Disaster Relief Committee. Disaster Relief Committee is divided into two parts:

(a) Central Disaster Relief Committee (CDRC)

The Central Disaster Relief Committee (CDRC) chief is the Honorable Home Minister for disaster relief management in Nepal. The membership of the committee consists of government secretaries of the different ministries, Inspector General of Nepal Police, Chief of Royal Neal Army as well as representatives of various other government departments and non-government agencies, universities and NGOs.

(b) District Disaster Relief Committee (DDRC)

The Chief District Officer (CDO) is the chairman of the District Disaster Relief Committee (DDRC). It is the most active body for coordinating the relief works and supports relief activities in the district in case of a disaster. The committee has a membership representation from public sector organizations like District Development Committee Office, District Health Office, Royal Nepal Army District Unit, District Police Office and Nepal Red Cross Society etc. DDRC is responsible for coordinating the district level relief works.

4. Government Institutions for Natural Disaster Management

There are other government offices and departments, which are directly, or indirectly involved and responsible for conducting works in aspects of disaster management in the contemporary sense of the term "disaster management". These government organizations are partly or fully responsible to study particular types of natural disasters in the country.

5. Professional societies NGOs Involved in Aspects of Natural Disaster Management

Several Nepalese professional scientists and professional societies also work in aspect of disaster management seeking to provide the technical inputs and the scientific/technical basis for public awareness. The society utilizes other forums and means such as public lectures and its publications (Journal and News Bulletin of the Nepal Geological Society, topical publication etc.) to disaster safety messages to the Nepalese public. There are other scientific and engineering professional organizations in Nepal who are involved in aspects of disaster management, especially in the mitigation aspects.

6. Non-Government Organizations Involved in Aspects of Natural Disaster Management

In Nepal, beside the government organization other non-government organizations (NGOs) are also helping the government agencies and the disaster victims during or after the disaster events especially in relief operations.

7. International Organizations for Natural Disaster Management

There are quite a few international organizations and INGOs, who are directly or indirectly involved in disaster management activities. In the past such organizations helped Nepal by providing funds or essential relief materials to the disaster victims. Out of these United Nations Disaster Management Secretariat (UN/DMS) has been delivering important services in this field in Nepal.

To support the activities of the United Nations Disaster Management Team (UNDMT) and the disaster related activities of the international community, a permanent Disaster Management Secretariat (DMS) has been established by the UN Resident Coordinator. Its main functions are:

- To provide secretarial services for the disaster response activities of the international community
- To maintain a library of disaster related reference materials
- To maintain a database of international community disaster related resource available both within and outside of Nepal.

Other international agencies like JICA, GTZ, USAID and INGOs liker Lutheran World Service (LWS), United Mission to Nepal (UMN), CARE Nepal etc. are directly or indirectly involved in aspects of disaster preparedness and mitigation in community level USAID has provided funds in the past to Nepal Administrative Staff College to organize Regional Scale Disaster Management Training in five development regions. About 169 offices of HMG were trained so far.

8. Types of Natural Hazard/Disaster of Nepal

Nepal is a small country. It is exposed to several types of natural as well as man-induced hazards of wide varieties of physiographic, geological, ecological, meteorological factors contribute to the high levels of hazards faced, while demographic factors such as rapid population growth, improper land use, slow economic development and the resulting rampant poverty, wide spread mitigation, lack of firm political and social commitment also make the country extremely prove to disasters. The major types of natural hazards of concern are listed in the Table 11.1.

Table 11.1: Types of Natural Hazard/Disaster

Types of Hazard	*Prevalence*
Natural Hazards	
Earthquake	All over the country
Flood	Middle mountains, Terai
Landslide	Mountain and hilly parts.
Debris Flow and Glacier Lakes Outburst Floods (GLOF)	Higher Himalayas. Higher Mountains and Middle mountains
Avalanche	Higher Himalayas
Forest Fire	Middle Mountains and Terai
Drought	All over the country
Storms/ Hailstorm	Mountainous parts
Man-Induced Hazards	
Epidemics	Mostly in Terai some in mountains
Fire	Terai
Accidents	Urban areas. Road Network
Industrial/Technological Hazards.	Urban/industrial areas
Soil erosion	Hilly and mountainous area
Social Disruptions	

Source: Dixit (1996)

9. History of Disaster Events in Nepal

(a) Earthquake

Nepal lies in the central part of Himalayan regions. It has a complex geology and geological structures, the country on the whole is vulnerable to earthquake. High and very high hazard zones fall in the vicinity of the well-pronounced epicentral cluster of past earthquakes such as in Bajhang, Darchula region and northern parts of the central and eastern Nepal (Dixit and Maskey 1994). It is known that sand rich parts in the whole Terai were the sites of liquefaction during the past earthquake. Therefore it is clear that Terai area is susceptible to a high degree of risk during earthquake. Historical records are the proof for it. Micro seismic records and information for central Nepal is available since 1910. Some of the records are given in Table 11.2.

Earthquake is a major disaster which may effect Nepal any time specially the Kathmandu_valley. The National Society for Earthquake Technology at Nepal (N-SET) has taken responsibility for creating, implementing a plan to promote awareness of earthquake risk and implementation of seismic risk reduction project in Nepal. HMG of Nepal has declared the First Earthquake Safety Day on Jan. 16, 1999 (Magh 2, 2055).

(b) Landslide and flood Disaster

Nepal lies in the southern slope of the Himalaya. Almost 83 per cent of the country is mountainous, and the rest 17 per cent is low flat land There are more than 6000 streams and rivers in Nepal Most of the bigger rivers are snow fed and originate from the Higher Himalaya (glacier) which is covered by snow. Because of the topographical condition, most of the rivers/streams flow from north to south direction with considerably high velocity due to high river gradient. Because of rugged mountain topography, high-angle slope, fragile geology and terrain condition and very high intensity rainfall during monsoon causes many landslides in the mountainous (hill) area and flood in the low lands. In Nepal almost 90 per cent of total deaths of people in 1993 disaster was due to flood and landslides, 6 per cent was caused by epidemics and 4 per cent was due to earthquake and others. Some of the landslides and flood records in Nepal are presented in the Table 11.3.

Flood is a recurrent problem in the Terai as well as in the river valleys. Most part of Terai faces the problem of floods during the monsoon periods (June-August). Most of the flood disasters take place along the banks of the larger rivers such as Mechi, Kankai, Koshi, Kamala, Bagmati, East Rapti, Narayani (Gandaki), West Rapti, Babai, Karnali and Mahakali rivers. Generally, the south facing slopes in the Churia range (Siwalik Hill) show the higher extent of slope instability causing numerous landslides. The landslides are well seen also along the road cut sections. In the lesser Himalayan region (Mahabharat Range) there are several faults discontinuity planes which are responsible for the development of Shear Zones. Deep erosion, landslides, debris flow and debris avalanches are common in this area. The rock/ice fall, rock/ice avalanche, debris slide and glacier lake outbrust floods are common in the higher Himalayan region.

Table 11.2: Historical Records of the Earthquakes (Earthquake Catalog)

Date	*Time*	*Mag. (Richter)*	*Loss of Life*	*Injured*	*House Collapsed*	*House Damaged*	*Area Affected*
15/1/1934 (1990BS)	14:22	8.3	8519	NA	80890	207,248	32 districts affected in C&MW Region. Kathmandu was worst affected
29/7/1980 2037BS	Night	6.5	103	NA	36,012	12,100	Bjn, Bjr, Btd & Dcl districts were affected, Cattle loss = 207, 248
21/8/1988 (2O45BS)	04:54	6.6	721	6,553	65,432	235,403	Eastern and Central Nepal were affected
27/7/1966 (2023 BS)	20:41	6.5–7(?)	24	NK	Over 1,300		Dcl, Bjn, Bjr, districts were affected
28/8/1916	-	High to medium	NK	-			-
1989 BS	-	Low to medium	NK	-			-
1890 BS	11:00	7.8		-	4214		Kathmandu Valley highly affected
1880 BS	-	Medium		-			17 shocks recorded; Less people were affected
1737 BS	Night	Medium		-			Exact damage figures not available; Loss of life and properties
1464 BS	-	High to Medium	Loss of life	-			Kathmandu Valley, properties, infrastructure, temples damaged
1316 BS	-	High to Medium	Loss of life	-			Kathmandu Valley, Second recorded, earthquake; Loss of properties
1310 as	-	7.7 (?)	-	-		.	Almost 33% of the people in Kathmandu valley were affecterd

The Department of Mines and Geology is preparing a landslide inventory. Water Induced Disaster Prevention Technical Center (DPTC) is also thematic studies on landslide and monitoring of two-three landslides. The Department of Soil Conservation is doing some protection works in different districts. In the Nepalese mountains, one can see all types of mass wasting. The most frequent and the one which cause the greatest destruction in terms of loss of lives and properties, are the debris slide, debris avalanches, rock fall and slumps (Dixit, 1990).

Table 11.3: Historical Records on Landslides and Floods Disaster in Nepal

Date	*Location*	*Extent of Damage*	*Cost of Damage*
1979	Vijayapur Khola	30m Bridge	Rs.8,000,000
1979	Karra Khola	60m bridge	?
1981	Arniko High Way	27 km part	Rs.62,000,000
1983/1984	Dharan-Dhankuta Road	500 m Damage	Rs.23,000,000
1987	Seti Bridge	Collapsed	Rs. 520,000,000 to 730,000,000
1991	Prithvi Highway, Tribhuvan Highway, E-W Highway and Phidim-Taplejung Road	350 Km Road & 41 Bridges Collapsed	Road Rehabilitation cost Rs. 2,250,000,000
1993 flood & Landslide	Bagmati Barrage, Kulekhani HP and Destruction of Bridges	2000 landslides, Tribhuvan Highway washed at 20 places; 1,612 people lost their lives; 8,500 families affected. Their houses and cultivated lands were destroyed	Rs.50,000,000
1993 Flood & Landslide		Malekhu, Belkhu and Agra Khola and Bhainse bridge collapsed	Rs.200,000,000

Source: Ministry of Home.

(c) Floods and Landslides of South Central Nepal–July 1993

The south-central part of Nepal was effected by great floods, landslides and debris flows following incessant rainfall lasting 19-21 July 1993. Maximum rainfall recorded was 54 mm in a day with the night time rainfall of 65 mm per hour. The disaster was followed by another event of floods and landslides on the 8-9 August 1993. The total effect of the two events was 1460 people dead or missing, 73,606 families seriously affected 39,043 houses destroyed fully or partially, about 43,330 hectare of cultivated land washed away or covered with debris, 367 km. of roads damaged, 213 bridges including six concrete bridges on national highways, 38 large to small irrigation schemes, 452 school and government offices etc. were destroyed within the couple of days. Vital supplies to the capital city, Kathmandu was virtually cut off for more than a month because of the road breaches and damage to the bridges. Damage to the big Kulekhani hydropower system, consisting of two power plants and providing 40 per cent of the national power production resulted in heavy load shedding which affected not only the normal life of the population but also adversely affected the whole of the national economy. The data of the most affected area in central Nepal is presented in Table 11.4.

(d) Weather Forecasting and Warning System

There is no effective weather forecasting and warning system in the Country. The extreme weather event was sudden and it was not possible to issue any effective warning in so short time. The sudden release of water from the project dam for its safety was the main cause of the flood. The flood reached the Terai during the night time.

Table 11.4: Damage due to Flood and landslide in July 1993

District	*Family Affected*	*People Affected*	*No. of Deaths*	*House Collap-sed*	*Land Washed (ha)*	*Land Affected (ha)*	*Livestock Lost*	*Infrastructure Damage/ Collapsed*
Makwanpur	14748	84196	247	3010	4112	NA	1872	Kulekhani Hydro power plant/ roads, schools/ houses
Sarlahi	16812	91110	687	16708	379	16681	11310	Bagmati Barrage / roads, schools/ houses
Rautahat	14644	89146	111	6411	1366	6748	3211	Schools and houses, roads
Sindhull	16163	83441	53	2718	5918	1418	2045	Schools and houses, bridges and roads
Kavrepal-anchok	3318	18915	24	885	1244	NA	114	Schools and houses, bridges and roads
Dhading	1113	6358	24	827	1066	NA	353	Schools and houses, bridges and roads
Chitwan	5293	34943	24	2206	741	2321	5880	Schools and houses, roads
Total	**72091**	**408109**	**1170**	**32765**	**14826**	**27168**	**24785**	

Source: Annual Disaster review, 1993, DPTC.

This event drew the attention of the government and other about the necessity of installing warning system in the country. Hydrology and Meteorology Department has started the initial works in this direction.

(e) Glacier Lake Outburst Flood (GLOF)

Glacier Lakes are recorded in the Higher Himalayan region. They contain huge volume of water in them Because of their unstable condition they can burst any time and natural catastrophe may cause loss of life, properties and infrastructure. About 12 such Glacier Lake outburst Floods already took place during the period of last 56 years (from 1935 to 1991), Table 11.5. Records of loss of life and properties are available only for the latter. To avoid such situation in near future precautionary measure in time is very essential. Inhabitants of these areas must be aware of the forthcoming situation and a timely warning system must be developed. Present level of awareness about the possible Tsho Rolpa Glacier Lake Outburst Flood is one of the examples of preparedness. Tsho Rolpa Glof Risk Reduction Project is under construction which will to lower the Glacier Lake level by 3 meters. For this project the Netherlands

Government is the donor country. Location of Tsho Rolpa Glacier Lake map is attached herewith.

Table 11.5: Some Historical Records of Glacier Lake Outburst Floods in Nepal

Year	Location	Lives Lost	Injury	Houses		Development Structures Damaged	Cost of Damage (Rs.)
				Des-troyed	Dam-age		
1935	Bhote Koshi (Terrace)	—	—	—	—	—	—
1964 & 1982	Arun River (Jinco GLOF)	—	—	—	—	—	—
1964	Trishuli River (GLOF of Longda)	—	—	—	—	—	—
1977	Ama Dablam (Nare Glacier lake)	—	—	—	—	—	—
1981	Barun Khola	—	—	—	—	—	—
1985 Dig Tsho	Bhote and Dudh, Koshi/Namche	5	NA	30	NA	Namche Hydropower plant, Agricultural land	40000000
1964 & 1981	Bhote/Sunkoshi	—	—	—	—	Friendship bridge, Arniko highway, Sunkoshi Hydropower Plant	NA
1980	Phuchan (Tamor River)	—	—	—	—	—	—
1970	Ayico GLOF	—	—	—	—	—	—
1991	Chhubung GLOF	—	—	6	—	Agricultural land, food tracks and suspension bridges	—

Source: Bulletin WECS. 1993.

NA: Not Available.

(f) Storm, Wind Storm and Thunderbolt Disaster

Nepal lies between two gigantic countries: China to the north and India to the south, east and west. It is a land locked country with its southern corner about 500 Km from the nearest sea the Bay of Bengal. It lies in the temperate zone. So the tropical cyclone which is generally violent and brings heavy rainfall and causes damage to life and property would not effect more in Nepal The wind storm and thunderbolt also generally occur during the dry season. It is equally common in all parts of Nepal.

10. Man Induced Hazards

(a) Fire Disaster

Fire Disaster is much more common in Terai areas than hilly and Mountain areas. It take place normally in the month of May and June when the temperature

Figure 11.1: Location of Tsho Rolpa Glacier Lake in the Head Water of Rolwalling valley (after Yamada 1988)

rises above 35^0 Celsius. The house in the villages of Terai region are very close to each other. The roofs of the houses are normally made up of dry hays which can be very easily caught by the fire during dry season. Every year Fire Disaster causes many more loss of human and properties in Nepal.

(b) Epidemic Disaster

Mostly the epidemic disaster takes place during the summer or rainy season. It is due to low quality of drinking water and poor sanitation. Cholera, Typhoid, Jaundice, and malaria etc. are the common epidemic disease in Nepal. These types of disaster are common mainly in urban areas and Terai region (South belt Nepal).

11. Conclusion

The Central Disaster Relief Committee first of all tries to get the real information through DDRC about the event and its effects on people and damage to the infrastructures. It gives advice to DDRC to conduct immediate rescue and relief operation and provide emergency help to the victims. The government has developed better capabilities in emergency response especially after the 1980 and 1988 earthquake and 1993 floods incidence in central Nepal. The people should be aware about the possible disaster. Responsible institutions have to be developed in local VDC level for emergency supplies of food, materials and to protect from possible disaster. There is an urgent need of specially trained personnel to deal with the management of specific disaster. Team of such specially trained experts should be formed and mobilized during disasters. Effective warning system must be developed for all types of disaster. For all types of disaster activities there is the need of sufficient funds. NGO also provide necessary help during the disaster. INGO and international organizations etc. provide various kinds of help in term of money and materials.

12

Forecasting, Early Warning and Reporting Procedure in Case of Disasters

Muhammad Munir Sheikh
Director and Chief Meteorologist, National Flood Forecasting Bureau,
Pakistan Meteorological Department,
46 Jail Road, Lahore, Pakistan

1. Introduction

Floods, Tropical Cyclones, Thunder and hailstorms and tornadoes are all weather related natural disasters. Earthquakes, Volcanoes, droughts and environmental disasters like ozone depletion, magnetic storms etc. are also natural disasters albeit not directly related to weather. With the exception of earthquakes, however, which are largely phenomena relating to the Earth's crust, the remainder are nonetheless related to atmospheric conditions, either for their initiation or for their subsequent dispersal and propagation. Despite the above, the monitoring of earthquakes, ozone and magnetic storms fall within the domain of Pakistan Meteorological Department.

The natural disasters wreak havoc and cause tremendous loss of life and property all over the globe. Although improved weather warnings and disaster preparedness now contribute significantly to the saving of life, yet loss of life and property is still very large in some cases. Several developing countries in the Asia and Pacific Region have large areas which are prone to, and hard hit by, natural disasters. Some 90 percent of deaths resulting from natural disasters occur in developing countries.

2. Natural Disasters in Asia and the Pacific

Nearly 60 percent of the world's natural disasters such as floods, earthquakes, tsunamis, tropical cyclones and volcanoes occur in Asia and Pacific region. A brief account of each disaster, its reporting system in Pakistan is given:

(a) Floods

Flood is defined as the high stage of a river at which the stream channel gets filled up and above which it overflows its banks and inundates the adjoining areas.

Floods have been recognized as a major natural hazard in Pakistan and the country has a long history of flooding from the Indus River and its tributaries. Floods of 1928, 1929, 1959, 1973, 1976, 1988 and that of 1992 are the sad yet memorable events entailing tremendous damages to the life and property. The loss of life and property associated with the floods has been colossal. In the year 1973, more than three million homes were destroyed and 160 persons lost their lives. The 1976 floods demolished over 10 million houses while 425 lives were lost with losses amounting to Rs. 6 billion. In 1988, an unprecedented flood occurred towards the end of September inflicting about Rs. 17 billion worth of damages to the country. The recent catastrophic flood of 1992 surpassed all the previous records with damages estimated at Rs. 50 billion. Historic floods with discharges in different years uptil 1998 are shown in the Table attached.

Impacts of floods are losses of life and property, inundation, deposition of silt and debris. Preventive measures include levees, drainage, retention works/dams, flood plain zoning, flood forecasting and warning and emergency preparedness.

Flood management in Pakistan is a multifunctional process involving a number of different Govt. organizations. National Flood Forecasting Bureau of Pakistan Meteorological Department is the sole agency responsible at the national level for the issuance and dissemination of flood forecasts and has the following constitution:

- Director, NFFB — Head
- Director, Hydrology WAPDA — Member
- Representative of Indus Water Commission — Member
- Director Floods (PIDA), Irrigation Department — Member

NFFB has taken in hand the dissemination of the flood forecasts/warnings to considerably large number of recipients directly or indirectly concerned with the flood mitigation process over and above the dissemination done by Flood Warning Centre of Punjab Irrigation Department. A schematic diagram indicating the dissemination by NFFB is attached.

(b) Earthquakes

Sudden shaking of a part of earth due to the release of accumulated stress developed as a result of the movement of tectonic plates or faults in earth's strata or volcanic eruption.

Earthquakes have been the subject of concern and awe through history. No other natural event is as disastrous over so large an area in so short a time. Lives lost as a result of single earthquakes often amount to tens of thousands, some times hundreds of thousands. Nearly all these losses are preventable as the main cause is the collapse of weak structures. Earthquake-resistant structures are becoming more common in Japan.

A network comprising of six seismic stations at Peshawar, Islamabad, Lahore, Quetta, Khuzdar and Karachi functions under Geophysical Centre, Quetta of Pakistan Meteorological Department.

Soon after the occurrence of an earthquake, the parameters like time of origin, epicentre, magnitude etc. are worked out which normally takes an hour or so and a press release is then issued.

A seismic zonic map has been prepared at the centre which is very helpful for the structural engineers and town planners.

(c) Tropical Cyclones

These are cyclones of the tropical latitudes. Classification used for different tropical disturbances in Pakistan is given below:

Type of Disturbance	*Corresponding Wind Speed*
Depression	22-27 knots
Deep Depression	28-33 knots
Cyclonic Storms	34-47 knots
Severe Cyclonic Storms	48-63 knots
Severe Cyclonic Storms of hurricane Intensity	64 knots or more

Severe cyclonic storms (S.C.S) are known as hurricanes in Atlantic Ocean, Typhoons in Pacific and S.C.S. in Indian Ocean. These are called Willy in Australia.

Location of Information

The more intense tropical cyclones are confined to fairly specific regions and seasons which broadly are the western sides of the great tropical oceans, beyond 5^0 from the equator, towards the end of the hot season or seasons. Main oceanic regions are:

Period	*Regions*
July to October	North Atlantic Ocean (West Indies)
	North Pacific Off the West Coast of Mexico
	North Pacific Westwards of 170^0 E (China Seas)
December to March	South Indian (Madgascar to 98^0 E and near north west Australia) and South Pacific (158^0 E eastwards to 148^0 W)
April to March and September to December	Bay of Bengal and Arabian Sea

The initial stage of a tropical cyclone's life cycle is not well-understood, due in part to the complexity of these storms. Another important factor is the lack of observations in regions where storms form. However, we do know that smaller tropical cyclones initiate the process. These initial disturbances are regions of low-level convergence and lifting. The U.S. National Weather Service labels such incipient storms as tropical disturbances.

Although many tropical disturbances occur each year, only a few develop into full-fledged hurricanes (severe cyclonic storms, typhoons etc) when their winds reach 119 Kilometers per hour.

The tropical storms diminish in intensity whenever they:

- Move over ocean waters that cannot supply warm, moist tropical air.
- Move onto land or.
- Reach a location where the large scale flow aloft is unfavourable.

Reporting of severe cyclonic storms is done by Pakistan Meteorological Department as was recently done for a S.C.S. which appeared in Arabian sea and hit the coastal areas of Sindh on 20th May, 1999. Polar orbital and Geo-stationary satellite pictures along with weather charts were the basis on which the forecasts were based.

(d) Thunderstorms

A small-scale phenomenon which results due to the vertical movement of the relatively warm unstable air. Thunderstorm activity is associated with cumulonimbus clouds that generate heavy rainfall thunder, lightning and occasionally hail.

Several thousand thunderstorms occur every day, mainly in the tropics. The number is smaller over oceans than over land, owing to lack of intense convection above water surfaces. In polar regions, these are virtually unknown. These are always associated with unstable air and strong vertical motion that produces clouds of the cumulonimbus type. A great deal of the energy for their development comes from the release of the latent heat of condensation in rising humid air. It is important to note in this connection that an unstable lapse rate and overturning of air may result from either warming of surface layers or introduction of cold air aloft.

Development of Thunderstorms

The common processes that initiate thunderstorm development are:

- Heating and convection in moist air over warm land surfaces.
- Passage of cold, moist air over warm water.
- Forced ascent of conditionally unstable air along zones of-convergence or at mountain barriers.
- Radiational cooling at upper levels or Advection of cold air aloft.

Moisture and rising are the essential elements for the development of a thunderstorm. Most thunderstorms consist of several convective cells that grow and dissipate erratically when the force of rising air is great enough, the storm can reach to heights from 4 to more than 20 Km. The height of a thunderstorm is related to latitude and season of the year, the greatest heights are achieved in summer and in the tropics. Typical diameters of thunderstorms vary from 3 to 40 Km. Precipitation from the mature storms is intense and composed of large raindrops, literally a cloud burst. If the thunderstorms have sufficient force and penetrate well above the freezing level, hail may fall from the cloud.

Thunderstorms caused by surface heating over land are most common in summer and in the afternoon or early morning.

For the purpose of meteorological records, thunder must be heard or overhead lightning or hail observed at station before a thunderstorm is reported. Thunder and lightening are the dramatic manifestations of the storms.

(e) Tornadoes

Tornadoes are most violent storms of the lower troposphere. A tornado is a tight vortex, gyrating around a center of extremely low pressure, usually associated with a severe thunderstorm. Accurate wind observations are impossible to be recorded within the storms but velocities of 200 to 300 knots are probably common. A tornado can be distinguished by its whirling, funnel shaped cloud which extends downward from the base at a cumulonimbus or a turbulent cloud layer.

Tornadoes are most likely to appear in spring and early summer when contrasts of temperature and humidity are at its maximum in the air masses along cold fronts. Although tornadoes are apparently less common elsewhere in the world, they have been reported at widely scattered locations in the mid-latitudes and tropics notably in Europe, Japan and Australia.

The vortex comprising the tornado is much more intense and occurs on the much smaller scale than the parent mesocylone. The tornado vortex is in fact too small to resolve in multiple doppler radar analyses, however it can often be detected in the single doppler data as a location of extreme wind shear from one data sampling volume to the next.

At sea tornadoes are known as water sprouts, having much the same characteristics except that they are usually smaller in diameter.

(f) Avalanches

Avalanches are, in a sense, a flash flood of water in the solid form. In other words, avalanche is a mass of snow and ice tumbling rapidly downs a mountain. The angle of repose of the snow cover and the underlying surface features are basic considerations in avalanches, they are set off naturally by conditions of snow structure, temperature, humidity and wind. Any disturbance of an unstable snow cover is likely to cause an avalanche.

Wind blasts known as avalanche wind frequently accompany severe avalanches. The more violent blasts have been known to break off trees several meters away from the main path of the avalanche. The phenomenon does occur in the mountains in the northern parts of country, but their forecasting and reporting is not done by the Pakistan Meteorological Department. Presently Ice and snow survey is the field given to WAPDA.

(g) Land Slides

These are sliding down of landmasses from the mountain sides or cliffs. The process of land sliding occurs either due to the earthquakes or due to the heavy precipitation. Such phenomena are mostly localized and are difficult to be forecast.

Landslide disasters are common in mountainous areas of the country. Landslides are either triggered by heavy rainfall or by the shaking of earthquakes. Human necessities like houses, highways, water supply, drainage, farm lands and forests get affected.

It is not known as to which agency in Pakistan is responsible for the forecasting and prevention of land sliding. However the velocity and displacement in the movement of the landmasses are considered important to be kept under watch. Mapping of the vulnerable sites needs to be carried out to mitigate the effect of this disaster.

(h) Tidal Waves

A popular term for a destructive type of wave motion in seas and oceans, associated either with strong winds or with under-water earthquakes. In technical term, they are classified as storm surge and Tsunami respectively.

There are many type of waves in the ocean with wavelengths ranging from an order of millimeter to several thousand kilometers, and causes of them are widespread. From the point of view of spectrum, the storm surge may be characterized as being sea-surface disturbance with dominant period ranging roughly from 10^3 to 10^5 second, falling between the tsunami and lower frequency astronomical waves.

In case storm surges are likely to be caused by the tropical storms, Pakistan Meteorological Department has the responsibility to issue the forecasts and inform the concerned agencies about the likelihood of the storm surges. Forecasts for the severe cyclonic storm which hit coastal areas of Sindh on 20th May, 1999 covered this aspect nicely.

(i) Ozone Depletion

The region of atmosphere lying above the troposphere (10 Km at equator and 15 Kms at poles) and below the Mesosphere is known as stratosphere. In the stratosphere, the temperature at first remains nearly constant to a height of about 20 Kilometers. It then records a rather sharp increase that continues until the straopause is encountered at a height of about 50 Kms above the earth's surface. Higher temperatures occur in the stratosphere because it is in this layer that the ozone is concentrated and it absorbs U.V. radiation from the sun. Consequently the stratosphere is heated. The maximum ozone concentration exists between 15 and 30 Kms maximum around 22 Kms.

The ozone gets depleted due to the release of CFC and other gases as is explained in the figure.

In a study conducted by the writer using data of Almata (Russia), New Delhi (India) and Quetta (Pakistan), it has been extracted that no ozone depletion at least exists over Pakistan.

Ozone monitoring is done by Pakistan Meteorological Department. It has the installations at its Quetta centre called Geophysical centre to monitor ozone both in stratosphere and in troposphere.

Ozone functions as a protective shield for the U.V. Radiations as it absorbs the ultraviolet radiations and do not let them penetrate and reach the surface. These ultraviolet radiations are harmful to life on earth, thus ozone is considered a desirable atmospheric component that is critical to life on earth and should be preserved.

Whereas ozone serves as a protective shield in the stratosphere, it is produced as a pollutant in the troposphere. Smog is a major environmental problem in big cities and ozone is the major component of this noxious mixture of gases and particles that forms as a result of reactions among pollutants emitted by motor vehicles and industries. During air pollution episodes, ozone levels are frequently used as an index to the poor quality of urban air. The higher the ozone concentration, the poor is the air quality. Therefore, ozone is an undesirable pollutant in Troposphere that threatens human health.

(j) Magnetic Storms

The sunspots which are huge magnetic storms appear over the sun and eject huge amount of charged particles from the sun. The appearance of the sunspots has a mean periodicity of 11 years on the average.

Somewhere within the interior of the sun, the conditions of the equilibrium are upset. Bright spots called faculas appear over the surface of the sun. When these expand, they look comparatively dark and are called sunspots.

The charged particles emitted from the sun, when interact with the ionosphere, disturb the short wave communication system.

The electrical structure of the ionosphere is not uniform. It consists of three layers of varying ion density. From bottom to top, these are D, E & F layers respectively.

Fast moving charged particles from the sun disturb the lowest D-lawer and consequently disturb the short wave radio communication.

Pakistan Meteorological Department has a network of two magnetic observatories at Quetta and Gilgit where round the clock recording is done. Besides their other role in mineral prospecting, these observatories can play an important role in giving forecasts for such magnetic storms. The observatories work under the Director, Geophysical Centre, Quetta.

(k) Drought

Drought is the dryness which occurs due to lack of rainfall. The definition of Drought given in the International cloud Atlas, Vol-I, W.M.O, 1956 is as under:

- An 'absolute drought' is a period of at least 15 consecutive days to none of which was credited 0.2 mm or 0.01 inches, or more of rainfall.
- A 'partial drought' is a period of at least 29 consecutive days, the mean daily rainfall of which does not exceed 0.2 mm or 0.01 inches.
- A 'dry spell' is a period of at least 15 consecutive days to none of which was credited 1.0 mm, 0.04 inches or more of rainfall.

At present no forecast for droughts are being issued, but these are indirectly covered in the seasonal rainfall forecast issued by the Pakistan Meteorological Department.

Of all the natural disasters, droughts have the greatest potential impact and can affect the largest number of people. In contrast to Earthquakes and Cyclone, Droughts affect large geographical areas, often covering whole countries or parts of continents. These may last for months and in some cases several years.

(l) Aviation Hazards

Aviation is the main beneficiary of the services rendered by the Pakistan Meteorological Department. Full-fledged forecasting offices exist at all the main airports which work round the clock and provide terminal and route forecasts to the flights. Aviation hazards like poor visibility, turbulence, thunderstorms, presence of jet streams and icing level etc are particularly taken care of in the forecasts.

RVR (Runway Visible Range) are installed at the airports for recording visibility.

13

Manageable Procedures to Encounter the Natural Disasters

Abdul Qader Melhem
Professor of Structural Engineering, Associate Dean, Faculty of Civil Engineering, University of Aleppo, Syria

1. Introduction

The natural phenomena, which we are living with, are numerous such as floods, volcanoes, hurricanes, and earthquakes. Although thousands of earthquakes, floods, cyclones occur each year, and although they are widely distributed over the world's surface, comparatively few of these cause significant damage to property or loss of life. Those that are of interest to the structural engineer are those that can cause human loses in addition to structural damage; these are called strong motion (or movement) natural disasters (1). Facing techniques to those natural disasters have been changed tremendously during the last two decades. Such changes have been prompted by high-speed computer technology.

2. Proposed Model for Flood Control

Since there have been occasional floods that have caused damage to human and properties, Artificial Guides (Barriers) will be presented to regulate the water course. Figure 13.1 shows how the flood widens the watercourse and threatens the bridge piers before using the Artificial Guides. Figure 13.2 shows how the Artificial Guides control the floodwater.

The economic analysis is to be based on an estimated n = 50-year project life assuming zero terminal salvage value and using average rate of interest i (usually 6 per cent). The analysis is based on Benefit/Cost ratio for the following two cases: No Flood Control (NFC) and Guides for Water Course (GWC). Let:

A_{NFC} = Annual cost due to flood damage

A_{GWC} = Reduction in annual cost of the flood damage due to GWC

P_{GWC} = First cost of building GWC at zero date

$A_{O\&M}$ = Annual operation maintenance of GWC

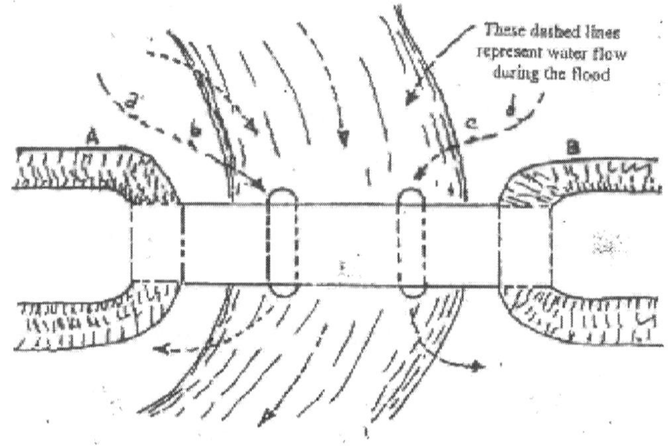

Figure 13.1: Flood Widens the Watercourse and Threatens the Bridge Piers Before Artificial Guides

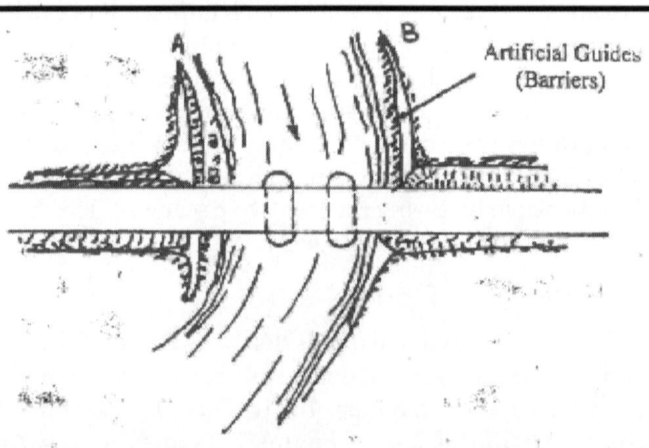

Figure 13.2: Artificial Guides which Control the Flood Water

$$\frac{Benifit}{Cost} \qquad \frac{A_{NFC} \quad A_{GWC}}{P_{GWC} \; A/P, i\%, n \quad A_{O\&M}}$$

Where: $(A/P, i\ per\ cent, n) = \frac{i(I \quad i)^n}{(I \quad i)^n \quad 1}$

If B/C d•I => *Construct the GWC*

If B/C e•I => *Do not construct GWC*

3. General Arrangement to Face the Hazards

(a) Training and Guidance

Goal

- ❖ Prepare the attention of the public on the necessity of "what to do to face the danger of natural disaster"

Procedure

- ❖ Public activities such as: lectures, seminars, workshops, etc.

(b) Regulate the Public Voluntarily and Support the Non Governmental Organizations

Goal

- ❖ Support cooperation between local people and special agencies which are dealing with the danger coming from natural disaster
- ❖ Find sort of integration to execute the requirements, instructions, roles, orders, etc. to counter the danger safely and easily.

Procedure

- ❖ Encourage enrollment of the public voluntarily in the local organizations to avoid the danger
- ❖ Perform regular training locally
- ❖ Prepare suitable environment to activate the non governmental organizations such as: Red Cross

(c) Improve and Develop means and Requirements to Avoid the Danger

Goal

- ❖ Performance of activities needed to avoid the danger fast and safe.

Procedure

Improve and develop the followings:

- Transportation (hovers, vehicles, ships etc.)
- Communications (radio stations, telecommunications etc.)
- Evacuation means (routes, roads, etc.)
- Accidental Equipment (fire extinguishments, water pools, energy generators etc.)
- Equipment and means for observation, inspection and measurement (ambuscades, radar, seismographs etc.)
- Headquarters for accidental management to counter the danger.

Appendix-I shows Procedures for Hazard Management in Syria

4. Investigation Procedures for Structure Subjected to Natural Disaster

This investigation procedure consists of three major stages (2):

(a) Assessment: Evaluation of the present state of the Structure

Gathering Information on the Structure

- Reviewing the design calculations and drawings.
- Studying the material properties (usually by non-destructive methods).

Diagnosis (Intuitive)

- Understanding of the structure behaviour.
- Knowing the trouble source and the trouble mechanism.

Diagnosis (Analytical)

- Structural analysis and design.
- Load tests (if necessary).
- Safety and serviceability analysis.
- Conclusions as regards the present safety level and measures methods needed.

(b) Re-Design: Designing of proposed intervention

Conclusions of the Preceding Stage may Indicate

- Satisfactory safety level (no problem)
- Minor deficiencies, which can be compensated by: protective measures, load limitations, change service type, and reduction of story number.
- Major problems, which necessitate structural interventions.

Repair (Strengthening)

- ❖ Development of re-design alternatives.
- ❖ Consulting with the owner, architect and contractor to evaluate the considered alternative (safety, practicality, economy, applicability, etc.)
- ❖ Finalizing the design on the basis of the structural analysis of the structure modified by the prescribed interventions.

(c) Construction: Application of the Designed Intervention

- ❖ Existing of an expert and responsible inspection: The repair (or strengthening) operations are far more complicated and troublesome than ordinary construction works.
- ❖ Existing of reliable consulting agency: The unexpected problems may arise any minute, and a single step in the wrong direction may lead to very undesirable consequences.

5. Methods of Repair (Strengthening)

It is useless to make a complete list of all the methods of structural repair (strengthening), since each case requires a unique solution and since there can be no limitations on the methods to be employed. Any method can be used if it is shown to be effective to produce the desired result, reliable and desirable from safety and serviceability points of view, applicable and economical.

The commonly used methods of structural repair (strengthening) are presented below in order to give a general idea:

- ❖ Repair (Strengthening) of individual members (locally and totally).
- ❖ Replacement of individual (damaged or inadequate) members.
- ❖ Use an additional member to share the existing or future loads with current weak members.
- ❖ Use of external pre-stressing to improve the over all behavior of the entire structure.
- ❖ Use of in-filled frames to improve seismic behaviour of reinforced concrete framed structure.

6. References

1. Uniform Building Code, International Conference of Building officials, Whittier, California 1994.
2. Tankut, A.T. and Ersoy, U. "Behavior of Repair/strengthened Reinforced concrete structural members" Proceedings, ACI International conference on Evaluation and Rehabilitation of concrete structures and innovations in design, Hong Kong, Dec.1991.

Appendix

Procedures for Hazard Management in Syria

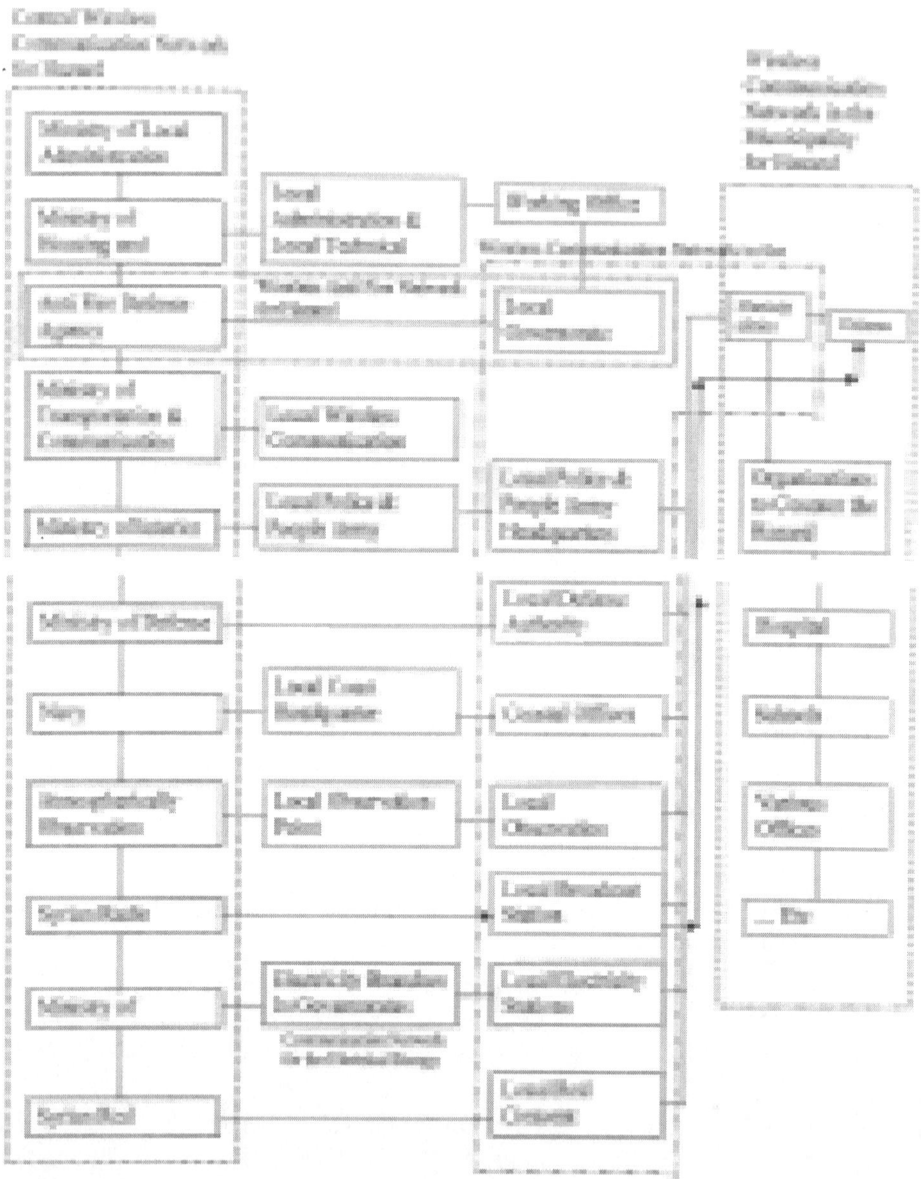

14

Channel Changes Using Satellite Data for Flood Mitigation, Watershed Degradation and Flood Plain Monitoring

Lal Samnarakoon[1], Kiyoshi Honda[1] and Akichika Ishibashi[2]

[1] *ACRoRS/SERD, Asian Institute of Technology, Bangkok, Thailand*

[2] *Nippon Koei Co., Ltd., Research & Development Center, Kukizaki, Japan*

1. Introduction

Nepal is a mountainous country, rectangular in shape extending 80° E to 88° E in NW–SE and 26.3° N to 30.4° N in the NS direction, of 147,181 sq. km in area. Two third of the total area of the country is occupied by hills and mountains. Population stands at 18.8 million (1992), with a growth rate of 2.1 per cent . Ninety per cent of the total population is dependent on agriculture, occupying most of the hill tops and valleys for cultivation. Forest serves as the fuel reserve for peasants, and food storage for animals that supply supplementary food and money, the nominal income. With the increasing population, burden on the forest land increases resulting further land degradation. The changes in the forest cover could have impact on climatic and weather patterns resulting intensive rainfall causing heavy soil losses, devastating floods, and high degree of sedimentation. The accelerating number of natural hazards and the their recurrence period would be a good indicator of the environmental degradation experiences Nepal today. The major natural disasters that occur in Nepal are glacier lakes out burst, earthquakes, floods, droughts, landslides, out of which glacier lakes out burst, floods, droughts and landslides are water induced disasters.

The recent flood disaster occurred in July 1993 is said to be one of the worst in Nepal. The total damage was more than 4000 million Nepal Rupees (ICIMOD, 1993). The occurrence of these extreme events could be very rare, but once occurred the impact on the society is very high. Events that are considered as natural and had little impact on the society are taking heavier tolls today as the flood plains and other marginal lands are cultivated, improved for living environments with little or no concern on the environmental degradation. The amount of land degradation that may have direct or indirect consequences on these devastating effects not be evaluated in monetary values, as the amount of soil loss, and the outcome of it on the society could be enormous. These escalating and devastating flood events cause heavier losses by washing away the topsoil. The related consequences are rapid siltation of reservoirs, abrupt changes in the courses of rivers, spread of sand and gravel across rich agricultural land on the plain. This would lead to another round of deforestation far croplands, fuel, and fodder, moreover increasing the burden on forest reserves. This further escalates the soil loss and other natural hazards. Ives, 1987 says that in the worst case the top soil which is the very basis for existence of life will virtually flow down to Bay of Bengal by the year 2000.

2. Objectives

Lack of knowledge of natural events, their occurrence and recurrence time could hinder proper disaster prevention planning and mitigation. This is specifically true where the distribution of information, and infrastructure is yet to develop. It was thought that satellite remote sensing data could offset the information gap, as they can provide timely and repetitive data of particular phenomena without physically visiting the area of interest.

In this study it was decided to investigate the applicability of satellite data for river management, land degradation assessment and monitor these phenomena. The objectives of the study can be enumerated as below:

- Estimate the river sedimentation and channel planform change using satellite data,
- Estimate the change of forest cover that could influence surface erosion using remote sensing technology,
- Establish a GIS database for watershed and flood plain mitigation works.

3. Study area and Data

(a) Outline of the Study Area

Ratu watershed, which is situated in the Siwalik area, was selected for the present study. Ratu river originates from a Churiya hills in central Nepal at an altitude of 700 meters and drains into Terai region, few kilometers north of Janakpur. The watershed lies west of Kamala river and south of Sun Koshi. Ratu river crosses the East-West highway (EWH) around 86E and 27N. River runs dry during the winter and transport sediments during the rainy season with the high water flow. The sediment unloading capacity said to be very high during a heavy rainfall or continuous rainfall during the monsoon. The riverbed gradient is very gentle, and the average bed slob from the EWH to its origin is only about 1 per cent . This indicates that the sediment transporting capacity may not be attained without considerable amount of precipitation.

Geology of Ratu watershed consists of Siwalik group, middle Miocene~Pleistocene, tertiary. Upper Siwalik formation, Middle Siwalik formation and Lower Siwalik formation are distributed in the northern part of the watershed from the EWH. Geological structure of this Siwalik group shows that the strike is Northwest-Southeast and the dip is changeable. In addition to these, it is pointed that this, area is moved by Neo-tectonics movements, Iwata (1988), and Matsuda (1983) showed that the Siwalik area is Neo-tectonic on comparison of many terraces.

The topography is predominantly steep except in the lower part of the watershed where some gentle sloping hills can be found. About 70 per cent of the watershed area is covered by forest with varying cover densities. *Shorea Robnsta,* locally called *Sal* is the major species found in the area. Remaining land could be grouped into croplands and barren land according to their land use practices. It is said that the depth of the soil layer is less than 20cm in the Churiya Hills, probably same in this watershed. This soil layer is very fragile and subjected to extreme erosion, making the regeneration potential is poor.

(b) Data Acquisition

It was decided to obtain satellite remote sensing data over a long time span to estimate the changes, specifically to observe the forest cover and its change that could be used as a key to land degradation. Also, field investigation was planed to identify the physical nature of the soil erosion, its transport and sedimentation to evaluate the volume of sediment production that could be used to compare satellite data evaluated soil yield. A major flood event was considered to estimate the volume of sedimentation by field observations, and to use in the model evaluation. The most recent flood event, 1993 July was selected for this as it could give the opportunity to collect the information on the extent and nature of the flood by visiting the field where no other means of information are available. Referring to available satellite sources, data shown in the Table 14.1 was selected for the study. In selecting data, special attention was given to choose data that are acquired in the same season of the year to minimize irradiance variations on the surface due to positional differences of the sun.

Referring to the availability of satellite data, and considering major flood events in the past, aerial photographs acquired in 1979 and 1992 were obtained for the study. The scale of the photographs are 1:40,000, and taken in the wet season limiting the comparison with satellite data due to seasonal variations. Therefore, it was decided to photograph the Ratu watershed using a helicopter. A normal camera that uses visible light with 50mm focal length was used to obtain vertical photographs. Further, some of the sub streams were surveyed to recognize the sediment formation, distribution and clues to differentiate the age of the deposits to establish the 1993 soil production process, and the amount of river aggradations and degradation.

Table 14.1: Information on the Satellite Data Obtained for the Study

Sensor	*Date*	*Sun Angle*	*Sun Azimuth*	*Processing Level*
MSS	1973.03.14	Not known	Not known	System
MSS	1977.03.20	Not known	Not known	System
TM	1993.03.16	47°	127°	System
TM	1995.03.22	46°	122°	System
LISS-	1995.03.15	47°	127°	System

(c) A GIS Database Creation for the Study

It was decided to handle all the information pertaining to the watershed digitally for analysis. The conventional maps, topographical and vegetation maps were digitized in establishing a Geographical Database (GIS) in the LTM map projection. The satellite data obtained from the receiving centers do not represent a common geographic projection restricting comparison without rectification. The procured satellite data were brought in to a common map projection by constructing functions which relate satellite data projections with map projection. First order transformation functions were established for all the datasets, and nearest neighbour re-sampling was used for re-mapping the satellite data into the UTM projection, and integrated into the same GIS database. Further, the aerial photographs and helicopter photographs were scanned, rectified and registered into UTM projection in the process of integrating them into the GIS database. Thus the completed GIS database for the present study included multi-sensor temporal satellite data, aerial photographs, elevation and land cover information. TM data sets were rectified with less than 20m rms. error, for MSS the rms. was 25. In the present study creation of the GIS database was carried out in the arc/info environment, and satellite data handling, classification and integration with the GIS data was accomplished by the ERMapper software package. The process of the GIS database creation and general outline of the analysis procedure is shown in Figure 14.1.

4. Results and Discussion

(a) Channel form Changes in the Watershed

With reference to the aerial photos and other conventional photographs, reference areas were established and corresponding digital counts were extracted for dominated cover classes, forest, crop lands and river sediments covering most of the study area. Statistical parameters of representative sample were calculated and analyzed for differentiation of these Comparatively high reflectance was observed for riverbed, followed by crop lands and forest. The riverbed materials in the upper stream showed less spectral response than the materials in the floodplain riverbed. These differences could be due to particle size or the composition of the materials, presence of moisture or the trace of the river flow. It could be said that any of the TM spectral bands, specially, band 1, band 3, band 5 and band 7 are very much suitable for classification of river bed degradation and aggradations or planform changes, and there is no necessity to establish any other derived index. For MSS, the best band would be band

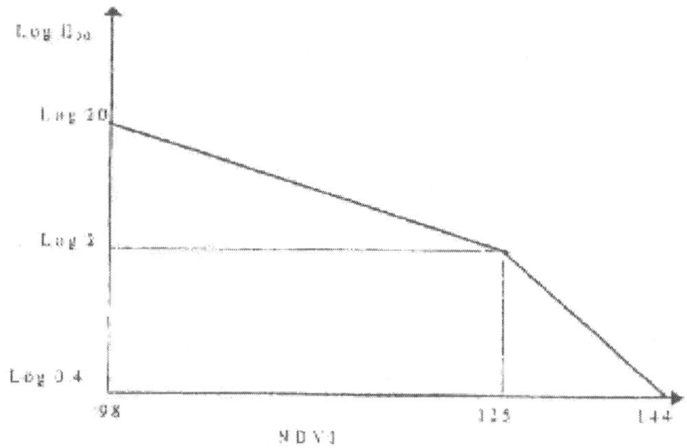

Figure 14.1: Relationship of NDVI and the Log E_{30}

4, band 5 or band 6. Band 7 may not be very much suitable due to its narrow dynamic range.

Using the statistical parameters of the samples selected over interested cover classes, satellite datasets were classified into sediment deposited and non-deposited areas. The riverbed extents obtained from these classifications are shown in Table 14.2.

Table 14.2: Extent of the Riverbed of the Ratu River in the Upper Watershed

73 MSS	93 TM	95 TM
11.67 Sq. km.	12.76 Sq. km.	12.66 Sq. km.

There was no appreciable change in the extents of the riverbed area of the upper stream except for some minute differences. Given the geometric resolution of the sensors, 79m, 30m, and 34m for Landsat MSS, TM and LISS-II, it is questionable to interpret these changes as actual riverbed expansions. These marginal differences might have occurred because of the limitations of the spatial resolution of the sensors, and the orientation of the sensor field of view at the time of satellite pass. In concluding, it could be said that there was no appreciable change in the riverbed in the upper watershed during the 1973 to 95 time span.

(b) Channel Changes and Sedimentation in the Floodplain

As for the upper reach of the river, the sediment deposition and its change was estimated for the floodplain using spectral patterns described earlier. The extents of the sediment deposition in the floodplain for the four dates datasets and for the LISS dataset is shown in Table 14.3.

Table 14.3: Floodplain Deposition of Sediment and its Change

73-MSS	77-MSS	93 -TM	95-TM	95- LISS

9.17 Sq. km.	11.58 Sq. km.	9.12 Sq. km.	9.61 Sq. km.	10.07 Sq. km.

These extents exclude the old riverbed deposits that were differentiable by respective sensors of the four dates corresponding to each data. The estimated extents for the four dates show that sediment deposited area is increasing gradually, with a drastic increase in the time span between 1973 to 1977. This increase could be a consequence of the comparatively high precipitation prevailed in the period of 1974 to 1975, where the total annual precipitation was over 6000 mm, (Karmacharya, 1995). The classification accuracy of LISS shows that LISS sensor data can also be used in lieu of Landsat TM data in sediment deposition estimations.

Four satellite images of different dates were integrated and the changes that have occurred during the three time spans were compared. Three types of changes, *newly deposited, unchanged* or *re-deposited,* and *unaffected* were observed in these multi-temporal classified datasets. A considerable increase during the period 73 to 79 was clearly visible in the most westward channel. This change could be due to continuous aggradations of the riverbed just below the EWH in the eastward channel resulting change of flow to west. Decrease in the sediment transportation in the lower portion of the most eastern channel would further support this assumption. Further, it was observed that the most westward channel, which was very active before 1977 had become inactive in sediment transportation. The width of the Ratu river just below the EWH, and eastern portion of the river above it has been decreased. This is as a result of a dike constructed in the eastern bank of the river, just above the bridge after 1977. Aggradations around the area just below the bridge in the west of the floodplain could have occurred due to different factors such as, an increase in material to be carried by the river, a loss of discharge or velocity flow, or a rise in base level. This caused the splitting the channel into two very distinctive river courses. Extension of the floodplain just below the EWH into few kilometers could support these reason, and high sediment activities just below the EWH. Similar explanation could be made to the division of the most eastern part of the river. Comparing the observations of these two time spans, it could be said that the planform deviation of the river was much active during the 1973 to 1979 period than the next 16 years.

These findings shows the potential of satellite data in identifying, and monitoring sedimentation process of a watershed, and tracing river channel planform changes.

(c) Land Degradation Assessment by Vegetation index

In estimating the change of forest cover in its extent and the density, it was decided to use a vegetation index, as a normalized vegetation index could partly compensate for differences in the external factors at the day of satellite pass. Most of the vegetation indices are based on empirical evidences, and nearly all of commonly used vegetation indices are concerned only with red and near-infrared regions of the electromagnetic spectrum. NDVI based on the equation 1 was used with multi-sensor digital data that were adjusted for bandwidth differences and compensated for atmospheric variations at the time of satellite passes.

$$NDVI \quad \frac{Infrared \quad red}{Infrared \quad red} \quad 1 \quad 100 \qquad (1)$$

Aerial photographs of 1992 were taken as ground truth information to classify 1992 Landsat TM data. Also, these photographic information were further compared with other dates of satellite data as the observation conditions were re-established to 1992 satellite pass. Aerial photographs covering the study area were classified, and digitally compared with NDVI images of fours dates for evaluation of forest land changes in the watershed. The observed size of the bareland within the forestland is relatively smaller than the spatial resolution of the sensors, therefore, photographs were overlaid and compared to investigate the possibility of identifying them using satellite data. Degraded mountain ridges, and soil deposited tributaries are very prominent in 1992 aerial photographs and helicopter photographs. These photographs were classified assigning a value zero for forest covered pixels, and 100 for non-forested pixels. Subsequently, original pixels were re-sampled into 100 x 100 meter to represent the average of original pixels fell in each new pixel. Thus the digital value of each newly created pixel represented the bareland or forest area percentage within the pixel concerned. Accordingly, the Landsat TM NDVI image of 1993 was re-sampled into same pixel size generating average NDVI values for each of the 100 meter pixels. The relationship of NDVI and the bareland ratio was compared to identify the potential of NDVI in recognizing the change of forest density. Categorized bareland percentages into 10 per cent intervals and the corresponding averages of NDVI values are shown in Table 14.4.

Table 14.4: Distribution of Photographs Derived Bareland Percentage and 1993 NDVI Values

Bareland %	0	1-10	10-20	20-30	30-40	40-50	50-60	60-70	70-80	80-90	90-99	100
NDVI 1993	125.37	124.44	122.77	120.91	120.04	118.9	114.65	113.1	107.07	104.58	100.93	98.71

This table shows that the NDVI decreases with the increase of bareland percentage. The highest NDVI for this area was 125, and lowest was 99 for complete forest and 100 per cent bare, respectively. This inverse relationship shows that NDVI can be used to represent the land degradation in the Ratu watershed.

Similarly, NDVI values of 1973, 1977, 1995 and 95-LISS data were compared with the bareland percentages. Distribution of the NDVI values and the aerial photographs established 1992 bareland percentages are shown in Figure 14.2. The 1979-MSS and 1995-LISS data are shown in break lines as they show some incompatibility with the other three dates data. 1977 MSS data shows higher NDVI values than others, and the deviation is irregular. It was found that there was a thin cloud cover in this dataset, and this might have formed higher level of scattering that was not presented in the other datasets. The LISS dataset also showed different trend of NDVI distribution. The reason for this is not clear, and requires study of internal calibration procedures of Landsat and IRS sensors. These two dates data, 1977 MSS and 1995 LISS were excluded in the proceeding analysis for land degradation.

Further, the helicopter photographs incorporated in the GIS database were compared with NDVI image of 1993 to investigate the degree of accuracy in identifying the denuded ridges and silted tributaries in the watershed. It was observed that most of the degraded ridges, and relatively larger sub-streams can clearly be identified with NDVI. Some of the tributaries were not visible on the NDVI image, especially, near the densely forested areas. This could be due to the spatial resolution limitation of the sensor and mixed land cover that could present in a single pixel of TM data. As a whole, the comparison of aerial photographs and helicopter photographs with satellite data showed that the remotely sensed data can satisfactorily be used in identifying degraded forest, denuded ridges and silted tributaries and main streams. Also, it was found that the continuous nature of NDVI facilitate the interpretation of forest density more realistically than classifying the forest cover into discrete density classes.

(d) Temporal Change of Average Annual Soil Yield

In the present watershed no field observation are carried out for surface runoff or soil loss for given land cover class. Current soil erosion models, Universal Soil Loss Equation and, most of the other models that are commonly used are developed by various authors on extensive field observations. Further, most of these equation requisite long term rainfall records, and measured denudation rates under different land use conditions.

Therefore, it was not possible to use a model that required parameters observed in the field for soil loss estimation in this watershed. Apart from these measurable external factors, the other major factor that highly contributes to the rate of soil erosion in this watershed is the surface topography. Therefore, a model that considered the surface slope as the main driving factor of intensive erosion in association with the surface coverage was considered. Honda, 1993 proposed a method for soil erosion in mountainous region by incorporating surface gradient. He has demonstrated the accuracy of the model applying in a well-monitored watershed in Japan. The annul average denudation E can be estimated as;

$$E \quad E_{30} \; \frac{S}{S_{30}}^{\;0.9} \qquad (2)$$

where,

E_{30}–rate of denudation at a slope of 30°

S–gradient of the pixel under consideration

S_{30}–tan (30°)

The denudation factor has to be identified for every spatial location of the watershed or, has to be measured for well-distributed points to apply the model as it is. This is not realistic even in a well-monitored watershed, hence an indirect estimation of the denudation factor using satellite measured vegetation index is suggested. As

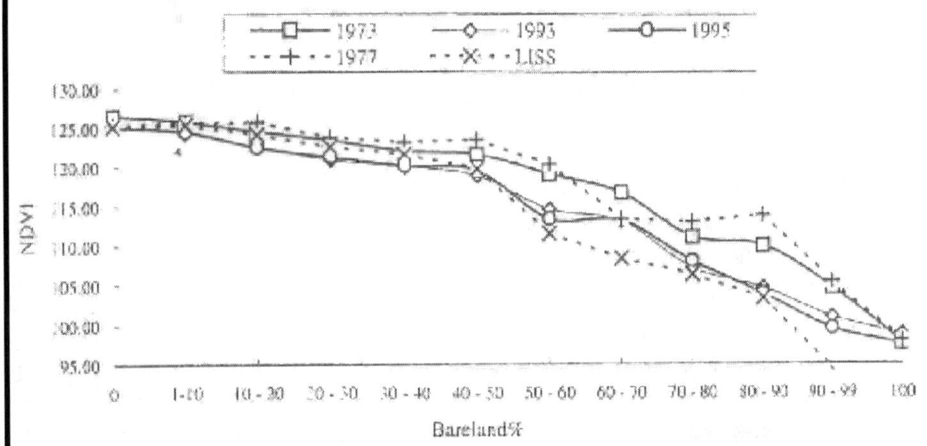

Figure 14.2: Distribution of Bareland Percentages and NDVI Values

no field measurements are carried out, denudation of dominant land cover types are extracted from documented materials, and a relationship was established with the respective NDVI values. Subsequently, denudation rate for a given location was estimated based on the relationship of denudation with NDVI. The base values that are required for establishment of the relationship were acquired from published materials. Estimation of soil yield in the Ratu watershed was carried out based on the equation 2. Table 14.5 shows denudation rate in the Himalayan region and in a regulated watershed in Japan.

Table 14.5: Land Denudation for Some Areas in Nepal and Japan

Description of the Site	*Rate tons/km/year*	*Reference*
Siwalik: East Nepal, 5-aspect, sandstone Foothills, landuse from forest to grazing lands	780-3.680 (0.4-1.8 mm/year)	Chatra, 1976
Siwalik: Far West Nepal, S-aspect, sandstone Foothills	2,000 (l mm/year)	Laban, 1978
Degraded Forest	4,000 (2 mm/year)	Laban, 1978
Degraded forest, gullied land	20,000 (10 mm/year)	Sahya
Severely degraded, heavily grazed	800 (0.4 mm/year)	Laban, 1978
Middle Mountains: Katmandu valley, steep slopes		
Japan: Asio region in Tochigi Prefecture for 30° slope		Honda, 1993
Bare lands	20 mm/year	
Grasslands	1mm/year	Honda, 1993
Forest	0.1 mm/year	Honda, 1993

In order to evaluate the soil yield, the denudation rate of each pixel has to be estimated using reference information given in Table 14.5, or otherwise. The values obtained by comparing aerial photographs in the Table 14.2 represent the average NDVI for forest density percentages in the Ratu watershed. The highest value of NDVI, 125 was for 100 per cent forest cover in this area, and the lowest value represented bareland. In establishing denudation rate in the Ratu watershed, three critical soil loss rates and corresponding NDVI values were recognized.

Publish documents identify the Siwalik area as severely degraded, hence the least degraded areas in the Siwalik area was assigned a denudation rate of 0.4mm/year (800 tons/km^2/year), which is similar to Middle Mountains. The average NDVI of the Middle Mountain forest coverage was 144, and this value was used in conjunction with this denudation rate of this area. Accordingly, the 100 per cent forest coverage within the watershed, which is an average for 400x100 meter pixel unit, was assigned a denudation rate of 2.0 mm/year (4000 tons/km^2/year), for which the average NDVI was 125. Finally; bareland having an average NDVI of 98 was assigned 20 ma/year which was used for a Japanese watershed. All of these denudation rates are assumed to be for land surfaces with 30° slope angle. In order to estimate the soil yield for the whole watershed, a relationship was considered for denudation and NDVI, (Honda, 1994). He has demonstrated that NDVI is related to common logarithm of the denudation rate. The interpretation of denudation with respect to NDVI for each pixel was carried out as shown in Figure 14.1.

This relationship gives the rate of denudation for any pixel in the watershed with respect to 1993 land cover condition. The other factor that is required for soil yield estimation is the slope gradient, and it was calculated from the digital elevation data incorporated in the GIS database. Considering no appreciable change of the topography during the 22-year period from 1973 to 1995, proposed equation for soil erodibility was used for estimation of the denudation rate and the volume of the soil production based on NDVI derived forest cover densities: The estimated values are tabulated in Table 14.6.

Table 14.6: Soil Yield and Denudation Estimated for the Ratu Watershed

Years	*1973*	*1993*	*1995*
Soil Yield m^3	271,110	321,156	293,096
Rate of denudation	3.29	3.89	3.55

Reliable data for comparison with satellite data estimation was not available. The estimated denudation rates are very much comparable with published materials presented earlier justifying the satisfactory application of present model in annual average soil yield estimation in Ratu watershed.

5. Conclusion

In concluding it can be said that satellite data can satisfactorily be used in land degradation estimations, and changes of planform of rivers. Historical satellite data are a valuable tool in evaluating the efficiency of flood protection measures carried out in the past. These evaluations would be an advantage in future flood management studies. The model proposed to estimate the average annual soil yield produced land denudation rate that is very much similar to the values published by intensive field works. This validates the potential of this model in estimating soil yield in a watershed where the accurate field measurements are scarce to find. Modification of the model for a storm event was suggested incorporating stream densities in the watershed. It is important to say that the present model was used in a watershed in the Siwalik area, and more case studies are required to identify it as a general model.

6. Acknowledgement

Financial aid for this project was provided by the Japan International Cooperation Agency. Authors are thankful to the Japanese Erosion Control Engineering Society for giving the opportunity to carryout this research project. The support of the DPTC also acknowledged.

7. References

1. Honada, K., S. Murai and R. Shibasaki (1993): *Prediction of vegetation restoration by erosion control works in Asio copper mine Japan,* 13th IGRSS.
2. ICIMOD (1993): *The Role of Extreme Weather Events, Mass movements, and Land Use Changes in Increasing Natural Hazards.*

15

Cyclone Disasters due to Heavy Rainfall

Suphat Vongvisessomjai
Professor and Director, Regional Environmental Management Centre, Water Engineering and Management Programme, School of Civil Engineering, Asian Institute of Technolog, Thailand

1. Introduction

The 1988 catastrophic flood in southern Thailand is one of the severest causing 356 dead, more than 1.3 million people affected and about 6 billion Baht damage. The damages were due to swift currents and land slides as well as inundation of the business center at Hat Yai.

2. Cyclone

In summer, air over sea surface near equator which is overheated will become lighter and rise, creating a low pressure center defined as cyclone. The outer cooler air blows towards the center in counterclockwise direction over the northern hemisphere due to coriolis effect, and clockwise in the southern hemisphere. This results in a system of cloud which precipitates when it passes over a mountainous area and thus produces flood.

There are five areas of origin for cyclones, namely, the South China Sea, the Andaman Sea, the Caribbean Sea, along coasts of Australia and Africa. Tracks of cyclone over the South China Sea and the Andaman Sea affecting Thailand are shown generally in Figure 15.1 and more specifically in Figure 15.2. It can be seen that the tracks shift from higher to lower latitudes as time elapses from the middle to the end of the year.

Characteristics of the three cyclones affecting Thailand are shown in Figure 15.3 for their variations of pressure and wind speed versus radial distance *r*. These cyclones can be seen clearly from weather satellite in form of huge clouds. These clouds cause heavy rainfalls and floods while strong winds cause destruction of houses, *i.e.* cyclone Harriet attacking Laem Talumpuk of Nakorn Si Thammarat province in October 1962 and cyclone Ruth causing damages to Ko Samui, Surat Thani, Chumphon and Prachuap Khiri Khan in November 1970.

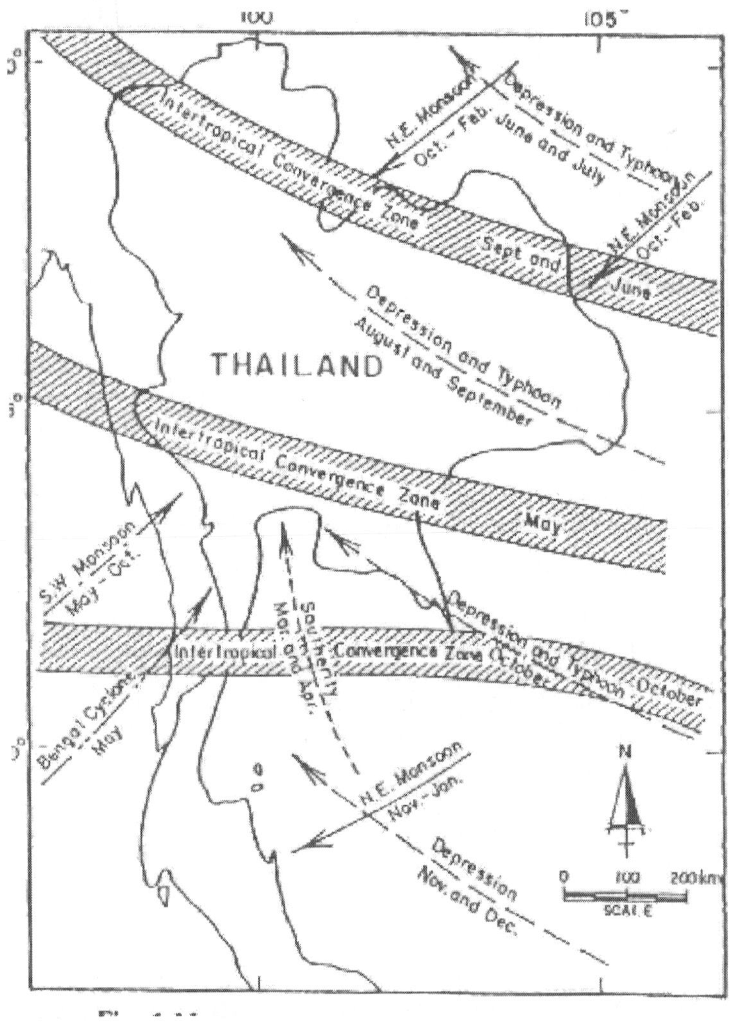

Figure 15.1: Monsoon and Storm Tracks in Thailand

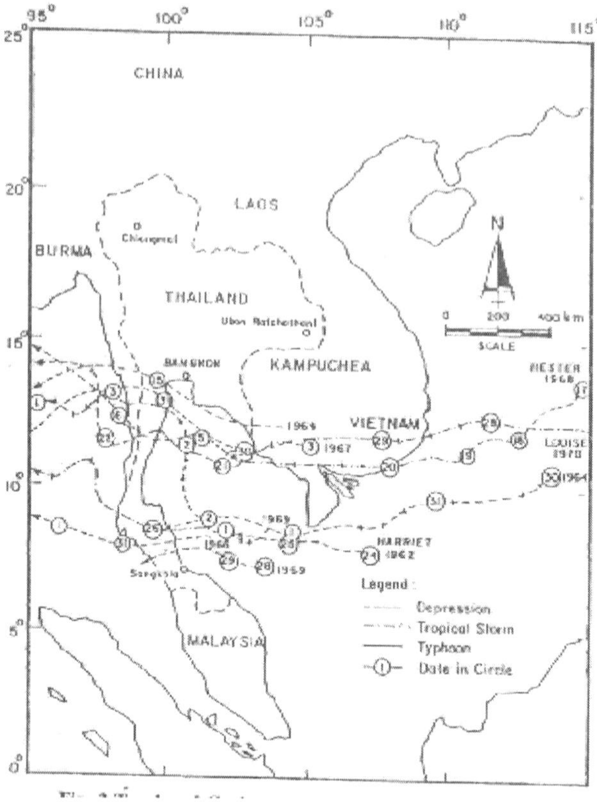

Figure 15.2: Tracks of Cyclones over the Gulf of Thailand in October 1961 to 1970

A tropical cyclone is characterized by four parameters, namely, its forward speed V_{F}, radius of the eye *R*, the minimum pressure at its center *Po* and the maximum wind speed at the radius of the eye U_{max}.

The pressure distribution of a cyclone *P* increases as a function of the radial distance *r* from its center from P_o to the atmospheric pressure P_n in the following manner.

$$P – Po = (P_n – Po) \exp(-R / r) \text{ for } 0 < r < “$$

$$\text{and Ug} \quad 0.868 \;\; 73 \;\; P_n \quad P_0 \;\; ½ \quad R \; 0.575 f$$

The maximum wind speed at the radius of the eye U_{max} in knots can be determined

$$U_{max} = 0.865 U g + 05 V_F$$

in which the unit of the pressure is in inches of mercury, that of the radius of the eye is in nautical miles and the coriolis parameter *f*= 2WsinÆ, where Æ is the latitude and the angular velocity of the earth W = *2À/24* radian per hour and U_g is the maximum gradient wind speed in knots.

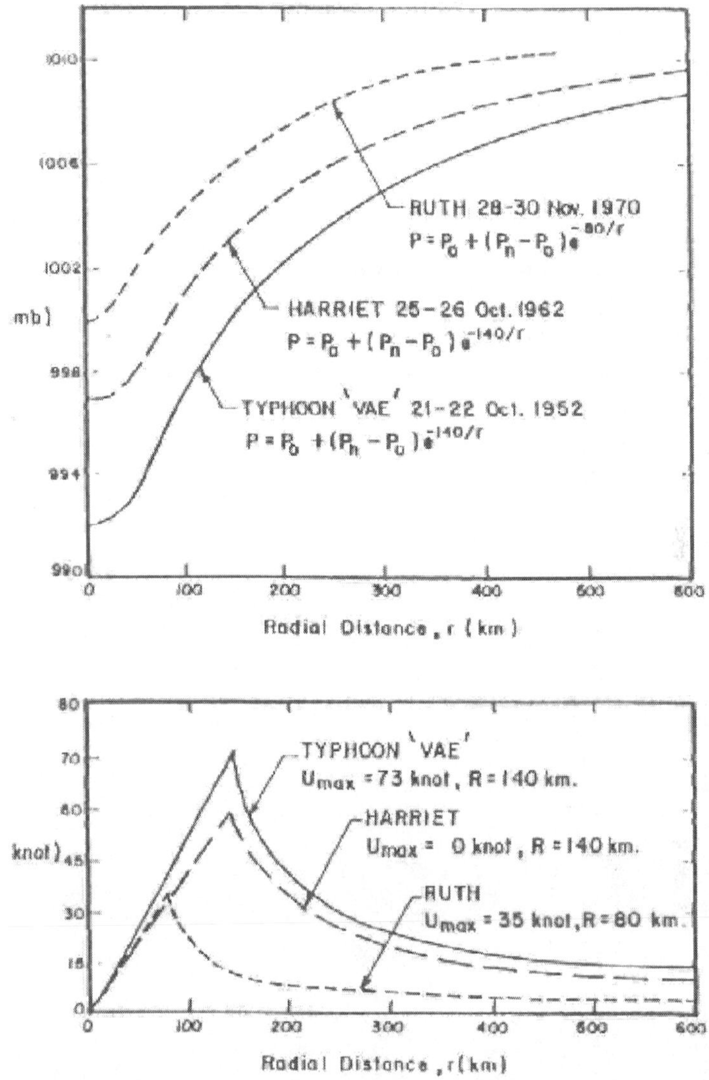

Figure 15.3: Radial Distributions of Pressures and Wind Velocity of VAE, HARRIET and RUTH

Tropical cyclones are designated according to the magnitudes of U_{max} as follows:

Tropical depression	$26<U_{max}<34$ knots
Tropical storm	$35<U_{max}<47$ knots
Severe tropical Storm	$48<U_{max}<64$ knots
Typhoon	$U_{max}>64$ knots

Under an international agreement, when the maximum wind speed U_{max} of a cyclone is greater than 35 knots, a name will be given to the cyclone.

3. Rainfall

Thailand has a tropical climate characterized by two major seasons. The southwest monsoon from mid-May through September during which hot moist equatorial air masses traverse the country bringing moderate to heavy rains all over the country. The northeast monsoon, from November to mid-March brings a reversal of air movement; bringing moisture from the Gulf of Thailand and causing heavy rains to southern Thailand while the rest of the country is dry. The mean annual rainfall in Thailand is shown in Figure 15.4. It can be seen from the Figure that there is more rain in the south which receives rain from both monsoons.

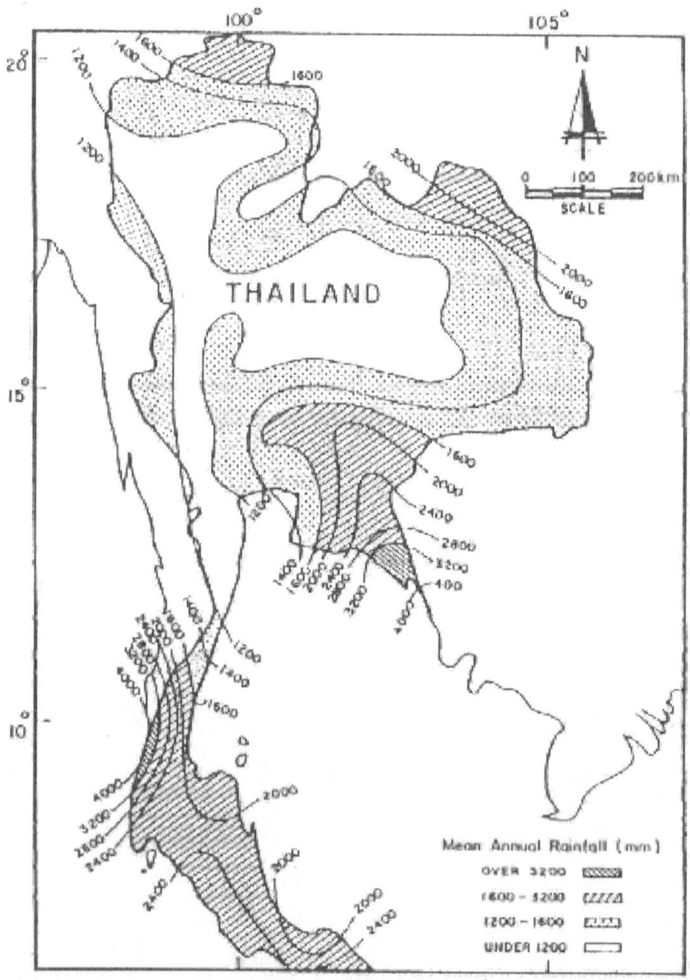

Figure 15.4: Mean Annual Rainfall in Thailand

Meteorological Department used maximum rainfall data in 1,2,3,4 and 5 days from 1951 to 1987 to determine their return periods (recurrence intervals). Figure 15.5a and 15.5b are for Surat Thani and Nakorn Si Thammarat respectively. Note that those of Chumphon and Prachuap Khiri Khan are quite close to Figure 15.5a while

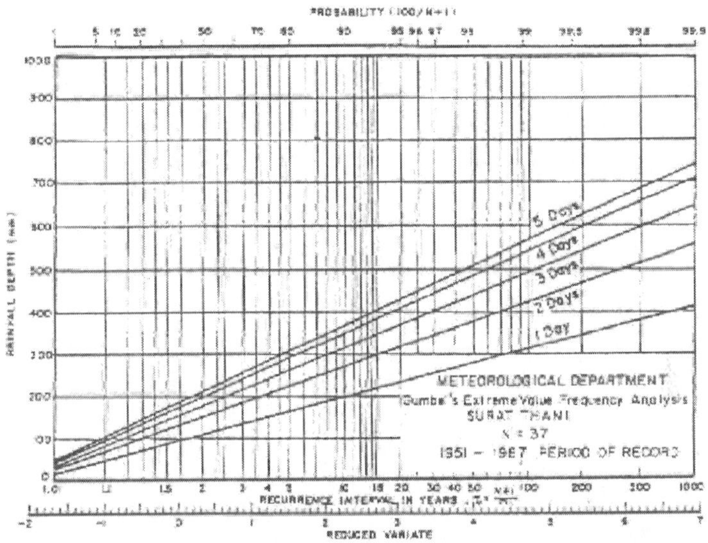

Figure 15.5(a): Recurrence Interval (Return Period) of Rainfall at Surat Thani (Meteorological Department, 1989)

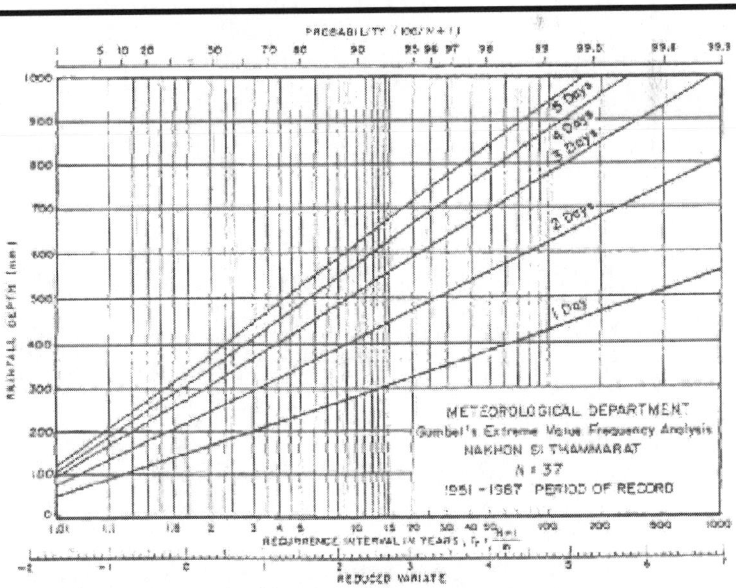

Figure 15.5(b): Recurrence Interval (Return Period) of Rainfall at Nakhon Si Thammarat (Meteorological Department, 1989)

those of Songkhla, Pattani and Narathiwat are quite close to Figure 15.5b. Yearly values of maximum rainfalls within 1 day of 6 southern provinces are listed in Table 15.1 which shows the date and month of the first three highest values of each station. Note that when rainfall within a day is more than 200 mm it will result in severe flooding with landslide from mountain.

4. Flood

When rainfall reaches ground, it changes to runoff. Rate of runoff depends upon intensity of rainfall and characteristics of catchment, *i.e.* infiltration, size, slope. Figure 15.6 shows provincial boundary of southern Thailand. The 1988 flood caused damages to all these southern provinces, however, the severest ones are Nakorn Si Thammarat, Surat Thani and Songkhla which can be grouped into the following 3 areas: on the west of Khao Luang mountain in the upper catchment of Tapi river at

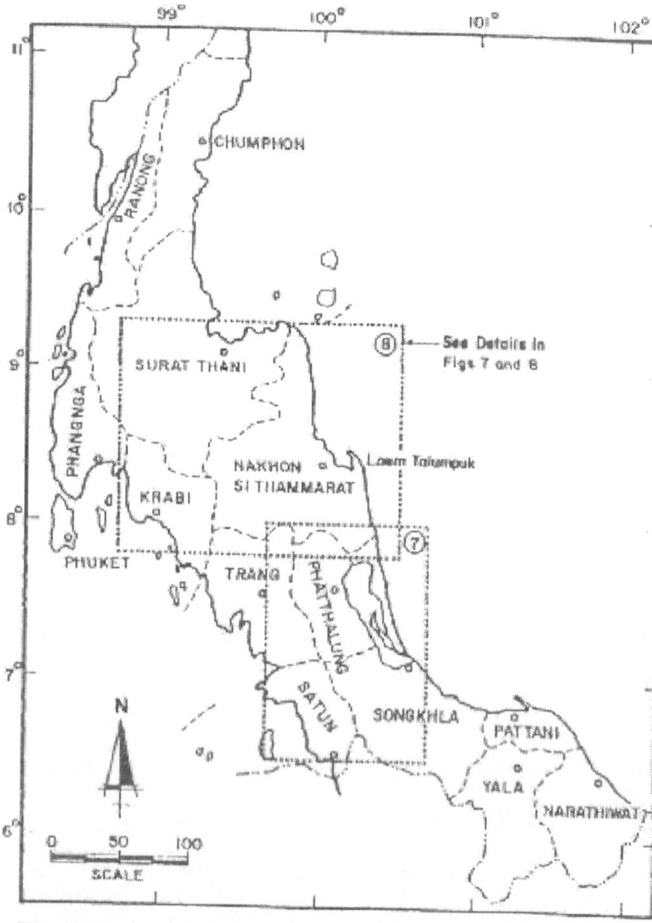

Figure 15.6: Provincial Boundary of the Southern Provinces

Ban Nasan and Ban Kathun Ban Huai Ko shown in Figure 158a; on the east of Khao Luang montain in the small catchment of Khlong Thadi at Ban Khiriwong shown in Figure 15.8b; and at Hat Yai of Khlong U-Thaphao catchment shown in Figure 15.7.

Table 15.1: Maximum Rainfall within One Day of Six Southern Provinces (Meteorological Department, 1989)

Year	*Chumphon*		*Surat*		*Nakorn*		*Songkhla*		*Pattani*		*Narathiwat*	
	mm	*D/M*	*mm*	*D/M*	*mm*	*D/M*	*mm*	*D/M*	*mm*	*D/M*	*mm*	*D/M*
1951	181.4		168.3		238.6		146.0				105.6	
1952	134.9		139.2		225.7		205.9				225.9	
1953	152.4		168.8		242.8		207.2				206.9	
1954	94.5		51.8		127.7		116.3				247.1	
1955	143.6		151.5		132.1		159.2				625.9	01/01
1956	238.8		101.1		145.3		206.6				142.8	
1957	83.3		46.0		171.1		85.5				77.7	
1958	55.6		192.5		206.4		121.8				133.2	
1959	125.8		57.9		133.6		148.2				366.1	
1960	81.2		85.3		87.0		94.5				116.4	
1961	208.8		48.2		179.6		159.7				172.4	
1962	116.3		177.3		122.6		133.7				124.4	
1963	143.8		130.8		271.7		210.4				103.2	
1964	148.7		457.1	12/11	183.7		72.3				111.9	
1965	69.6		51.6		149.0		211.8				236.6	
1966	120.9		152.8		237.7		142.2				291.5	04/12
1967	114.1		216.6	07/01	143.8		131.6				424.6	
1968	62.3		46.7		77.8		132.3				126.4	
1969	84.0		147.1		149.2		242.6				312.1	
1970	264.1	29/11	147.4		174.1		169.9				152.7	
1971	242.1	03/11	133.2		241.5		247.7	25/11	194.8		120.3	
1972	93.1		62.1		72.2		119.5		55.0		67.2	
1973	65.0		75.3		190.6		160.2		106.4		238.4	
1974	73.1		95.0		177.4		228.5		226.3	18/11	144.9	
1975	423.4	08/01	274.4	02/11	433.3	05/01	167.3		191.0		244.8	
1976	75.2		92.4		414.0	23/11	329.4	20/11	206.2		233.2	
1977	138.3		117.1		142.6		116.5		88.6		135.6	
1978	123.1		87.3		69.6		60.0		121.5		120.5	
1979	95.9		92.1		125.6		147.0		101.5		176.5	
1980	153.5		119.2		244.2		82.4		76.4		132.3	
1981	144.5		91.0		190.0		286.0		142.8		244.4	
1982	102.0		66.3		108.7		107.9		73.8		129.4	
1983	104.7		86.2		102.9		153.9		102.7		177.2	
1984	83.9		116.5		352.4	27/11	201.7		105.7		224.7	
1985	83.4		72.7		105.2		77.0		124.2		111.9	
1986	96.1		116.2		205.6		390.6	27/11	266.2	27/11	442.7	27/11
1987	91.7		131.4		157.9		189.0		233.4	03/12	181.8	

(a) Tapi River

The severest flooded areas on the west of Khao Luang mountain in the upper catchment of Tapi river are at Ban Nasan of Khlong Chawang catchment and at Ban Kathun-Ban Huai Ko of Khlong Kathun catchment shown in Figure 15.8a. Rainfall started on November 20, 1988 and on November 22 at 5:45 a.m. water level exceeded the banks of Khlong Chawang which has a catchment area of 214 square kilometers. The water rose rapidly and flooded many roads with flood-depth of 1.5 to 2 meters at 11:30 p.m.; the swift current carried many floating debris, sand, silt and logs into Ban Nasan.

The Royal Irrigation Department (RID) of Thailand had gauging at stations 1, 2, 3 and 4 with the following details.

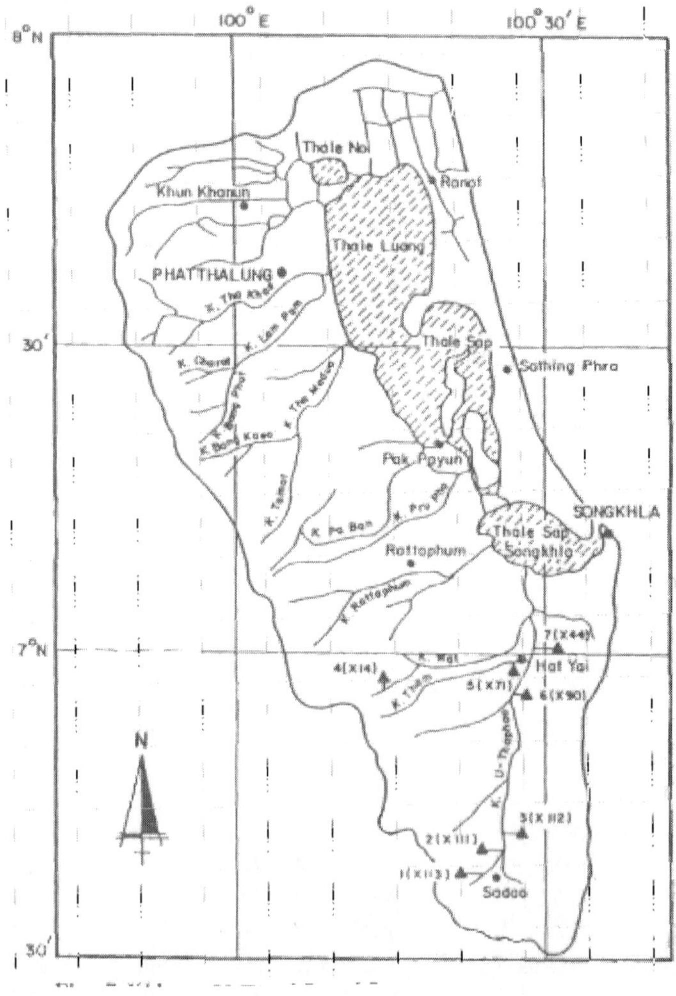

Figure 15.7: Khlong U-Thaphao Basin and Thale Sap Songkhla

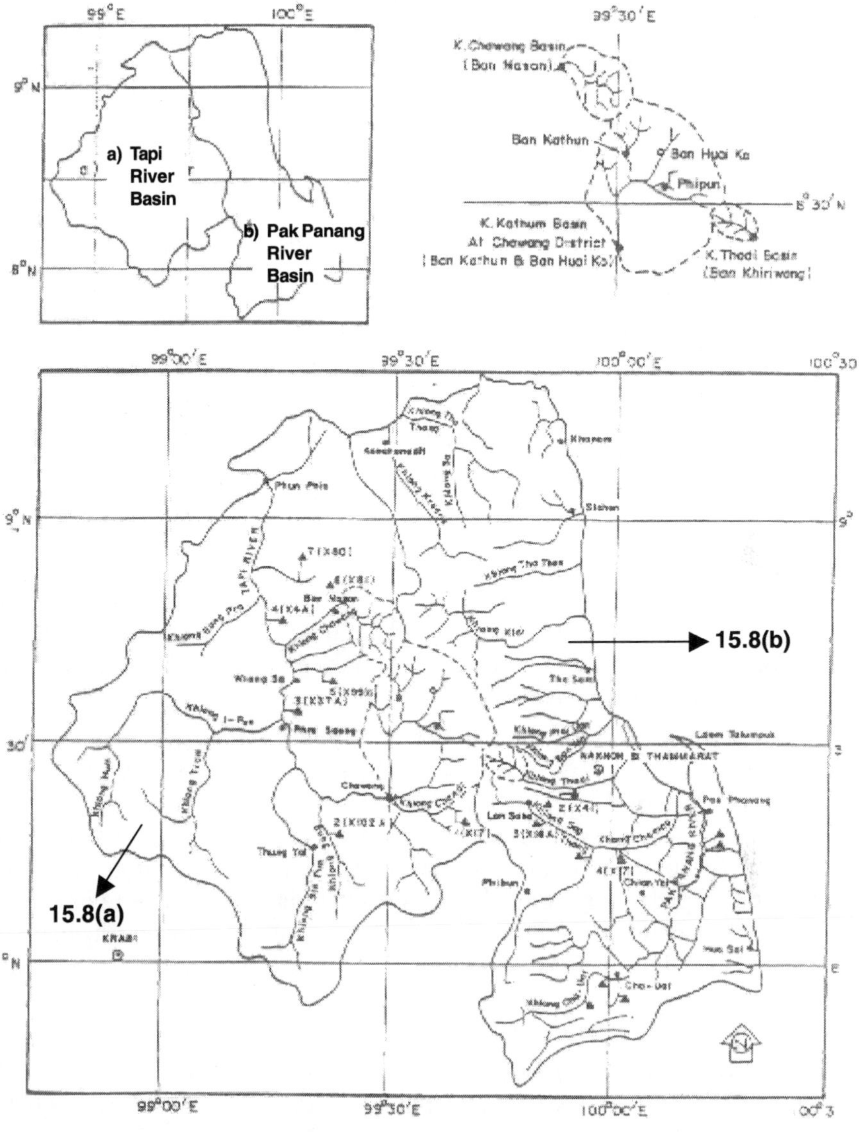

Figure 15.8(a): Tapi River Basin

Figure 15.8(b): Pak Panang River Basin

Station (Figure 8a)	*River orKhlong*	*District*	*Province*	*Code*	*Catchment (km^2)*	*Period*
1	Chandi	Chawang	Nakorn	X17	16	1956-1959
2	Sang	Thung Yai	Nakorn	XI02	179	1977-present
3	Tapi	Wiang Sa	Surat	X37A	5,200	1963-1969
4	Tapi	Nasan	Surat	X4A	6,202	1950-1962

(b) Pak Phanang River

The severest flooded area on the east of Khao Luang mountain in Ban Khiriwong of Khlong Thadi with catchment area of 70 square kilometers is shown in Figure 15.8b. Heavy rainfall started here on November 20, 1988; the heaviest rainfall on November 21 was 447.8 mm. Disaster came in the morning of November 22 with swift current and landslide destroying all infrastructure and communication system in the area.

The details of RID's gauging stations in this area are as follows.

Station (Figure 8b)	River orKhlong	District	Province	Code	Catchment (km^2)	Period
1	Khao Kaeo	Lan Saka	Nakorn	X15	47	1956-1959
2	Sao Thong	Lan Saka	Nakorn	X41	149	1966-1969
3	Sao Thong	Lan Saka	Nakorn	X18A	163	1961-present
4	Chamao	Chain Yai	Nakorn	X17	660	1949-1960

(c) Khlong U- Thaphao

The business center of southern Thailand, Hat Yai, was flooded for two days (November 22 and 23, 1988). The flood-depth was almost 2 meters above the highway due to the flood water from Khlong U-Thaphao in which RID had established the following gauging stations listed below.

Examples of hydrographs of stations XI02, X37A and X4A of Tapi river recorded by RID during the floods in 1981 and 1984 are shown in Figure 15.9a while those in 1986 and 1988 are shown in Figure 15.9b. The amount of daily rainfall which caused the flood is also shown in the figures which revealed a clear picture of chronological flooding, first at the upstream station and later at the downstream station. The rise of hydrograph at the upstream station is higher which is. more dangerous. For Khlong U- Thaphao catchment, they are shown in Figures 15.10a and 15.10b. It can be seen in the figures that the flooding at Sadao occurred for about one day earlier than at Hat Yai, therefore, if there would be good communication, severe damages could have been alleviated through warning of the arrival of the flood.

Due to lack of on-going gauging stations around Khao Luang mountain where severe flooding occurred in 1988, NAM model developed by Nielsen and Hansen (1982) is used to compute flood discharges at Ban Nasan, Ban Kathun and Ban Khiriwong as well as that at Chawang district using rainfalls at Nakorn Si Thammarat as plotted in Figure 15.11 which revealed that there were more rainfalls in the upper south at Ko Samui, Surat Thani and Nakorn Si Thammarat than those in the lower south at Hat Yai, Songkhla, Pattani and Narathiwat. The computed results thus obtained are plotted in Figure 15.12 which showed that the discharges of Khlong Thadi at Ban Khiriwong and Khlong Kathun at Ban Kathun are higher than 300 and 400 m^3/s respectively. Before the flood the widths of these two canals are less than 20 meters; after the flood, they were wider than 200 meters due to the high discharges.

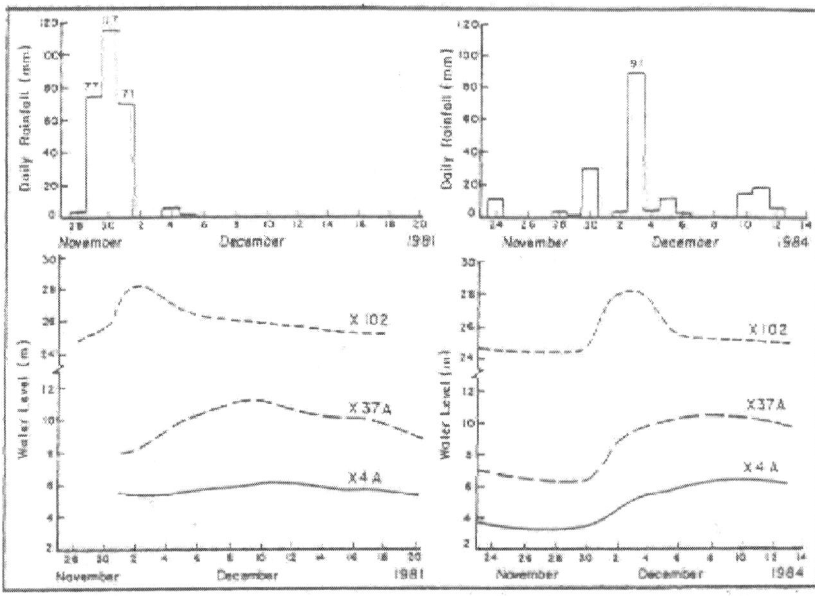

Figure 15.9(a): Hydrographs of Tapi River during Floods in 1981 and 1984

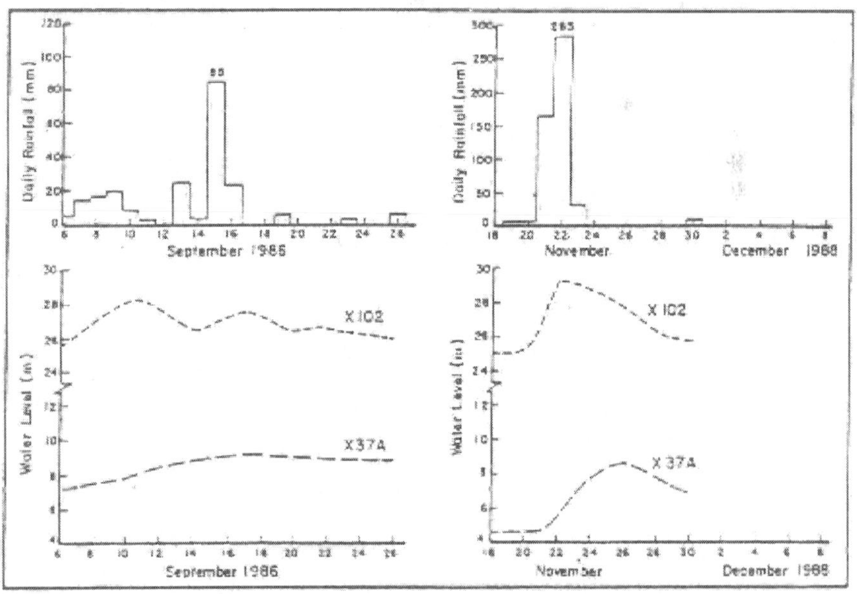

Figure 15.9(b): Hydrographs of Tapi River during Flood in 1986 and 1988

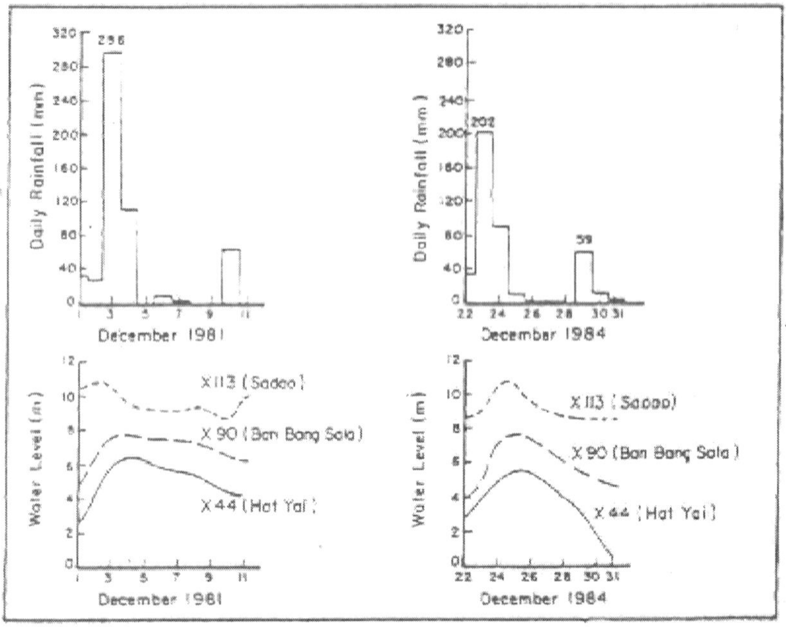

Figure 15.10(a): Hydrographs of Khlong U-Thaphao during Floods in 1981 and 1984

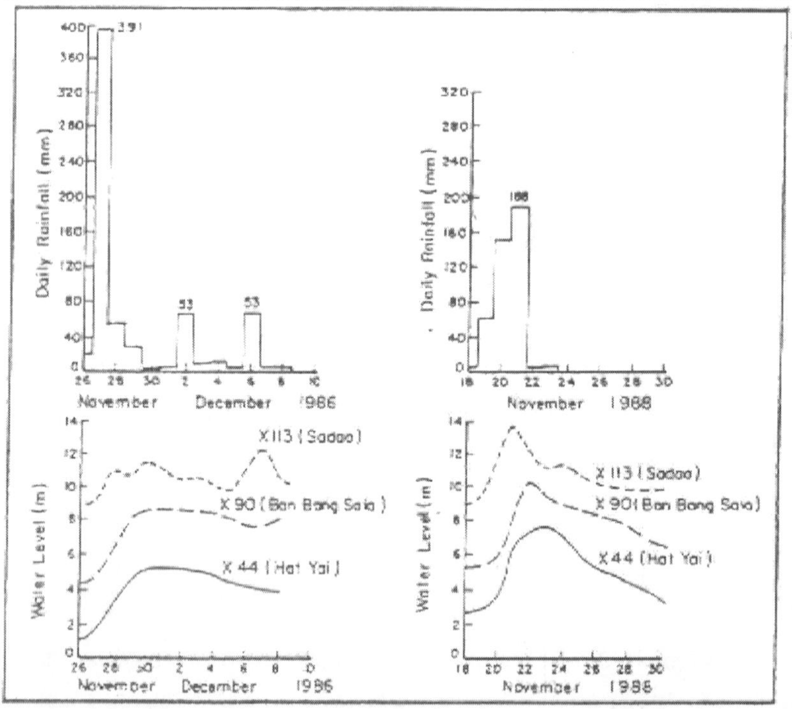

Figure 15.10(b): Hydrographs of Khlong U-Thaphao during Floods in 1986 and 1988

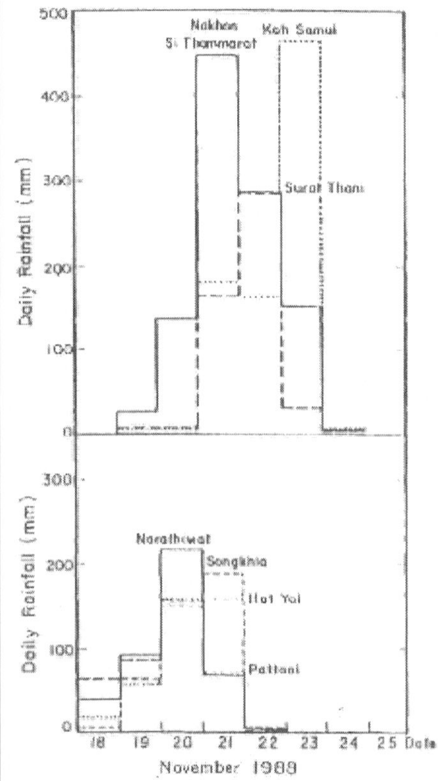

Figure 15.11: Daily Rainfall in the South during 1988 Flood

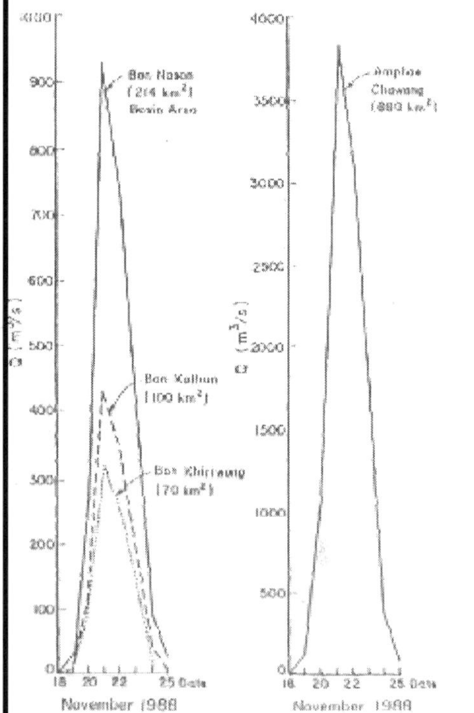

Figure 15.12: Computed Discharges of Four Critical Basins

Severe erosions of river-beds and banks occurred due to these huge discharge. The casualties and damages caused by this catastrophic flood were summarized in Table 15.2 and its resulting landform due to land slides were shown in Figure 15.13.

Station (Figure 7)	*River or Khlong*	*District*	*Province*	*Code*	*Catchment (km^2)*	*Period*
1	Sadao	Sadao	Songkhla	X113	129	1979-present
2	Lum	Sadao	Songkhla	X111	256	1979-present
3	Lumphan	Sadao	Songkhla	X112	493	1979-present
4	Wat	Hat Yai	Songkhla	X14	71	1954-1971
5	Tham	Hat Yai	Songkhla	X7l	127	1967-present
6	U-Thaphao	Hat Yai	Songkhla	X90	1,425	1971-present
7	U-Thaphao	Hat Yai	Songkhla	X40	1,441	1967-present

Figure 15.2: Summar of Casualties and Damage Caused by Floods in Southern Thiland during November, 1988 (Damage as of December, 1988)

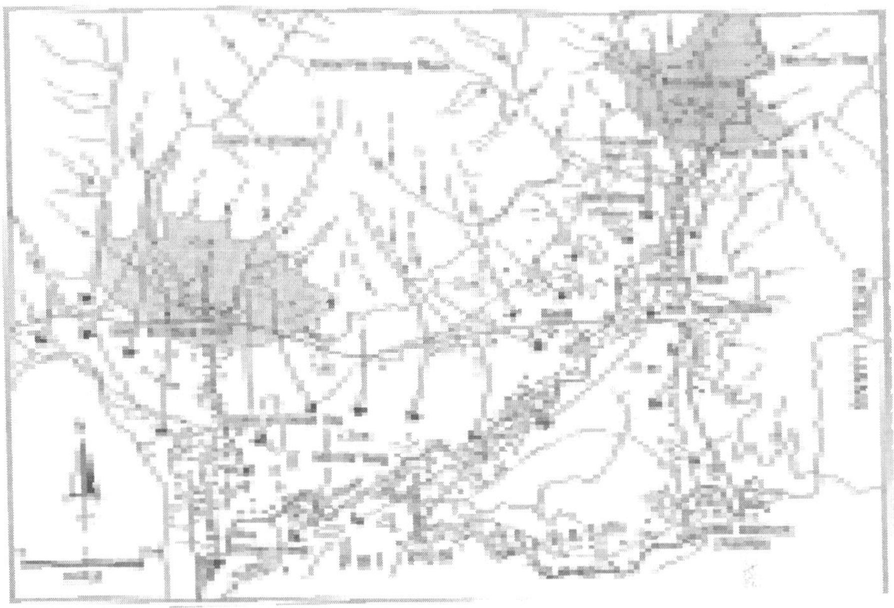

Figure 15.13: Sketch of Landforms in Phi Pun Basin, Amphoe Phi Pun, Nakorn Si Thammarat Province. Stippled Area Covered by Sheet of Water and Sand during the Height of the Rainstorm Event of 20-23 November 1988. Thickness of Sand is shown (Meters). Approximate Directions taken by Floodwaters shown by Large Arrows. Dashed Arrows in Mountains show General Direction taken by Sand slides and Rockslides (from United Nations, 1989).

5. Conclusion

The following conclusions could be drawn from this study.

1. The 1988 catastrophic flood was due to heavy rainfall over the Khao Luang mountain which resulted in swift currents and land slides.
2. Flood warning by radio would be extremely useful to alleviate flood damage. Warning could start when low pressure center would be detected by weather satellite and subsequent warnings could follow when heavy rainfall and rising water level would be observed.

6. References

1. Meteorological Department (1989) "Floods in Southern Part during 19-23 November 1988", (in Thai) February 1989.

2. Nielsen, S. A. and Hansen, E. (1982) "NAM Model Documentation and Users Guide", Danish Hydraulic Institute, Technical University of Denmark, Denmark.

3. Nutalaya, P. and Sophonsakulrat, W. (1989), Floods in the Southern Part of Thailand", (in Thai) Vol. 1, Proc. Seminar on Flood Protection in the Southern Part of Thailand, Bangkok, Thailand, Jan. 18-19, 1989.

4. United Nations (1898), "ESCAP Technical Assistance to the Flood Affected Areas in Southern Thailand", Mission Report, Economic and Social Commission for Asia and the Pacific (ESCAP), Bangkok, Thailand.

5. Vongvisessomjai, S. (1989), "Analysis of Flood Conditions in the South of Thailand", (in Thai) Vol. 1, Proc. Seminar of Flood Protection in the Southern Part of Thailand, Bangkok, Thailand, Jan. 18-19, 1989.

16

Cyclone Disasters due to Strong Wind and Surge

Suphat Vongvisessomjai
Professor and Director
Regional Environmental Management Centre,
Water Engineering and Management Programme,
School of Civil Engineering,
Asian Institute of Technolog, Thailand

1. Introduction

Cyclone disasters in Thailand due to strong winds and surges are those (i) in 1952 when typhoon Vae attacked the Upper Gulf, (ii) in 1962 when typhoon Harriet caused disaster at Laem Talumpuk of Nakorn Si Thammarat Province due to its devastating winds and surges causing 800 deads, (iii) in 1970 when cyclone Ruth attacked Ko Samui and coastline of Surat Thani and Chumphon, and (iv) in 1989 when typhoon Gay caused disaster at Patiew and Tha Sae of Chumphon province due to strong winds and surges, 580 dead were mostly fishermen, 620 boats sunk, 40,000 houses destroyed and about 11 billion Baht damage. This paper presents the characteristics of these cyclones.

2. Cyclones over Thailand

In summer, air over sea surface near equator which is overheated will become lighter and rise, creating a low pressure center defined as cyclone. The outer cooler air blows towards the center in counterclockwise direction over the northern hemisphere due to coriolis effect, and clockwise in the southern hemisphere. This results in a system of cloud which precipitates when it passes over a mountainous area and thus produces flood.

A tropical cyclone is characterized by four parameters, namely, its forward speed V_F, radius of the eye R, the minimum pressure at its center P_o and the maximum wind speed at the radius of the eye U_{max}.

(a) Pressure Distribution

The pressure distribution of a cyclone p increases as a function of the radial distance r from its center from Po to the atmospheric pressure P_n in the following manner.

$$p-p_o = (P_n-p_o)exp\,(-R/r) \text{ for } o<r< \text{“} \quad (1)$$

(b) Velocity Distribution

The wind velocity distribution of a cyclone V varies as a function of the radial distance r, that proposed by Jelenianski (1965) is given below.

$$V= V_o(r/R) \quad \text{for } r \text{ d” } R \quad (2)$$

$$V = V_o(R/r) \quad for\ r > R \quad (3)$$

where,

V_o = the maximum sustained wind in a cyclone;

R = the radius of maximum sustained speed;

r = distance between eye of the cyclone and the point where V is desired.

Tracks of 4 disastrous cyclones over the South China Sea affecting Thailand are shown in Figure 16.1. Characteristics of the first three cyclones affecting Thailand are shown in Figure 16.2 for their variations of pressure and wind speed versus radial distance r. These cyclones can be seen clearly from weather satellite in form of huge clouds. These clouds cause heavy rainfalls and floods while strong winds cause destruction of houses, *i.e.* typhoon Vae attacking the Upper Gulf of Thailand in October 1952, typhoon Harriet attacking Laem Talumpuk of Nakorn Si Thammarat province in October 1962 and cyclone Ruth causing damages to Ko Samui, Surat Thani, Chumphon and Prachuap Khiri Khan in November 1970. In 1989 typhoon Gay caused disaster at Patiew and Tha Sae of Chumphon province where 580 people were killed.

The observed surges and tides at Ko Prap and Ko Mattaphon are shown in Figure 16.3.

(c) Cyclone Wave Characteristics

The stress of surface winds produces surges along shoreline and waves in bodies of water, and the sea-level pressure deficit in the inner part of a cyclone permits a corresponding rise in the water level by hydrostatic equilibrium principles.

For a slowly moving cyclone, the following formulae given by CERC (1984) can be used to obtain a good estimate of the deepwater significant wave height and period:

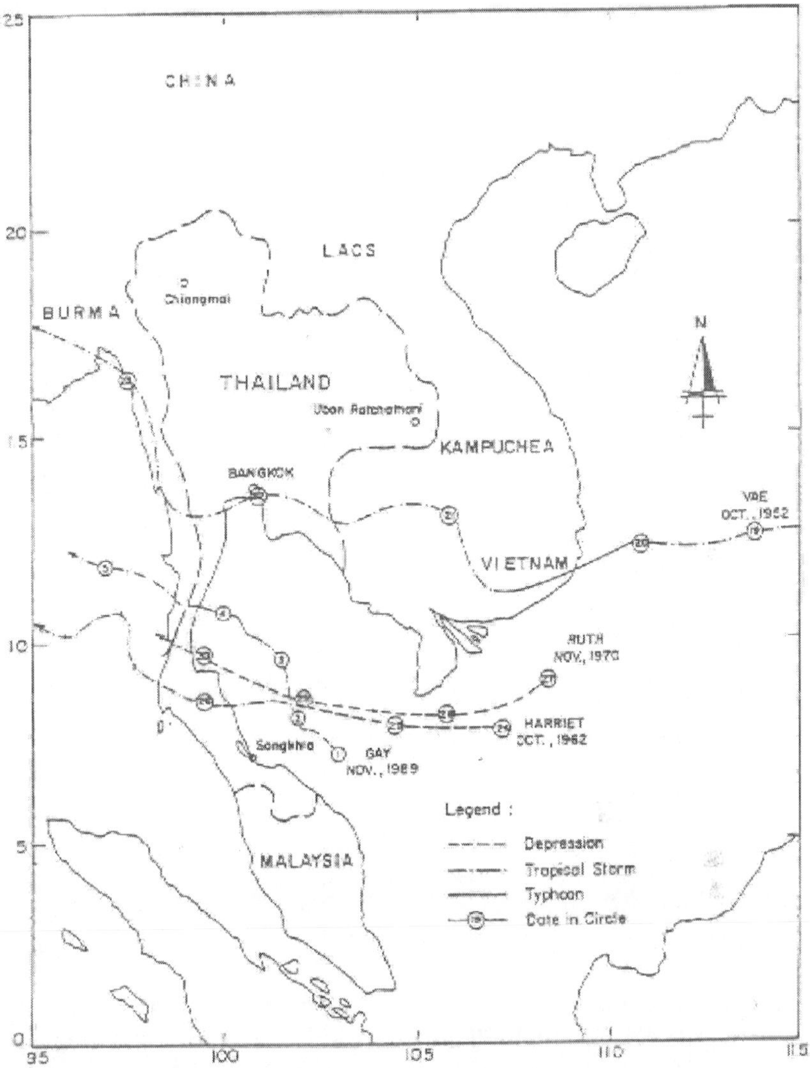

Figure 16.1: Tracks of 4 Most Disastrous Cyclones over Thailand

$$H_0 \quad 5.03\exp \frac{R \ \ p}{4700} \quad 1 \quad \frac{0.29 \quad V_F}{\sqrt{U_R}} \qquad (4)$$

and

$$T_s \quad 8.6\exp \frac{R \ \ p}{9400} \quad 1 \quad \frac{0.145 \quad V_F}{\sqrt{U_R}} \qquad (5)$$

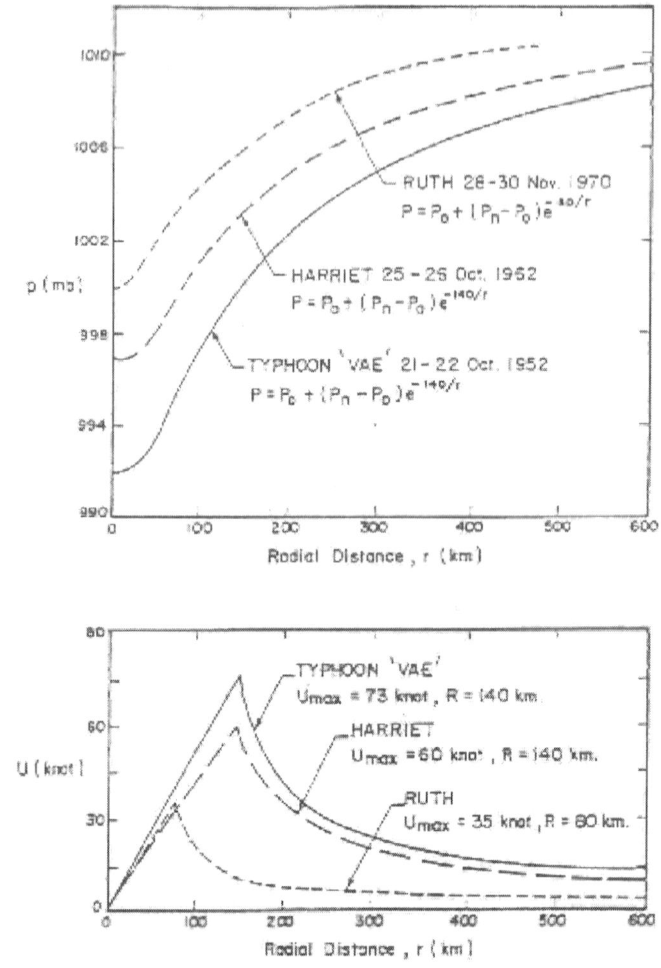

Figure 16.2: Radial Distributions of Pressures and Wind Velocity of Typhoons Vae, Harriet and Ruth

where,

H_0 = deepwater significant wave height in meters

Ts = the corresponding significant wave period in seconds

R = radius of maximum wind in kilometers

$p = p_n - P_0$, where p_n is the normal pressure of 760 mm of mercury, and P_0 is the central pressure of the cyclone in mm of mercury.

V_F = the forward speed of the cyclone in knots

U_R = the maximum sustained wind speed in knots, calculated for 10 meters above the mean sea surface at radius *(R)* where

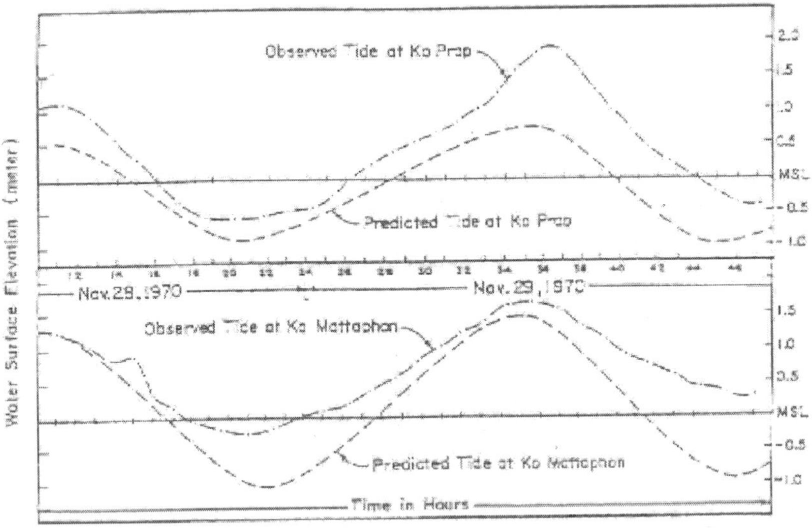

Figure 16.3: Comparison of Water Surface Elevation to Show Surge Height

$$U_R = 0.865\, U_{max} \text{ (for stationary cyclone)} \qquad (6)$$

$$U_R = 0.865 U_{rmax} + 0.5 V_F \text{ (for moving cyclone)} \qquad (7)$$

U_{max} = maximum gradient wind speed in knots 10 meters above the water surface

$$U_{max} = 0.447\,[14.5(p_n - p_0)^{1/2} + -R(0.31f)] \qquad (8)$$

f = Coriolis parameter (2w sin) in radians per hour where

Latitude ( )	25°	30°	35°	40°
f	0.221	0.262	0.300	0.337

= is a coefficient depending on the forward speed of the cyclone, V_F, and the increase in effective fetch length because the cyclone is moving. It is suggested that for slowly moving cyclone = 1.0.

Once H_0 is determined from Eq. (4), it is possible to obtain the approximate deepwater significant wave height H_0 by use of Figure 16.4 for other areas of the cyclone. The corresponding approximate wave period may be obtained from

$$T_s \quad 12.1\sqrt{\frac{H_s}{g}} \qquad (9)$$

It is these large waves and surges induced by the strong winds of the cyclones that cause casualties of people living along the shorelines.

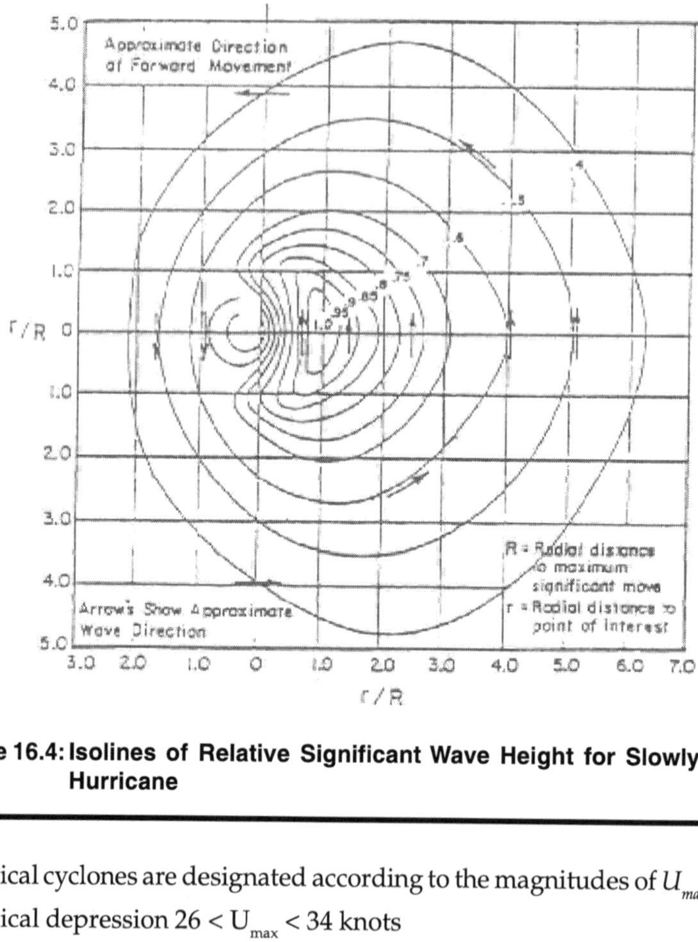

Figure 16.4: Isolines of Relative Significant Wave Height for Slowly Moving Hurricane

Tropical cyclones are designated according to the magnitudes of U_{max} as follows:

Tropical depression $26 < U_{max} < 34$ knots

Tropical storm $35 < U_{max} < 47$ knots

Severe tropical storm $48 < U_{max} < 63$ knots

Typhoon $U_{max} > 64$ knots

Under an international agreement, when the maximum wind speed U_{max} of a cyclone is greater than 35 knots, a name will be given to the cyclone.

3. Cyclonic Surge and Wave at Ao Phai

Planning and design of a power plant at A_0 Phai requires knowledge on probable maximum and minimum sea levels as well as surge and wave generated by cyclonic from the South China Sea.

(a) Cyclonic Surge Analysis

In determining the Probable Maximum Cyclone and the 250 year cyclone (Cyclone associated with value of central pressure index of once in 250 years) for further computation of cyclonic surges and waves, several tracks as known (Figure 16.1) are tried and the most severe cyclonic effects is 35 nautical miles (radius of the eye) north of A_0 Phai with movement of the storms center east to west by Vongvissessomjai et al. (1977). It is generally assumed that the Central Pressure Index (CPI) or the minimum central pressure (P_0) values of storms belong to a normally distribution population. This permits the extrapolation of the CPI to theoretically high recurrence interval so as to get the corresponding values of the CPI for PMC. The inherent parameters adopted for PMC and the 250-year cyclone from Figure 16.5 are given in Table 16.1.

Table 16.1: Historical Cyclone Characteristics

No.	*Year*	*Month, Date*	*Name (millibars)*	*CPI or P_0 U_{max} (mph)*	*Max. Velocity Speed, V_F miles)*	*Forward R(nautical (mph)*	*Radius,*
1	1952	Oct 21-22	VAE	992	84	14.97	76
2		Oct 24-25	TRIX	998	44	17.27	60
3	1960	Oct 03-04	-	992	52	3.45	8.4
4	1962	Oct 25-26	HARRIET	997	69	18.45	76
5	1966	Jun 17-18	-	-	-	12.67	-
6		Oct 25-26	-	990	48	9.21	49
7	1967	Jun 17-18	-	978	62	12.67	140
8		Oct 05-06	-	996	49	11.52	16
9		Oct 09-10	-	998	44	17.27	90
10		Nov 10-11	-	-	-	12.67	-
11	1968	Sep 05-06	BESS	992	44	2.30	115
12		Oct 21-22	HESTER	998	46	11.52	10
13	1967	Jun 24-25	-	998	46	6.91	7.5
14		Sep 20-21	-	992	51	12.67	57
15		Nov 02-03	-	1000	45	16.12	10
16	1970	Sep 20-21	-	994	52	13.82	20
17		Oct 25-26	KATE	1000	27	13.82	314
18		Nov 29-30	RUTH	1000	42	11.52	43
19	1972	Jun 03-04	NAMIE	990	48	6.91	123
20		Sep 06-07	-	990	49	4.61	16
21		Sep 18-19	-	-	-	-	-
22		Dec 04-05	SALLY	994	50	5.76	5
23	1973	Nov 12-13	-	1002	38	5.76	4
24		Nov 17-18	THELMA	998	45	5.76	39
25	1974	Oct 09-10	-	1002	34	6.91	15
26		Nov 05-06	-	998	45	13.82	60

Illustrated (Figures 16.6 and 16.7) respectively are the designed PMC wind field and typical four hourly values of the wind field over the Gulf. Plotted (Figure 16.8) are

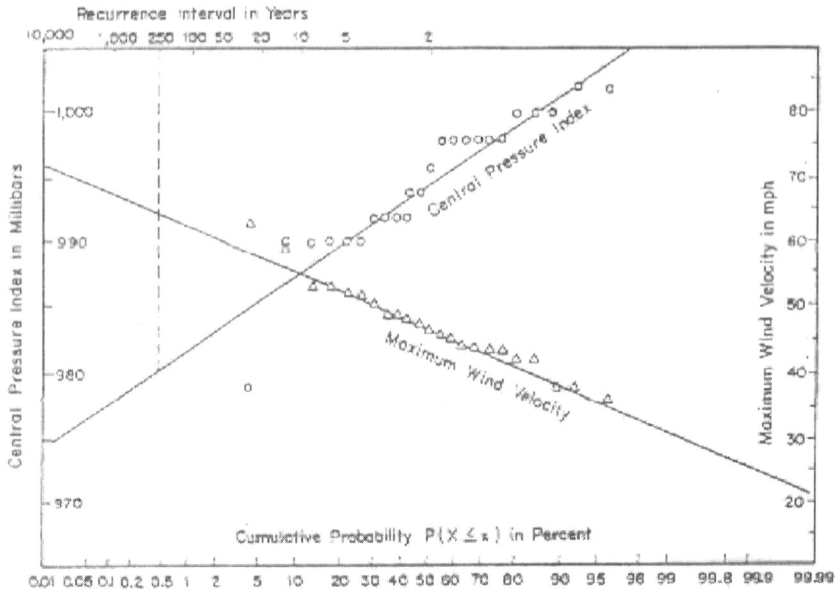

Figure 16.5

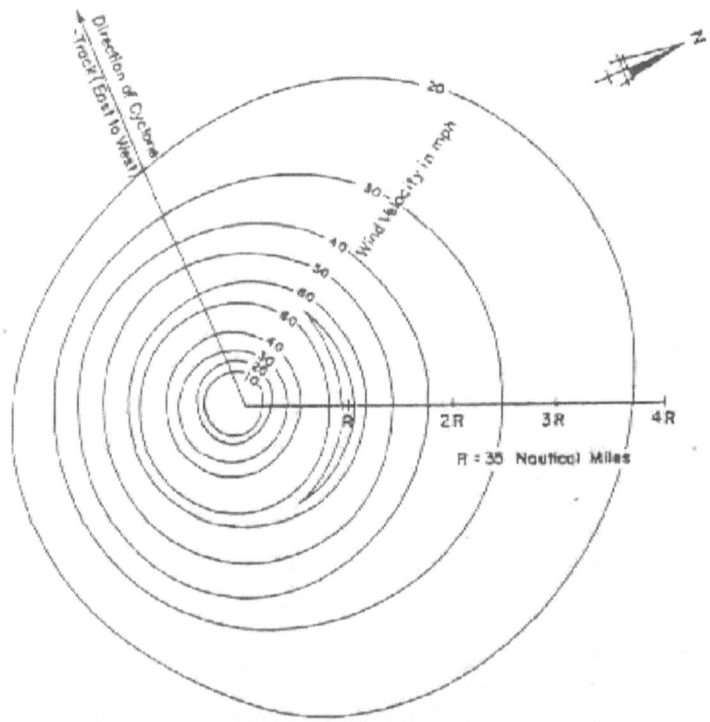

Figure 16.6

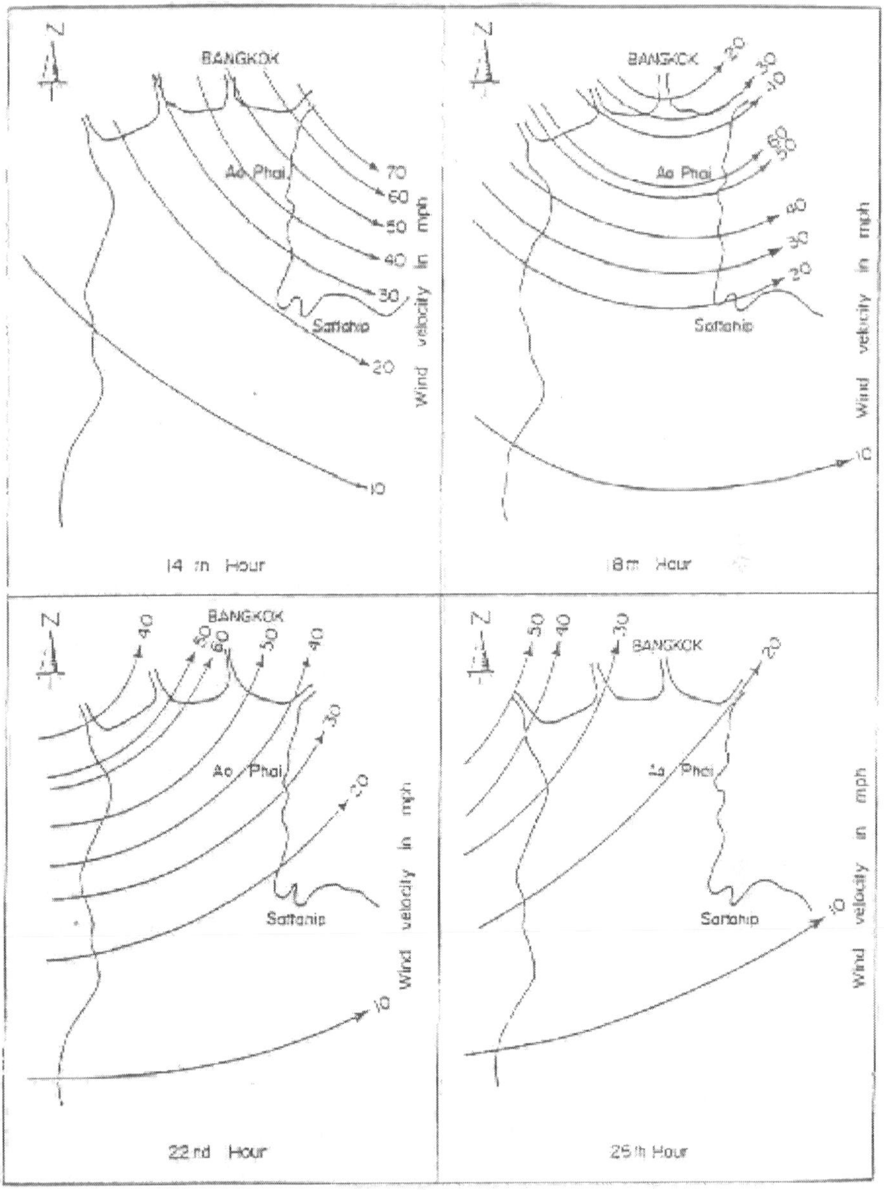

Figure 16.7: PMC Wind Field over the Gulf of Thailand

the magnitudes and directions of wind as would be observed at different radial distances from the centers of the PMC and of the 250 year cyclone, for a span of 46 hours. The surge computation is then performed on an IMB-370 computer using the derived PMC data. The surge hydrography is then obtained (Figure 16.9).

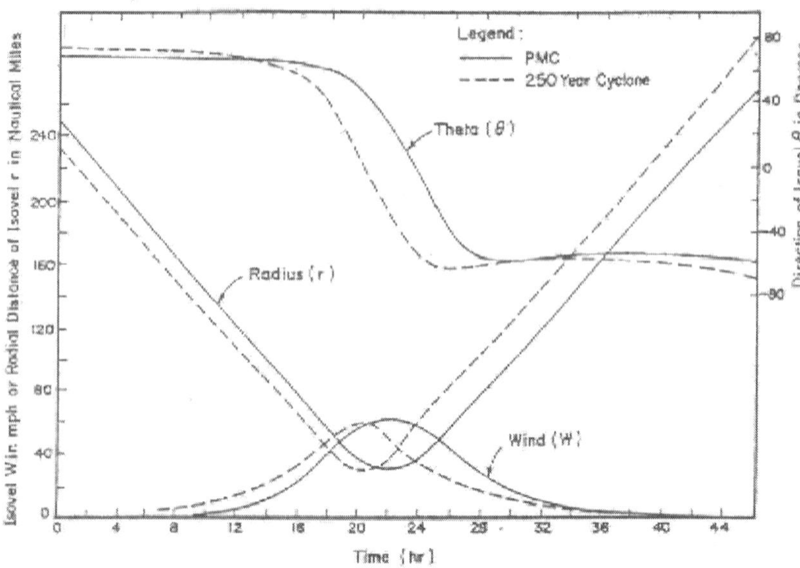

Figure 16.8: PMC and 250-Year Cyclone Characteristicsas would be Observed at AO Phai

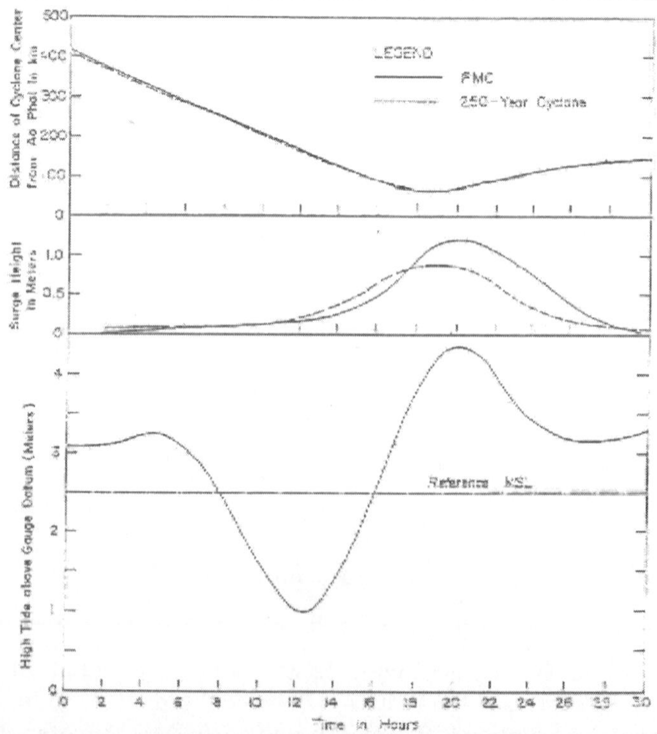

Figure 16.9: Probable Maximum Cyclonic Surge (PMC and 250-Year) and High Tide at Ao Phai

The observed seasonal waves are found to be insignificant in height and period. However, short-duration waves generated by cyclones, known as "cyclonic waves" are important aspects of cyclones occurring in the near shore zone and in the immediate neighborhood of coastal front structures. They can be prominently superposed on the surge levels. Quantitative estimates of the waves associated with cyclones are forecast and included here.

(b) Cyclonic Waves

A procedure for present computation of cyclonic waves is developed (Day, 1977). Two design cyclones; the PMC and the 250-year cyclone as used for the surge computation, are adopted. The results are shown (Figure 16.10).

In Figure 16.10 the starting time of computation is taken to be that when the iso-velocity line of zero wind velocity touches the shoreline at the west side of the Gulf.

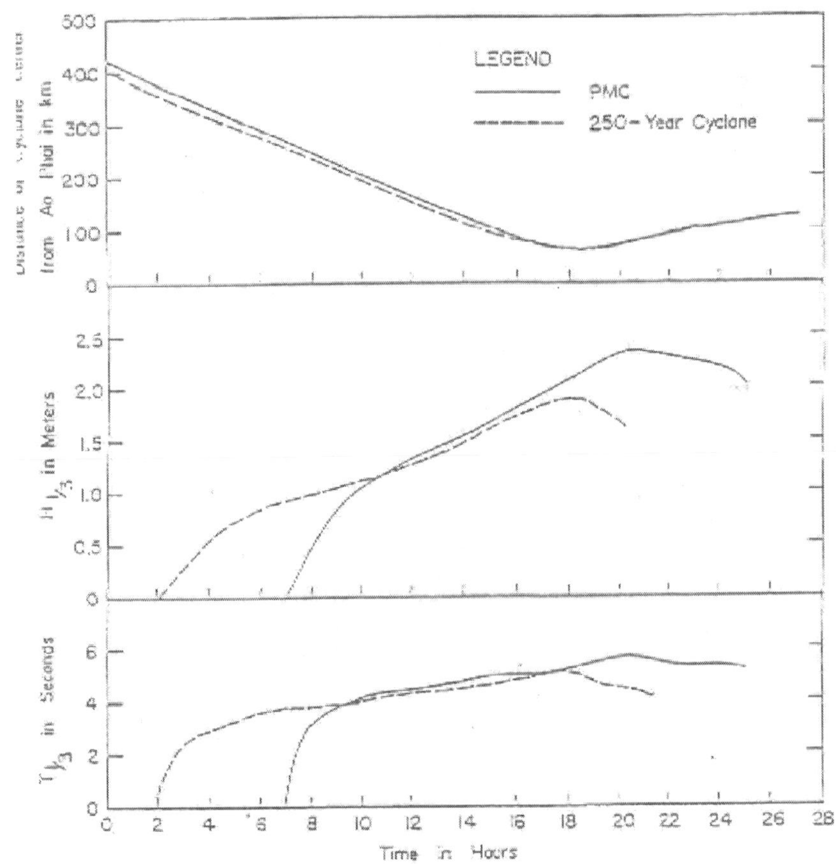

Figure 16.10: Probable Maximum Cyclonic Wave (PMC and 250 Year) at Ao Phai

The distance of the cyclone center from Ao Phai shown in this same Figure indicated that the cyclone center is nearest to Ao Phai at about the 18th hour. At this time, the cyclonic waves would be the most severe; this would be particularly so if the track of the cyclone is about 35 nautical miles north of Ao Phai. The severest cyclonic wave characteristics were found to be 2.3 m in height and 5.9 sec in period at PMC condition. For the condition of the 250-year cyclone, the severest cyclonic wave characteristics were found to be 1.9 m and 5.1 sec. No cyclonic waves have been actually recorded to permit comparisons. However, this cyclonic wave model has been successfully applied to tropical cyclones in Hong Kong and Taiwan (Day, 1977), and the computed order of magnitudes obtained above are within this expectation.

4. Conclusions

Due to the fact that severe cyclones rarely reach the Gulf, result in quite small values of extreme surges of 1.17 m and 0.90 m for PMC and 250 year cyclones respectively while their corresponding significant waves are 2.3 m, 5.9 s and 1.9 m, 5.1s at Ao Phai. When typhoons Harriet and Gay attacked southern shorelines which are open sea, the resulting surges and waves were much larger which caused much more damages and casualties.

These disasters can be alleviated from known characteristics of cyclones and through proper warning

5. References

1. Bodine, B.R. (1971), Storm Surge on the Open Coast: Fundamentals and Simplified Prediction, U. S. Army, Corps of Engineers, Coastal Engineering Research Center, Technical Memorandum No. 35.
2. Coastal Engineering Research Center (CERC, 1984), Shore Protection Manual, Department of the Army, Waterways Experiment Station, Corps of Engineers, Vicksburg, Mississippi, Vol. 1, Chapter 3.
3. Day, Ching-Her (1977), Cyclonic Wave in South China Sea, AIT Master Thesis No. 935, Bangkok, Thailand.
4. Jelenianski, C.P. (1965), A Numerical Calculation of Storm Tides Induced by a Tropical Storm Impinging on a Continental Shelf, Mon. Weather Rev., Vol. 93, June.
5. Vongvisessomjai, S., Thinaphong, S., and Balasubramaniam, K. (1977), Prediction of Probable Maximum and Minimum Water Levels, AIT Research Report No. 69; Asian Institute of Technology, Bangkok, Thailand.

17

Mitigation of Typhoons and Flood

Daong Quang San
Expert,
Ministry of Science, Technology and Environment, Vietnam

1. Natural Hazards

Vietnam is a tropical country subject to the Southeast Asian Monsoon with an annual rainfall of roughly 2000 mm. About 80 per cent of this falls in summer (May-October) causing rivers to flow full.

At the same time, the Northern and Central parts of Vietnam are subject to about 4 to 6 typhoons a year on average. Whenever the intense rain added from one of these typhoons, monsoons flows in these rivers causing flood. About one year in five, a typhoon will be so large that it crosses the mountains into the lower Mekong Basin causing very severe floods in Laos, Cambodia and South Vietnam.

The intense rainfall also causes flash floods, landslides and mud flows in the mountains, erosion and siltation of river beds and water-retaining structures further downstream. The typhoons generate high waves and raise the water level of the sea, inundating ports settlements and coastal agricultural land with saline water.

These losses from water disasters in Vietnam are large. Every year, hundreds of people die and the damage to property runs into hundreds of millions of dollars.

2. Causes, Impact of Typhoons and Flood

Since 1954, there have been 212 typhoons landing in or directly influencing Vietnam. On average there are about 30 typhoons originating in the Western Pacific Ocean each year, of which about 10 are generated in the South China Sea. Of these, an average of 4 to 6 hit affects Vietnam. There are years where at least 10 typhoons arrived in Vietnam recently are 1964 (18 typhoons), 1973 (12), 1978 (12), 1989 (10) and 1996 (10).

The areas most affected by typhoons are the coastal Province of the North and Central Regions. However, typhoons in the South, though less frequent, can still be extremely damaging.

About 62 per cent of the population and 44 per cent of the whole are frequently affected by typhoons, which on average kill some 250 people every year. The worst in this century were the 1904 typhoon in the South which caused death and injury to 5000 people, and the 1985 typhoon in Binh Trt Thien Province which killed 900 people. Typhoons are normally accompanied by storm surges. During the past 30 years, half the typhoons have caused a storm surge of over 1 m, 30 per cent of typhoons over 1.5m, and 11 per cent of typhoons over 2.5m. These typhoons and storm surges have often overtopped and frequently destroyed sea dykes, flooding lowland coastal areas.

3. River Bed Clearance

Over a 10-year period (1971-1981) 45 per cent of the people living outside the dyke were resettled. Some 7 million m^3 of earth have been removed from high river banks, and a number of fallen bridges and sunken ships have been taken out.

However, during recent years, the situation has again worsened. Construction materials have been dropped in the waterways, new residential areas have been established on the river lands and sand bars along the rivers and the estuaries have not been dredged through lack of funds.

4. Food Diversion

Works for flood diversion, through augmented channel capacity and for flood storage have been installed, but they have always been able to work at their designed capacity.

For example, the Day river channel has been planned to divert floods from the Red river without endangering the Day River Dyke. The designed discharge of the Day Diversion Spillway is 5000 m^3/s, but only around 3000 m^3/s is possible for flood diversion because areas within the floodplain have been settled for agriculture during the long period since the last flood. The most difficult problem for flood diversion in the Day River is that too many people (nearly 500,000) would now have to be resettled and about 200 km of dykes need to be more frequently repaired.

5. Upstream Reservoirs

In the 1971 flood, Thac Ba Reservoir helped to reduce the water level by 0.10-0.15m in the Red river. Since that time, it has been estimated that the new Hoa Binh Reservoir could lower the repeat of 1971 flood by 1.2-1.4 in at Hanoi city.

On the other hand, the Hoa Binh Reservoir, by holding back sediment, is inducing erosion in the lower basin, and lengthening the period of flooding. The former effect increases the danger to the dykes while the latter stretches the resources of the dyke management and repair teams during flooding, especially in trying to ensure continued protection of the banks.

6. Dyke Monitoring and Repair

Our experience so far has been that dykes are the most important structural measure for flood mitigation and control of damage from typhoons. Our late President Ho Chi Minh once said, "All people must take care of the dykes".

Even when other measures are implemented, the dykes will remain an essential and indispensable structural measure to protect life and ensure continued agricultural production. However during large floods, dyke monitoring and repair needs to be undertaken quickly and reliably.

Vietnam now has nearly 8000 km of dykes, including 6000 km of river-dykes and 2000 km of sea-dykes. There are 3000 km of dykes along our larger rivers and 1000 km of major sea-dykes. About 600 revetments of various types and 3000 under-dyke sluices have been built. In addition, there are 500 km of embankments for controlling major floods and preventing salinity in the Mekong Delta.

Over the last two thousand years, techniques for combating failures in the dyke systems have been developed. In particular since 1971, MOST has worked hard to formulate new strategies for detecting zones of weakness for strengthening crucial areas of the dyke system, and for more effectively responding to alarms. However, we are still facing a number of serious problems:

- The existing river dykes were built long ago by hand using local materials and without much understanding of geo-technical principles. Because the earth fill and foundations were neither carefully selected nor treated, there are frequent sand boiling, piping seepage and slides, along nearly every section of dykes. Thus during large floods of long duration, there can be dyke breaches and embankment failures, especially where the dykes have poor foundations and water ponds on both sides because of unauthorized earth excavations in the past. There are also many termite nests and rodent holes creating large cavities inside the dyke and other causes of weakness in the embankments,
- Changes in the river channels during floods can cause bank erosion, threatening the safety of the dykes. Bank protection by revetments and groins are very costly, sometimes it is difficult to construct upto a satisfactory standard.
- Most sluices which allow water to pass through the dykes are out of date and seriously damaged, though they remain operational. In the flood season, many sluices have to be tendered inoperative in order to maintain the security of the dykes,
- The sea-dyke systems, especially in the Central Provinces are very low, overtop frequently and wash away. The sea-dyke systems in the North,

although larger are able to withstand typhoons up to level 10 at mean sea level. However it is difficult to remain operational when typhoons and storm-surges come,

- Resources and equipment for dyke monitoring and repair have been minimal and frequently insufficient. Dyke monitoring has been mainly visual even though most defects are located inside the dyke or in the foundations, thus difficult to discover. Fortunately, this situation is yet to improve substantially with the new dyke monitoring and repair technology being introduced under the UNDP's Project VIE/88/015,
- Although the Council of the State of Vietnam has promulgated an ordinance to protect dykes, violations of this ordinance are increasing, especially where the dykes pass through densely populated areas.

In an attempt to maximize the use of its own resources, Vietnam also applies structural and non-structural measures for mitigating floods, such as:

- Some of our coastline is expanding seawards as sediments is brought down from the mountains, and people seeing the new lands emerging, seek to colonize it. Very soon, they press for defense against the sea, and because the land becomes economically productive, it becomes difficult to deny them. Small sea dykes may then be erected but when their weight is insufficient, they demand higher and stronger ones.
- Should we agree to this? Economic studies tell us that many of these sea dykes are worthwhile. But the higher we go, the safer people feel and the more they invest in making their land productive. When the sea dyke overtops again, the losses will be much greater than before.
- In other parts of the coast, where there has been an interruption to the supply of sediment, the coastline is receding. The impact on the people, who are displaced because of this, is horrendous. Sometimes, this interruption of sediment results from natural processes and sometimes it is because of works, which divert the water to other economic uses such as irrigation.
- Which problems should we address first? Indeed, which is more important, irrigation or the protection of the coast?
- Much of Vietnam's coastline used to have mangroves which were very effective in reducing energy from waves. But now most of these mangroves have been cut down, while many of our coral roots, which can also provide protection, are being destroyed.

7. Mitigation of Typhoons and Floods

Since the historical flood in August 1971, the Vietnamese Government has applied six general measures for short-term and long-term flood control as follows:

- Reforestation and watershed protection;
- Construction of medium and large-scale reservoirs in upstream areas;

- Strengthening of the dyke systems;
- Flood diversion whenever necessary;
- River dredging and clearance for flood discharge channel;
- Dyke monitoring and repair.

As can be seen below the success of these strategies have not been all that might be desired.

(a Reforestation

During the past years, although reforestation has been promoted, the forest area is being reduced by about 100,000 ha/year. In Vietnam the losses caused by floods and typhoons seem to be increasing over time, as in the rest of the world. For example, due to floods and typhoons about 540 people were killed annually in the period 1985 to 1989, whereas in the years 1976 to 1979, the Figure was 225.

The uneven distribution of rainfall is the main cause of floods in the rivers. The river network in Vietnam has a total length of about 25,000 km, concentrated into three rather clearly defined networks the Red and Thai Binh river system in the North, the coastal river system in the Center, and the Mekong-Dong Nai river system in the South.

Due to the different topography in each area, each network has its own different characteristics. The rivers in the South are gentle, those in the North are fairly steep and those in the Center are both short and very steep. Some of the big rivers such as the Red river in the North and the Mekong River in the South, originate from neighbouring countries, running across Vietnam and into the sea. In the rainy season all the rivers cause flooding though the severity may be different from year to year.

Red River Delta

In this century alone, the Red and Thai Binh river systems had 26 major floods, the biggest being the great flood of 1971. Before that, a flood in 1945 had been considered to be the historic maximum. To give an appreciation of the magnitude of this flood, it might be noted that the level of the 1971 flood was 5-10m higher than the level of the fields inside the dykes.

Within a period of 45 years (1900-1945), there were 18 years in which dykes failed, or one has failure with crop losses every two to three years on average. In the 1945 flood the dyke system failed in 79 places, flooding N. Provinces over a cultivated area of 312,000 ha and affecting about 4 million people. The 1971 flood caused the dykes to fail in 3 large sections, inundating 250,000 ha and seriously affecting 2.7 million people. The most recent large flood was in 1986- the fifth-largest of this century. Where a section of dyke along the Red River was destroyed and a sluice under the Can River collapsed. Were it not for timely emergency works by the local people, the damage incurred would have been far greater than it was.

(b) Central Provinces

In the Central Provinces, there is regular annual flooding. Some of the more tragic have been the major floods in 1960 in the Quang Tri Thua Thien Region, in

Quang Nam in 1962, in Binh Dinh in 1932, in Hue in 1983, in the Eastern Provinces of the South in 1952, and in most of the Central Provinces in 1964.

Serious Flood in Central Provinces in Vietnam 1999

On 01-03 November 1999, due to the effect of strong cold air front in combination with the activities of a tropical conversion, there were heavy-to-very heavy rains in the Central Provinces from Quang Binh to Binh Dinh. On early morning, 03 November1999, there were still very heavy rains. Notably, in provinces from Quang Binh to Quang Tri, mean rainfall was 300-500 mm, and even over 2000 mm in some places.

Heavy rain, concentrating in a short period or time, caused flash flood in some places in mountainous areas of Quang Nam Province & Thua Thien-Hue Province, caused large flooding on river-banks from Quang Nam to Binh Dinh Provinces. Notably, there were very large floods on rivers from Quang Tri to Quang Nam Provinces. On the Huong River in Thua Thien Hue Provinces and on the Thach Han River in Quang Tri Provinces, there were historical floods. Flood levels were the biggest in 40 years. At 14:00 on 02 November 1999, the flood water level on the Huong River at the Hue gauging station reached its peak of 5.94 m (1.06 m above the historical flood level in 1983). After falling 0.20 m, on 03 November 1999, the flood water level rose again due to continuing rain on the upstream. Flood water levels in Quang Binh, Quang Ngai, and Binh Dinh continued to rise. The flood situation was very complicated and there was heavy inundation on a large scale.

According to Thua Thien Hue Province's report, heavy rain concentrating in a short period of time, caused flash floods in Xuan Loc (Phu Loc District) and Binh Dien (Huong Tra District). On the Huong River, in just 1 hour, the flood water level rose by over 1m; the whole province was less than 1-3m of water. The entire communication system and electric system were paralyzed.

(c) Mekong Delta

Flooding in the Mekong Delta is well known throughout the world. Recent examples of large floods (1961, 1966, 1978, 1984, 1991, 1995 and 1996) have seen hundreds of thousands of hectares of crops destroyed.

(d) Highlands

Although most of the land in the Highlands of Vietnam is well above flood level, there are still many developments in the floodplain. Since people value this land for agricultural production as well as it induces people from all over the world to settle.

Unfortunately, floods seem to have been on the increase in the highlands in the recent years: in Lang Son and Cao Bang (1986); in Lai Chau, Dak Lac and Bac Thai (1990); in Son La and Lai Chau (1991, 1994, 1995 and 1996) and in Ha Giang, Kon Turn (1996). The floods in 1990 and 1991 affected some densely populated areas of the two provincial towns of Lai Chau and Son La, and 1994, 1996 in Lai Chau, damaging most of their infrastructure.

(e) Coastal Disasters

Our country is currently classified as one of the poorest in the world. As a result, the poorest of our people have few choices in where they live, and where they can grow food. They have to do the following:

- ❖ Establishment of operation plans for flood mitigation and typhoon emergency action;
- ❖ Promulgating laws, ordinances and regulations for flood control;
- ❖ Improving the forecast and warning systems;
- ❖ Building typhoon and flood-resistant structures;
- ❖ Promulgation of design standards.

(f) Catchment Management

In common with many other developed and developing countries, the socio-economic circumstances or many of our people make it difficult for them to value forests, because they provide them with few short-term benefits.

As a result, trees are cut down to provide fuel and timber or to make room for more agricultural production. The resulting deforestation results in increased runoff and a greater rate of erosion. This leads to the flash floods, landslides, mudflows and siltation which have been mentioned earlier.

The work to rectify deforestation is a slow process, because of its complex nature. It entails the cooperation of many government agencies at the national, provincial and district levels, as well as local communities. It can require a change in economic activities, and sometimes a change in cultural practices.

Laws of Vietnam in the field of Disaster Mitigation

Since 1946 the flood and typhoon committee were formed from the central level to local level. These organizations have acted effectively in reducing natural disasters.

Vietnam also has promulgated the law on dyke and the law on flood and typhoon.

In this year Vietnam has also new law on flood diversion and flood retaining in the Red River systems to protect the safety of Hanoi capital

A strategy and action plan has also been established as well as implemented.

8. Interaction between the Organizations, Strategy and Action Plan for Mitigating Disasters.

Consequently in 1992, to support the goals of the International Decade for Natural Disaster Reduction (IDNDR), the Ministry of Water Resources of Vietnam and the Vietnam National Committee for the IDNDR had organized an International Workshop on Flood Mitigation, Emergency Preparedness and Flood Disaster Management in Hanoi, in association with the United Nations Development Program (UNDP), the United Nations Department of Development Support and Management Services (DDSMS/DESD), and the United Nations Department of Humanitarian Affairs (DHA/UNDRO) in 1994. This workshop was a great success as it was helpful in framing comprehensive national *strategy and action plan for Mitigating Water Disasters in Vietnam*. Based on recommendations of the workshop and over 100 written contributions received from 46 provinces and national government bodies, the Plan addresses the water disaster with a special impact on Vietnam:

- River floods
- Flooding from the sea
- Increased runoff
- Erosion and siltation of river beds
- Slope instability, mud flows and landslides
- Torrential rains in combination with strong winds
- Failures of water-retaining structures
- Seawater intrusion into ground water.

The Strategy and Action Plan has since served as the principle IDNRD framework in Vietnam for mitigating disasters. The strategy has three main task areas:

- Forecasting and Warning Systems
- Preparedness and Mitigation
- Emergency Relief

Each task area is further divided into physical solutions which focuses on structures, equipment and materials and non-physical solutions, which are predominantly to do with organizations, institutions, laws, procedures, investigations and training.

9. Recommendations

In order to have more effective results in the field of disaster management, Vietnam needs to mobilize not only the national resources but also international resources from UN organization and non-government organizations to build a rehabilitate construction concerned with the area of disaster management such as:

- Flood fighting
- Dyke maintaining and operation
- Flood warning system
- Local training for communities on disaster mitigation.

(a) Urgent works

Emergency spillways on primary dykes for Flood control in the North of Vietnam

(b) Extreme climate events

Over the past 10 to 15 years, Vietnam and some Southeast Asian countries appear to be most vulnerable to disasters resulting from both El Nino and La Nina events.

The typhoon Linda in 1997 and the severe drought in early 1998 in Vietnam and big flood in 1998 in China and again big flood in central of Vietnam were the result of unusual weather.

(c) The big flood may occur in 1999 or the next coming year

According to some hydrometeorology specialists, the tropical converge range, the main reason of causing big flood in China is tendency to move to the south of China, it means to the North of Vietnam. Meanwhile the central of Vietnam the big flood coming right after severe drought and the drought is moving to the North of Vietnam. These unusual events are warning, a big flood may be occurred.

In the Report No. 1064 dated 22 November 1998 submitted to the Government of the General Department of hydrometeorology, there is a comment. "In coming years due to the change of climate especially La Nina event is developing, there will be unpredictable dangerous changes of weather and hydrology in Vietnam." In fact the big flood occurred in central Vietnam with historical records.

(d) What are different discharges in the past and in the near future

Due to the unusual development and un-predicted climate there could be extreme flood in the 1999 flood season and coming years in Vietnam. The maximum discharge in the Red river at Son Tay during the flood period of August-September 1971 was around 37,800 m^3/s. (the highest historical flood recorded). According to hydraulic specialists the extreme flood could reach the discharge of 57,000 m^3/s at Son Tay gauging station and since 1971 the riverbed has been changed by human intervention. Therefore, extreme flood water levels are estimated much more higher than the historical flood water level at Hanoi.

(e) Urgent options

In order to respond timely and effectively to complicate development of flood and to minimize damage caused by disaster. Vietnam Government has recognized the importance of flood control and confirmed that "to find out the way for flood defense, it is not only priority but also urgent problem". The Government has authorized The Ministry of Agriculture and Rural Development to review and to put projects of emergency spillway.

The Ministry of Agriculture and Rural Development also considers the better management of the existing flood control structures as well as enhancement of public awareness of flood and storm control and disaster mitigation.